GRIMM UNIV

JOE BRUSHA A

MW00780301

Grimm Fairy Tales presents:

Wonderland

VOLUME **SIX**

THIS VOLUME REPRINTS GRIMM FAIRY TALES PRESENTS WONDERLAND ISSUES #26-30

PUBLISHED BY ZENESCOPE ENTERTAINMENT. FIRST EDITION, APRIL 2015 • ISBN: 978-1-939683-97-7

zenescope

WWW.ZENESCOPE.COM

ZENESCOPE ENTERTAINMENT, INC.

Joe Brusha • President & Chief Creative Officer
Ralph Tedesco • Editor-in-Chief
Jennifer Bermel • General Manager
Christopher Cote • Art Director
Jason Condeelis • Direct Market Sales & Customer Service

Grimm Fairy Tales presents Wonderland Volume 6 Trade Paperback, April, 2015. First Printing. Published by Zenescope Entertainment Inc., 433 Caredean Drive, Ste. C, Horsham, Pennsylvania 19044. Printed in Canada.

FACEBOOK.COM/ZENESCOPE • TWITTER.COM/ZENESCOPE • YOUTUBE.COM/ZENESCOPE

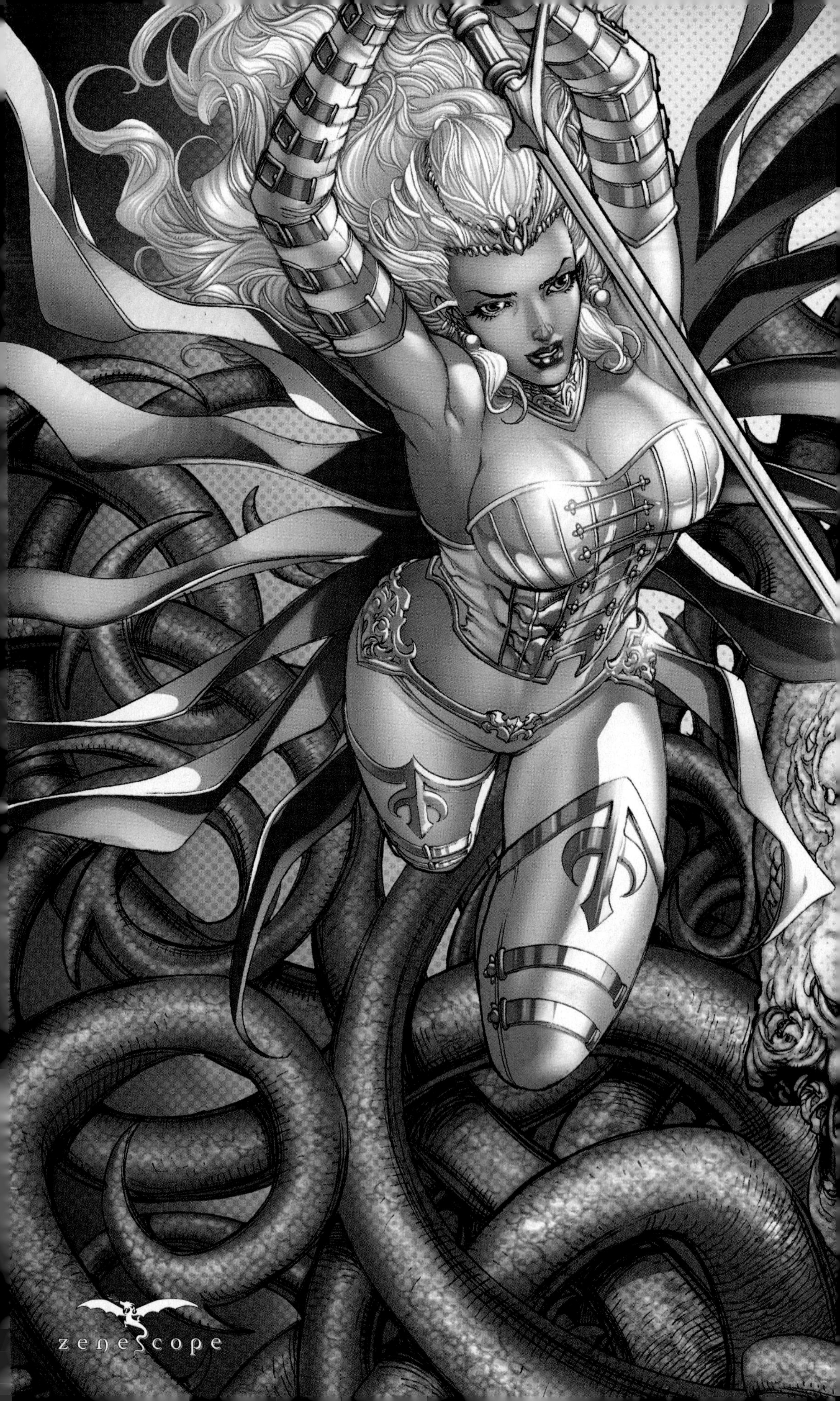
zenescope

RENAISSANCE

WRITER
ERICA J. HEFLIN

ARTWORK
VINCENZO RICCARDI

COLORS
BEN SAWYER

LETTERS
JIM CAMPBELL (PARTS 1-4)
CHRISTY SAWYER (PART 5)

EDITOR
PAT SHAND

TRADE DESIGN
CHRISTOPHER COTE

THE STORY SO FAR...

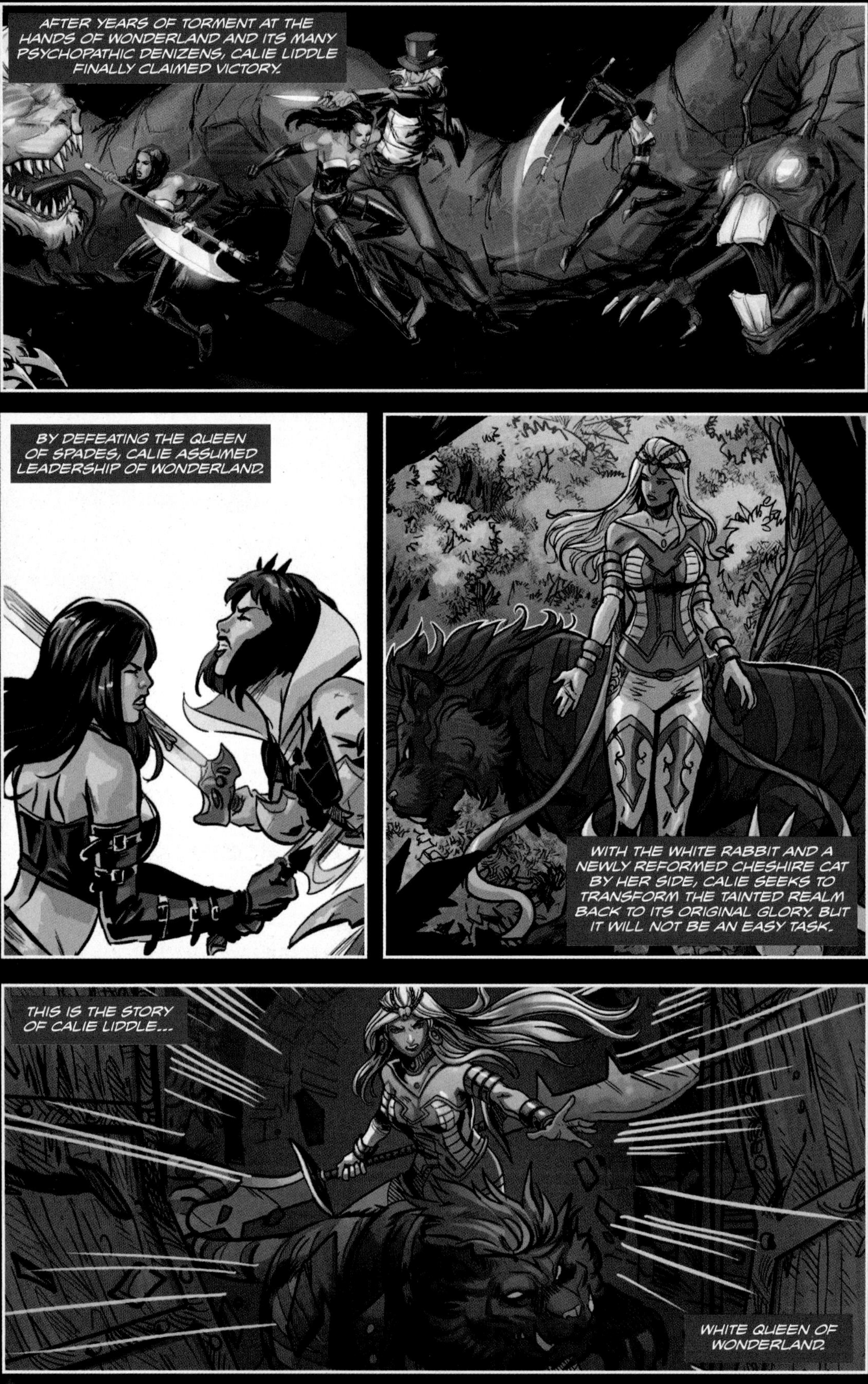

AFTER YEARS OF TORMENT AT THE HANDS OF WONDERLAND AND ITS MANY PSYCHOPATHIC DENIZENS, CALIE LIDDLE FINALLY CLAIMED VICTORY.
BY DEFEATING THE QUEEN OF SPADES, CALIE ASSUMED LEADERSHIP OF WONDERLAND.
WITH THE WHITE RABBIT AND A NEWLY REFORMED CHESHIRE CAT BY HER SIDE, CALIE SEEKS TO TRANSFORM THE TAINTED REALM BACK TO ITS ORIGINAL GLORY. BUT IT WILL NOT BE AN EASY TASK.
THIS IS THE STORY OF CALIE LIDDLE...
WHITE QUEEN OF WONDERLAND.

THE CAST

Calie Liddle

Violet Liddle

Dark Cheshire

White Rabbit

One-Eyed Jack

The Surgeon

RENAISSANCE

PART ONE

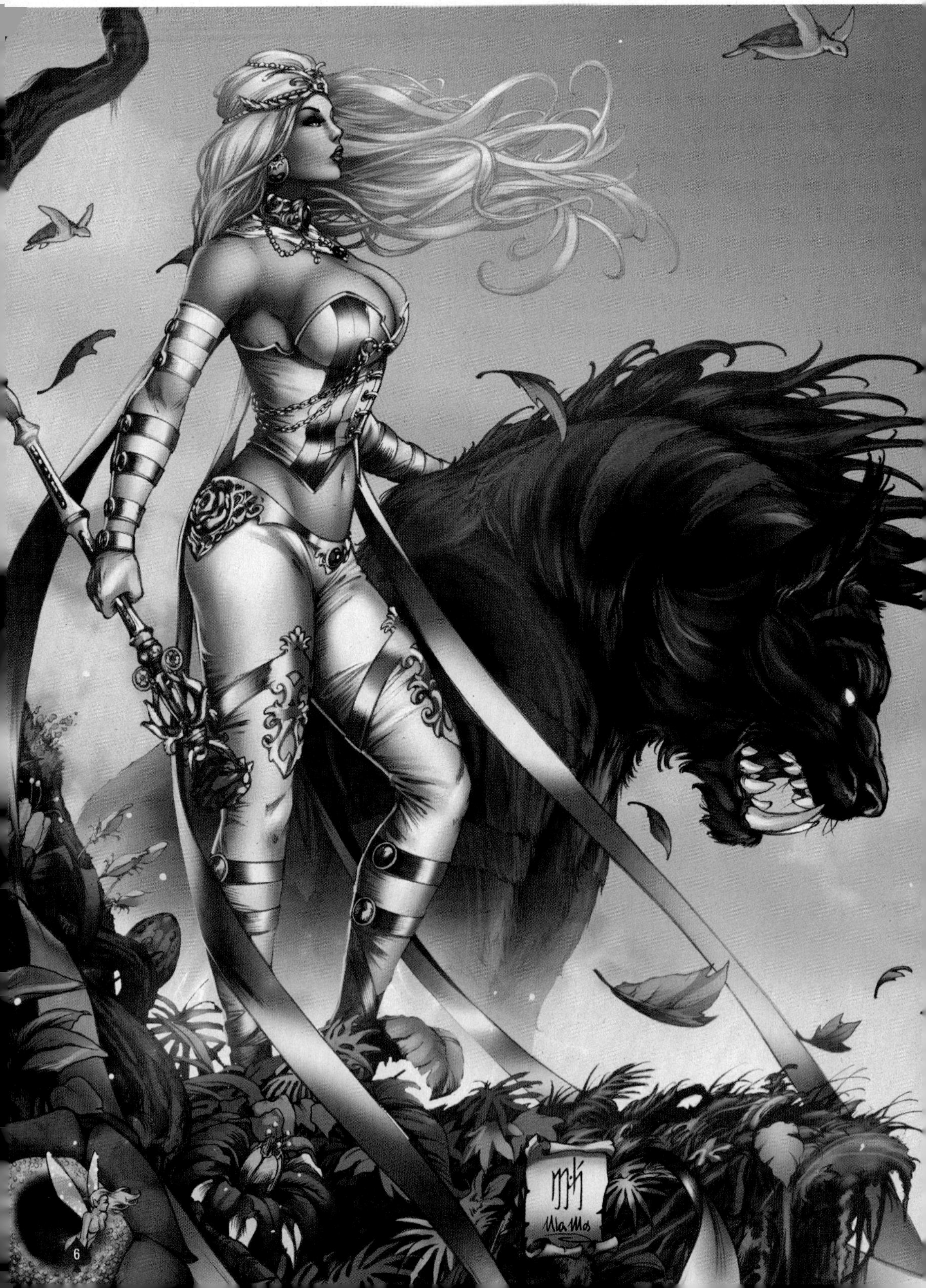

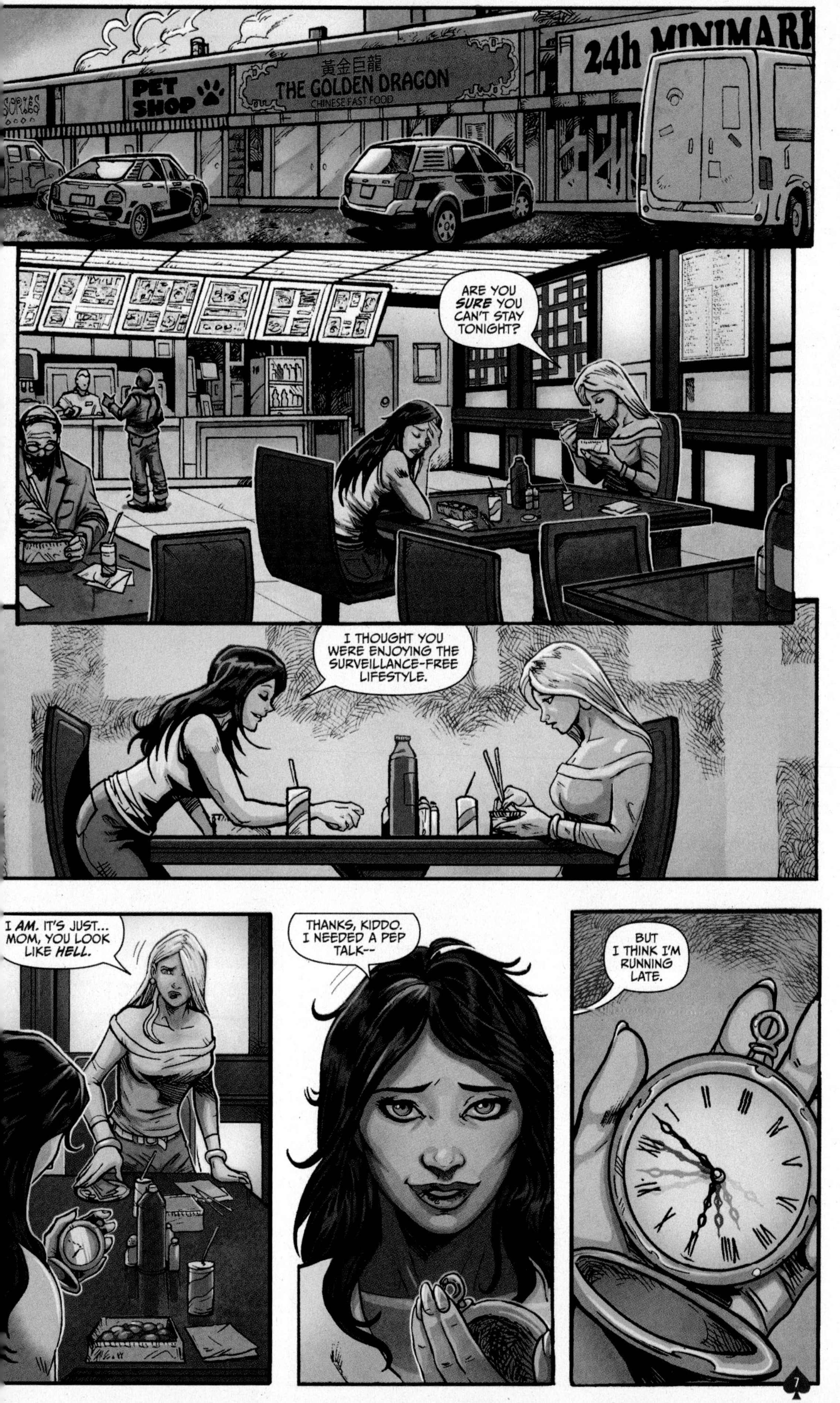
24h MINIMARK
PET SHOP
黃金巨龍
THE GOLDEN DRAGON
CHINESE FAST FOOD
ARE YOU SURE YOU CAN'T STAY TONIGHT?
I THOUGHT YOU WERE ENJOYING THE SURVEILLANCE-FREE LIFESTYLE.
I AM. IT'S JUST... MOM, YOU LOOK LIKE HELL.
THANKS, KIDDO. I NEEDED A PEP TALK--
BUT I THINK I'M RUNNING LATE.

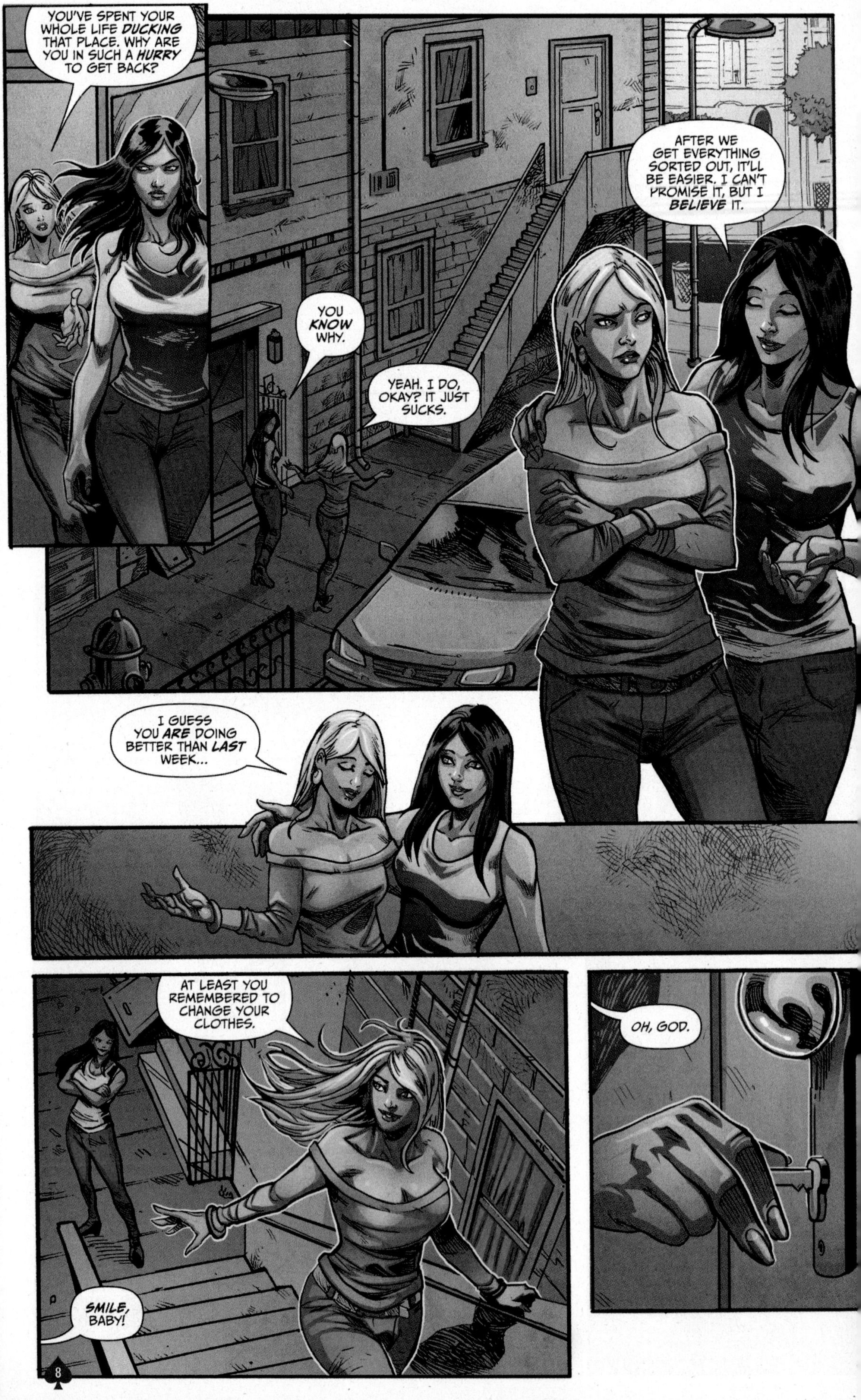
YOU'VE SPENT YOUR WHOLE LIFE DUCKING THAT PLACE. WHY ARE YOU IN SUCH A HURRY TO GET BACK?
YOU KNOW WHY.
YEAH. I DO, OKAY? IT JUST SUCKS.
AFTER WE GET EVERYTHING SORTED OUT, IT'LL BE EASIER. I CAN'T PROMISE IT, BUT I BELIEVE IT.
I GUESS YOU ARE DOING BETTER THAN LAST WEEK...
AT LEAST YOU REMEMBERED TO CHANGE YOUR CLOTHES.
SMILE, BABY!
OH, GOD.

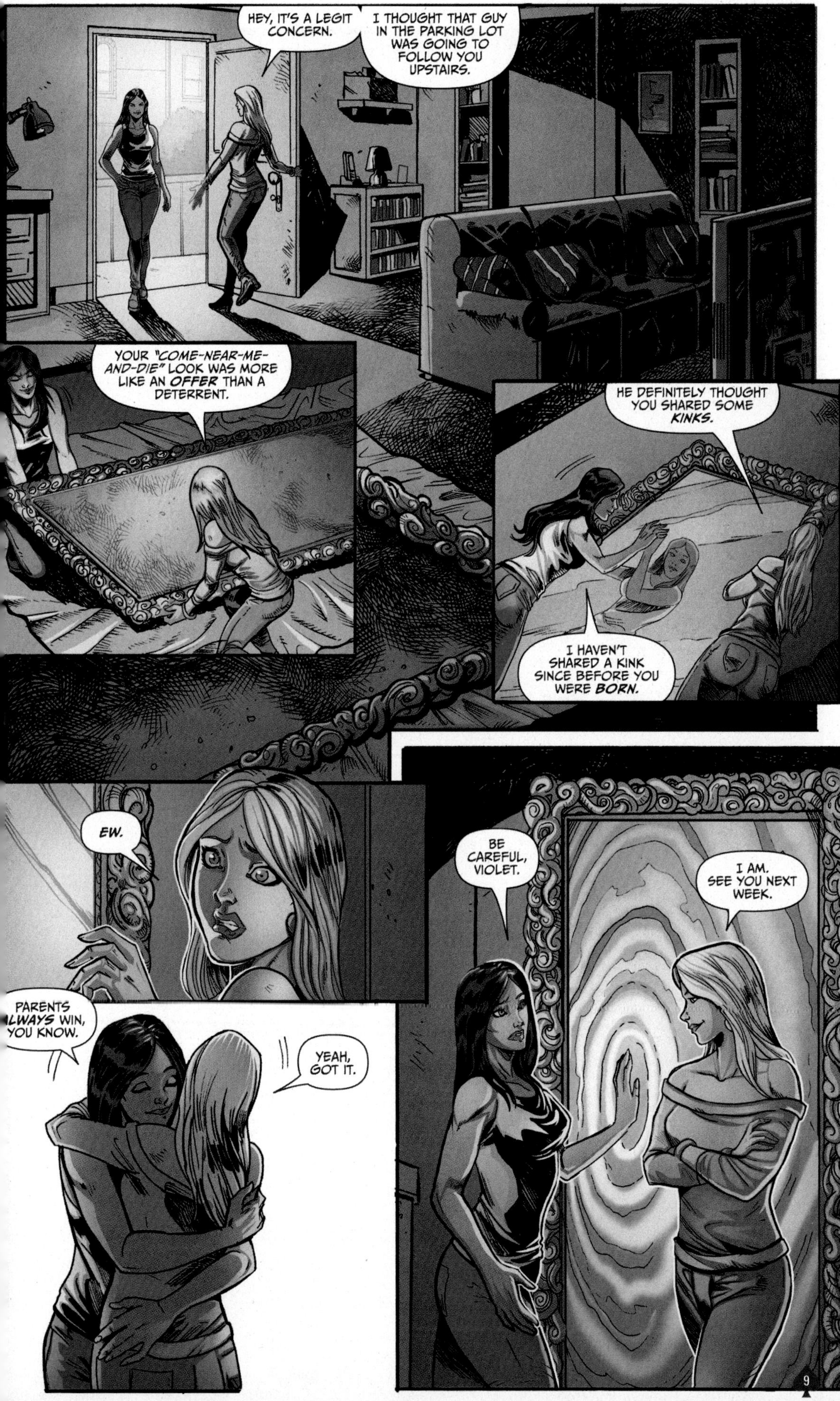
HEY, IT'S A LEGIT CONCERN.
I THOUGHT THAT GUY IN THE PARKING LOT WAS GOING TO FOLLOW YOU UPSTAIRS.
YOUR "COME-NEAR-ME-AND-DIE" LOOK WAS MORE LIKE AN OFFER THAN A DETERRENT.
HE DEFINITELY THOUGHT YOU SHARED SOME KINKS.
I HAVEN'T SHARED A KINK SINCE BEFORE YOU WERE BORN.
EW.
PARENTS LWAYS WIN, YOU KNOW.
YEAH, GOT IT.
BE CAREFUL, VIOLET.
I AM. SEE YOU NEXT WEEK.

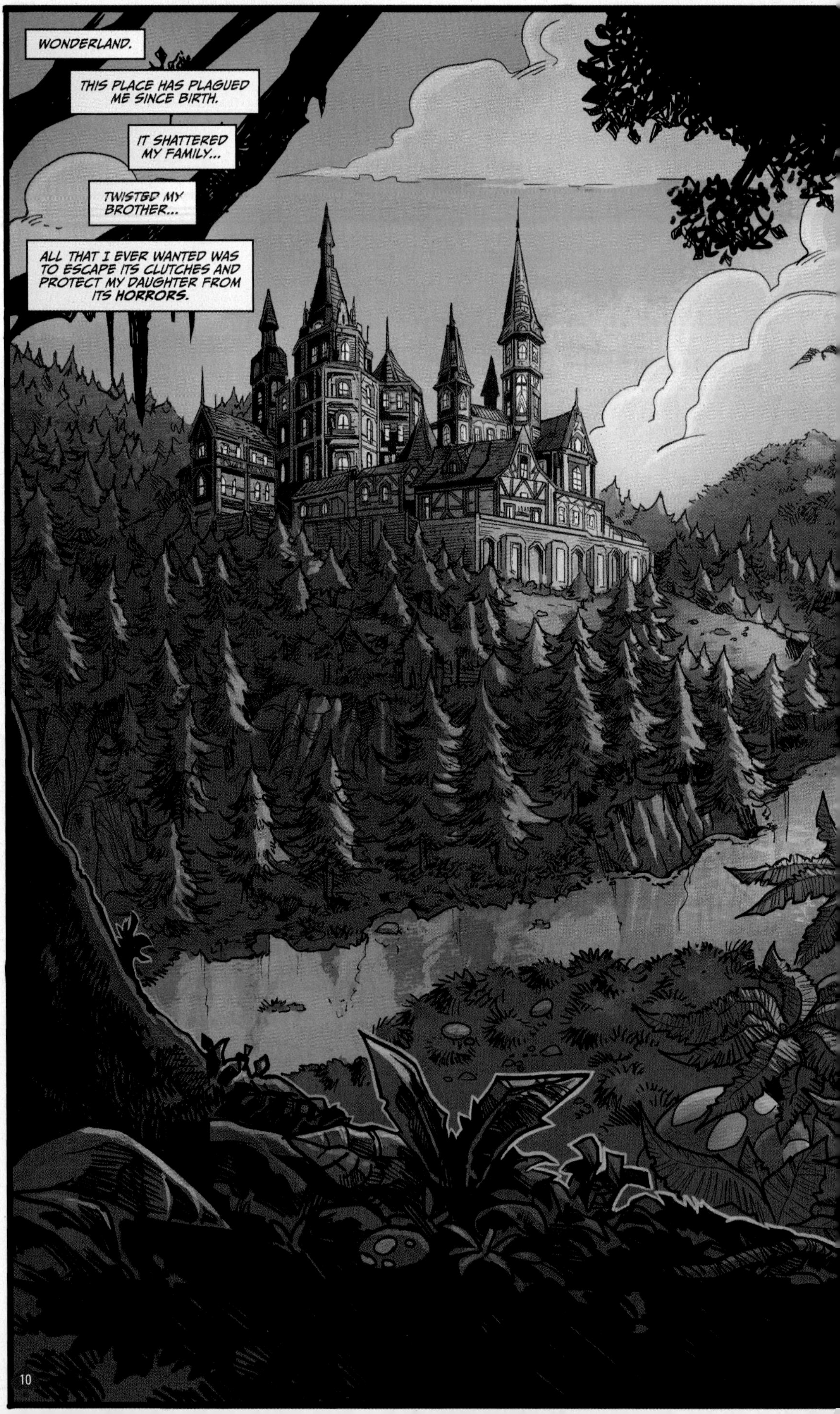
WONDERLAND.
THIS PLACE HAS PLAGUED ME SINCE BIRTH.
IT SHATTERED MY FAMILY...
TWISTED MY BROTHER...
ALL THAT I EVER WANTED WAS TO ESCAPE ITS CLUTCHES AND PROTECT MY DAUGHTER FROM ITS HORRORS.

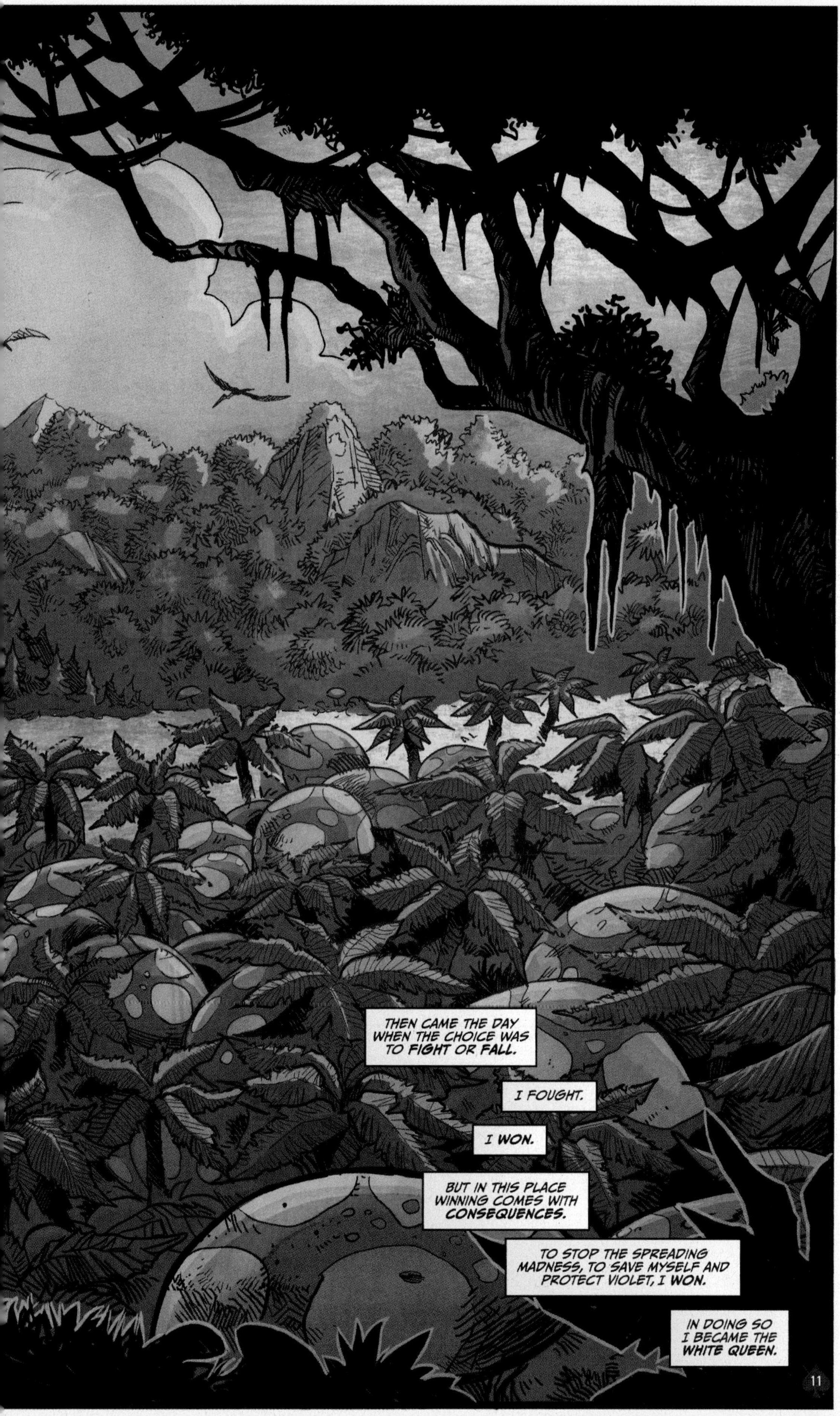
THEN CAME THE DAY WHEN THE CHOICE WAS TO FIGHT OR FALL.
I FOUGHT.
I WON.
BUT IN THIS PLACE WINNING COMES WITH CONSEQUENCES.
TO STOP THE SPREADING MADNESS, TO SAVE MYSELF AND PROTECT VIOLET, I WON.
IN DOING SO I BECAME THE WHITE QUEEN.

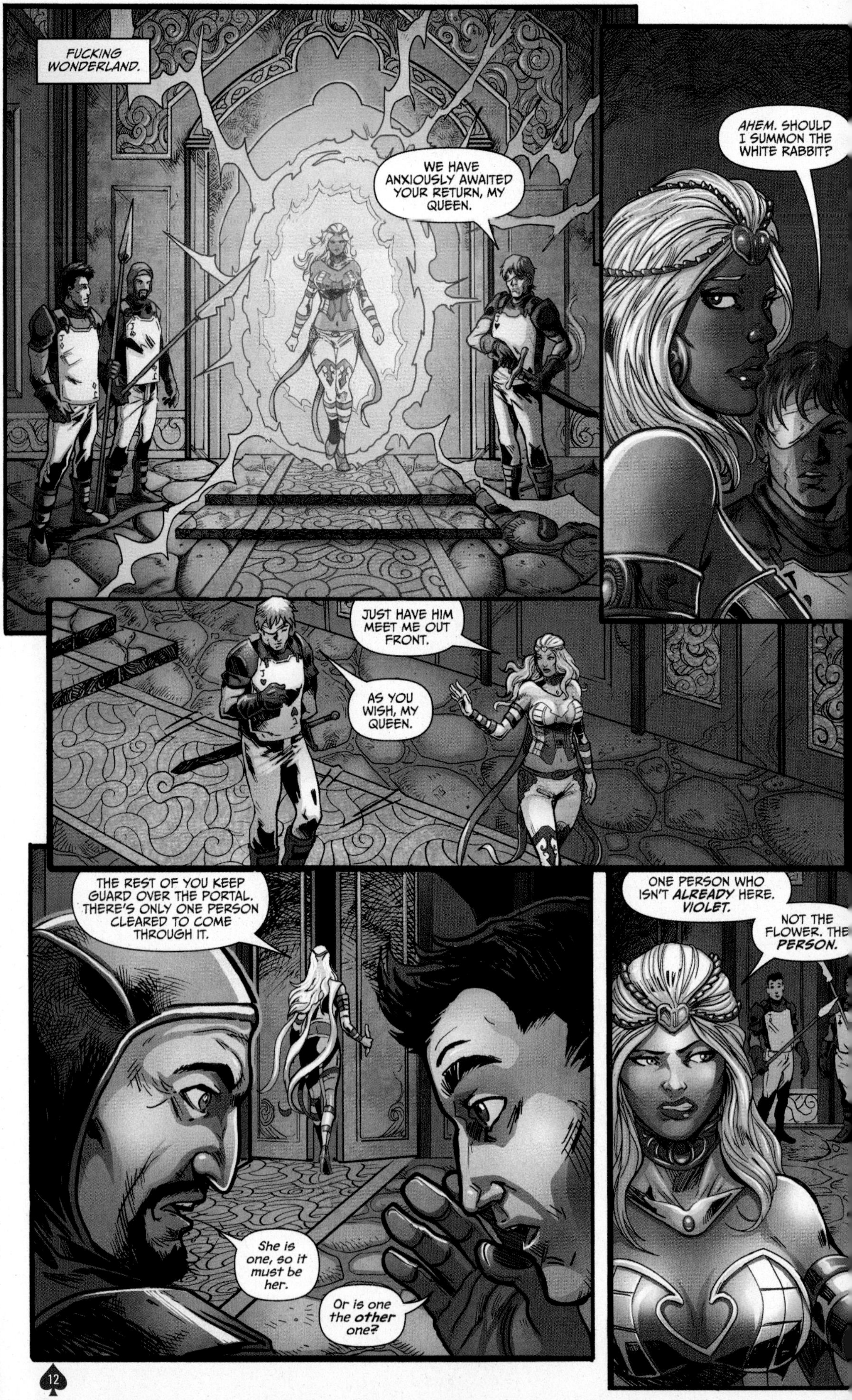

FUCKING WONDERLAND.
WE HAVE ANXIOUSLY AWAITED YOUR RETURN, MY QUEEN.
AHEM. SHOULD I SUMMON THE WHITE RABBIT?
JUST HAVE HIM MEET ME OUT FRONT.
AS YOU WISH, MY QUEEN.
THE REST OF YOU KEEP GUARD OVER THE PORTAL. THERE'S ONLY ONE PERSON CLEARED TO COME THROUGH IT.
ONE PERSON WHO ISN'T ALREADY HERE. VIOLET.
NOT THE FLOWER. THE PERSON.
She is one, so it must be her.
Or is one the other one?

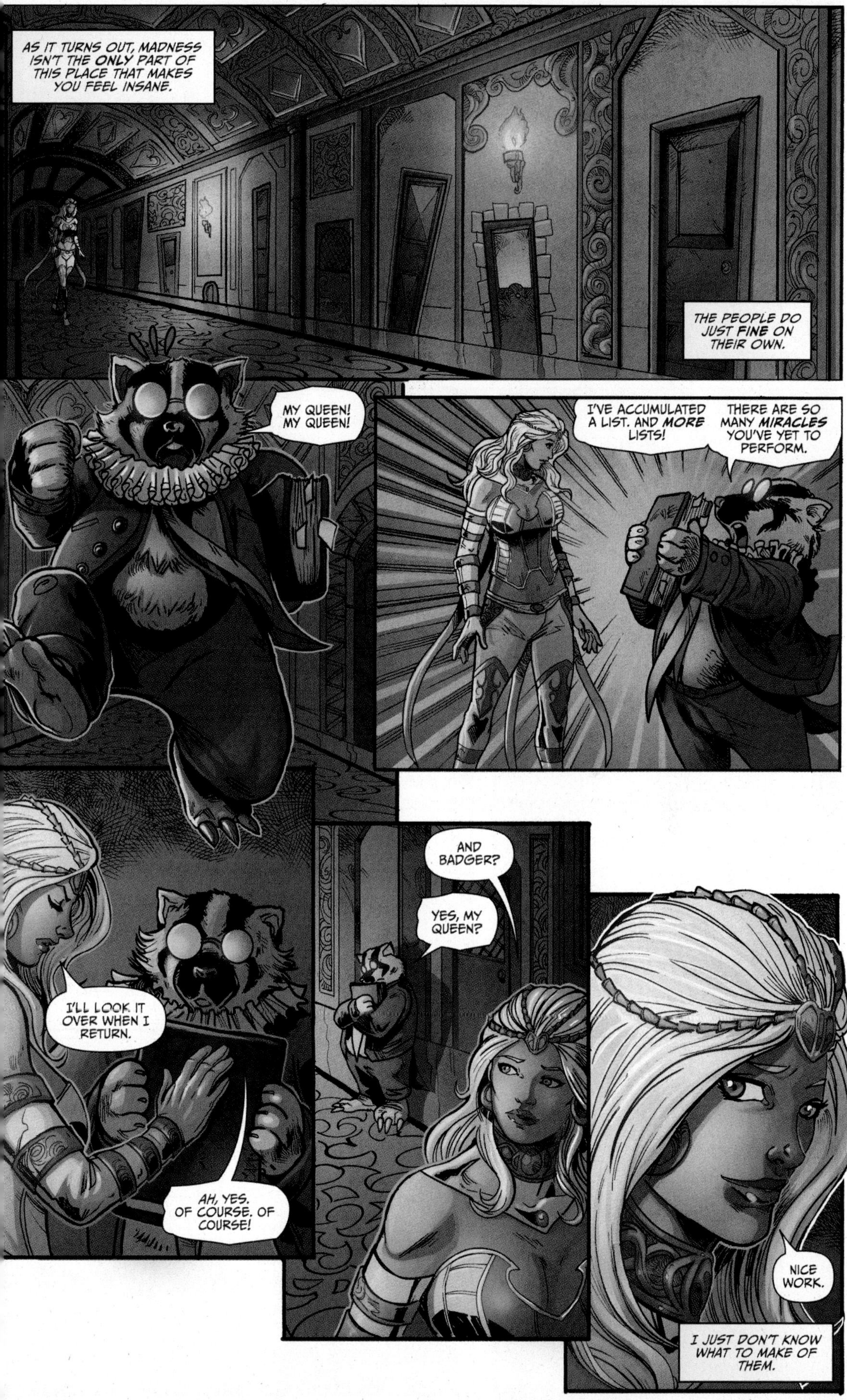
AS IT TURNS OUT, MADNESS ISN'T THE ONLY PART OF THIS PLACE THAT MAKES YOU FEEL INSANE.
THE PEOPLE DO JUST FINE ON THEIR OWN.
MY QUEEN! MY QUEEN!
I'VE ACCUMULATED A LIST. AND MORE LISTS!
THERE ARE SO MANY MIRACLES YOU'VE YET TO PERFORM.
I'LL LOOK IT OVER WHEN I RETURN.
AH, YES. OF COURSE. OF COURSE!
AND BADGER?
YES, MY QUEEN?
NICE WORK.
I JUST DON'T KNOW WHAT TO MAKE OF THEM.

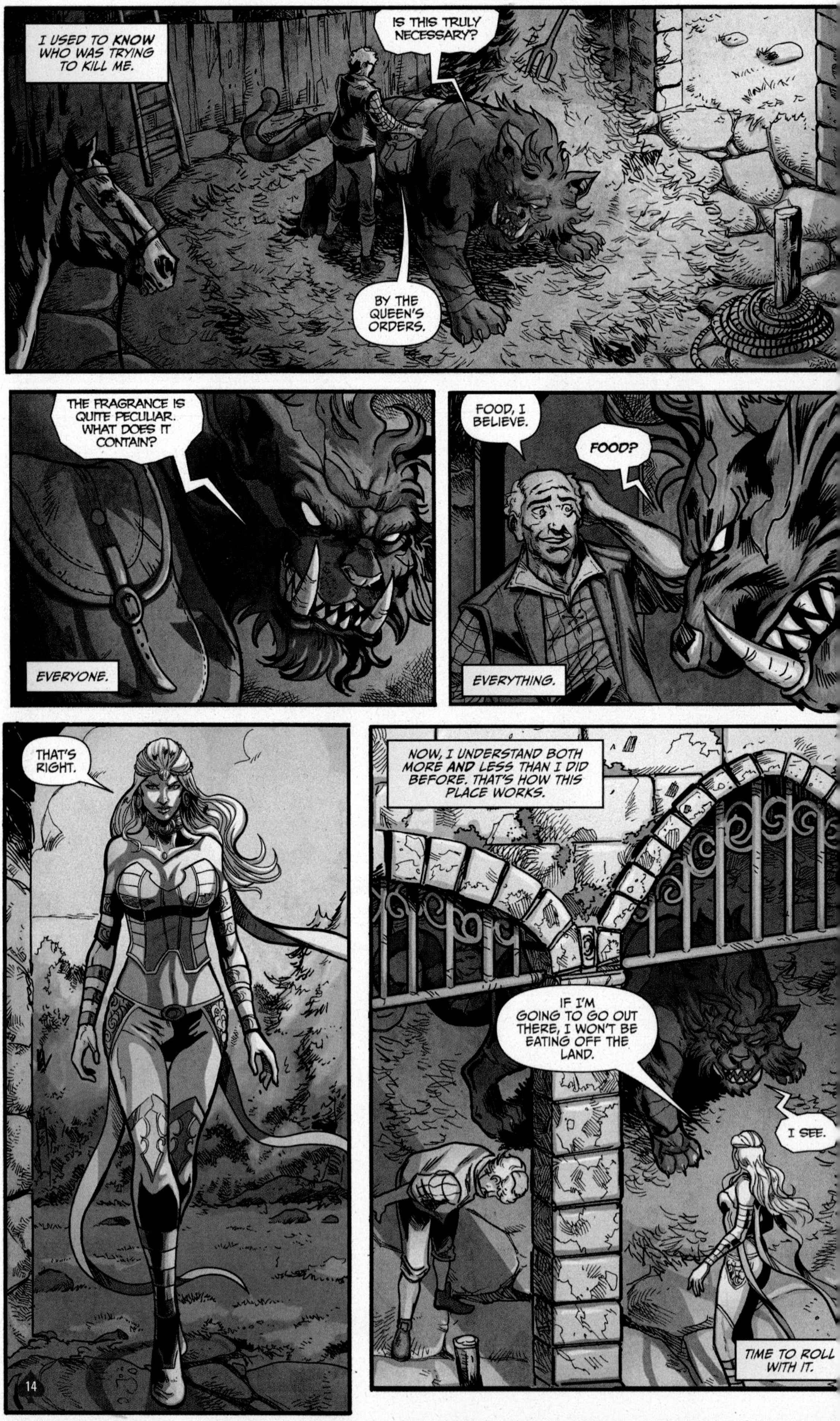

I USED TO KNOW WHO WAS TRYING TO KILL ME.
IS THIS TRULY NECESSARY?
BY THE QUEEN'S ORDERS.
THE FRAGRANCE IS QUITE PECULIAR. WHAT DOES IT CONTAIN?
EVERYONE.
FOOD, I BELIEVE.
FOOD?
EVERYTHING.
THAT'S RIGHT.
NOW, I UNDERSTAND BOTH MORE AND LESS THAN I DID BEFORE. THAT'S HOW THIS PLACE WORKS.
IF I'M GOING TO GO OUT THERE, I WON'T BE EATING OFF THE LAND.
I SEE.
TIME TO ROLL WITH IT.

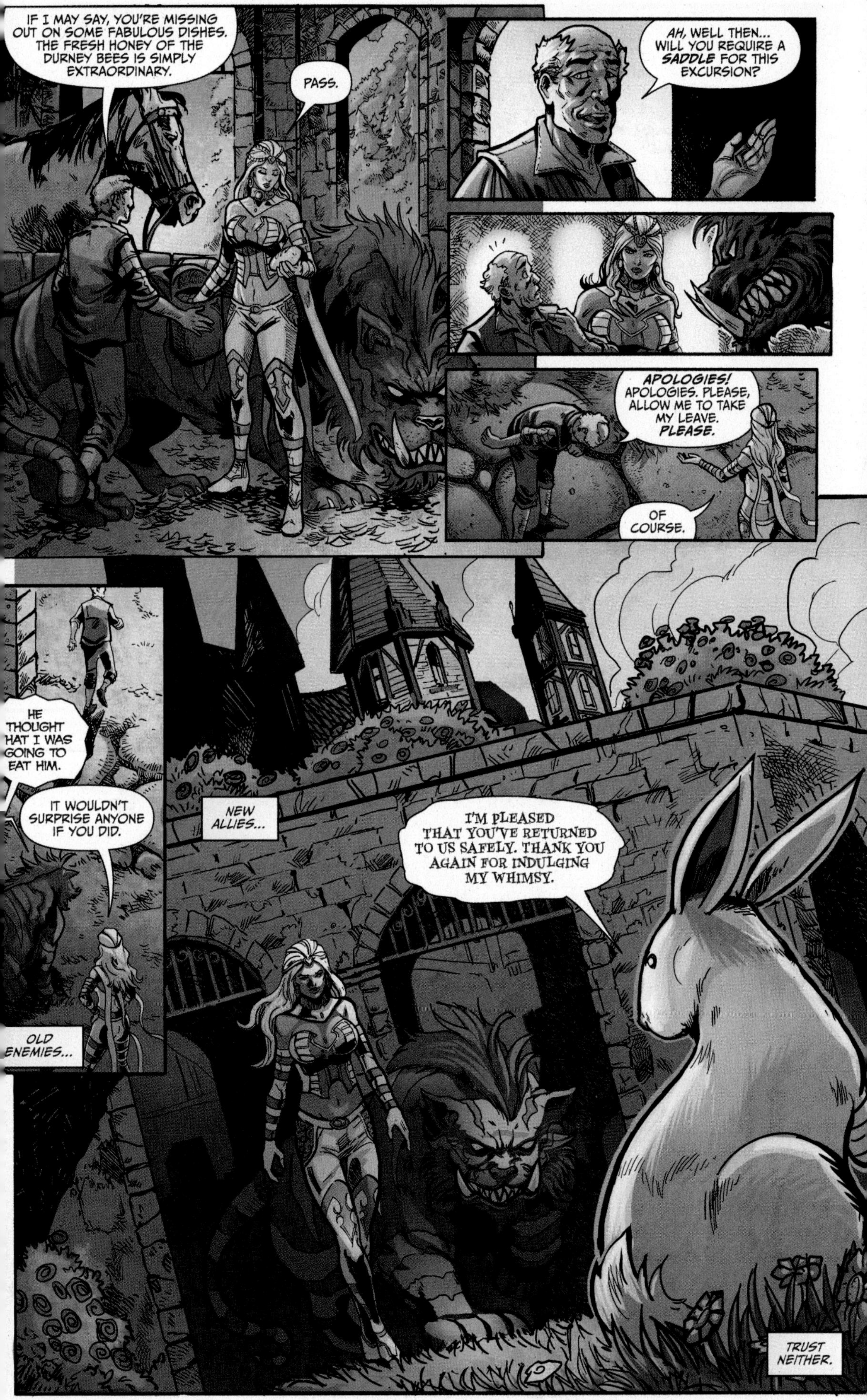
IF I MAY SAY, YOU'RE MISSING OUT ON SOME FABULOUS DISHES. THE FRESH HONEY OF THE DURNEY BEES IS SIMPLY EXTRAORDINARY.
PASS.
AH, WELL THEN... WILL YOU REQUIRE A SADDLE FOR THIS EXCURSION?
APOLOGIES! APOLOGIES. PLEASE, ALLOW ME TO TAKE MY LEAVE. PLEASE.
OF COURSE.
HE THOUGHT HAT I WAS GOING TO EAT HIM.
IT WOULDN'T SURPRISE ANYONE IF YOU DID.
OLD ENEMIES...
NEW ALLIES...
I'M PLEASED THAT YOU'VE RETURNED TO US SAFELY. THANK YOU AGAIN FOR INDULGING MY WHIMSY.
TRUST NEITHER.

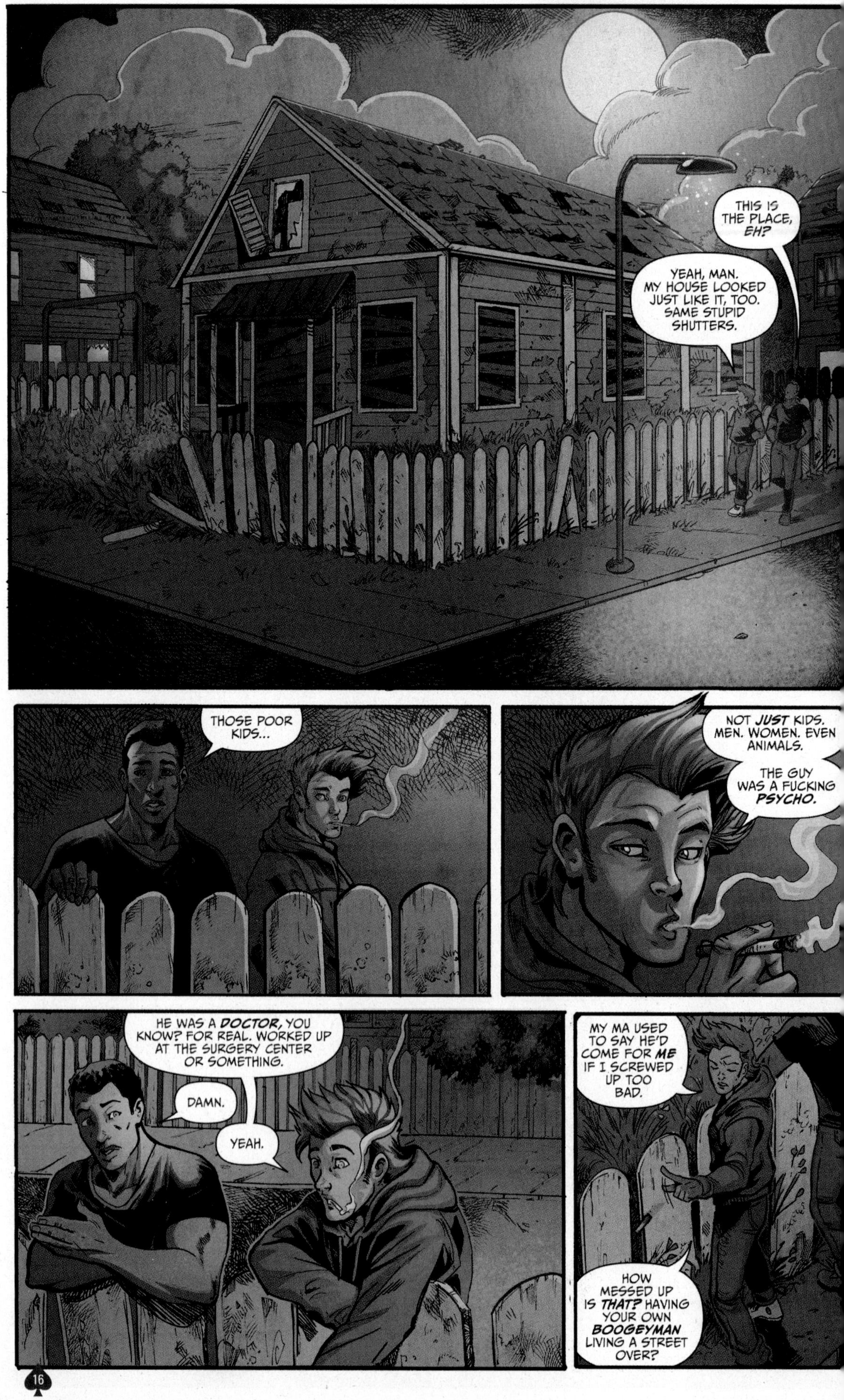

THIS IS THE PLACE, *EH?*
YEAH, MAN. MY HOUSE LOOKED JUST LIKE IT, TOO. SAME STUPID SHUTTERS.
THOSE POOR KIDS...
NOT *JUST* KIDS. MEN. WOMEN. EVEN ANIMALS.
THE GUY WAS A FUCKING ***PSYCHO.***
HE WAS A ***DOCTOR,*** YOU KNOW? FOR REAL. WORKED UP AT THE SURGERY CENTER OR SOMETHING.
DAMN.
YEAH.
MY MA USED TO SAY HE'D COME FOR ***ME*** IF I SCREWED UP TOO BAD.
HOW MESSED UP IS ***THAT?*** HAVING YOUR OWN ***BOOGEYMAN*** LIVING A STREET OVER?

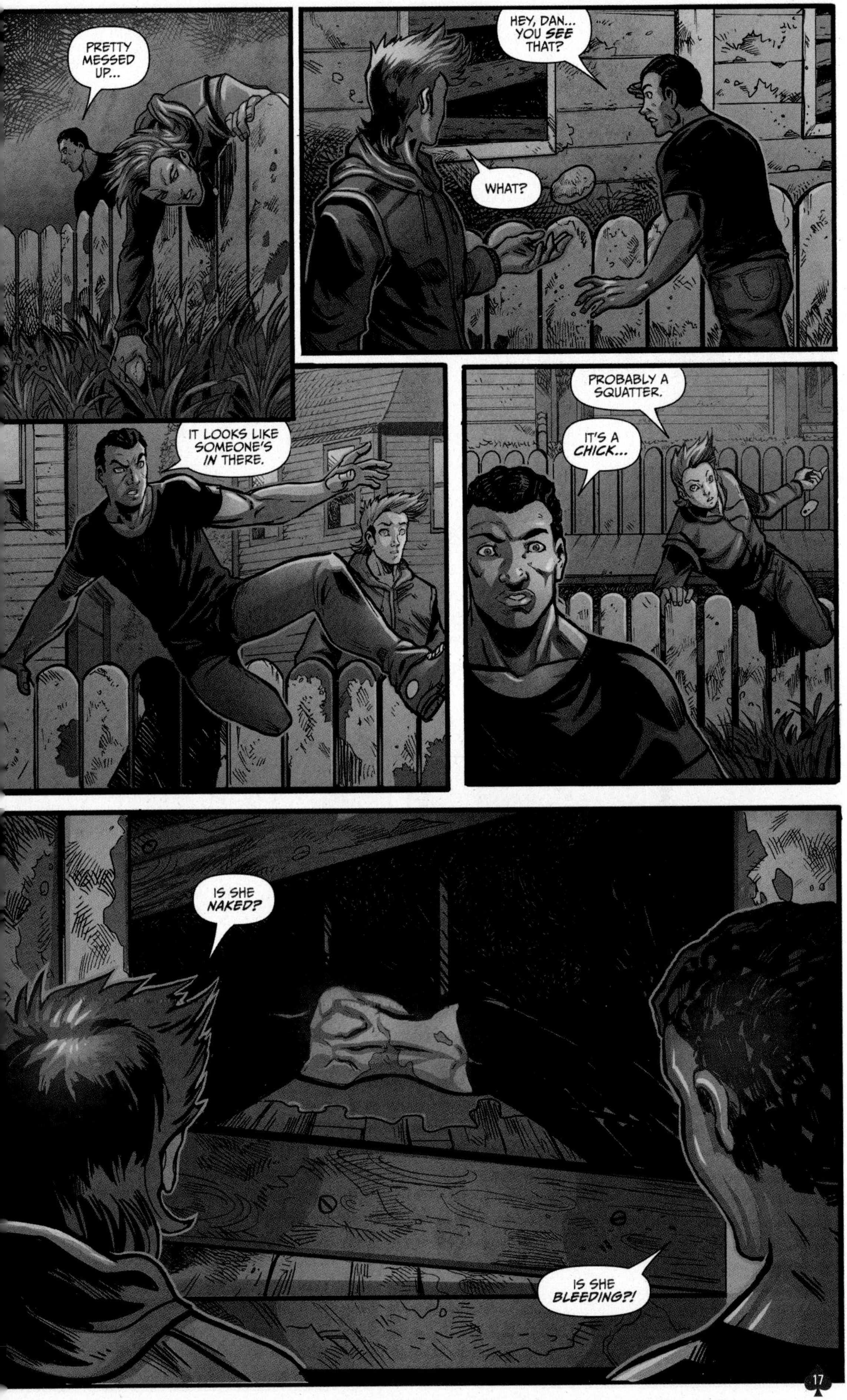
PRETTY MESSED UP...
HEY, DAN... YOU SEE THAT?
WHAT?
IT LOOKS LIKE SOMEONE'S IN THERE.
PROBABLY A SQUATTER.
IT'S A CHICK...
IS SHE NAKED?
IS SHE BLEEDING?!

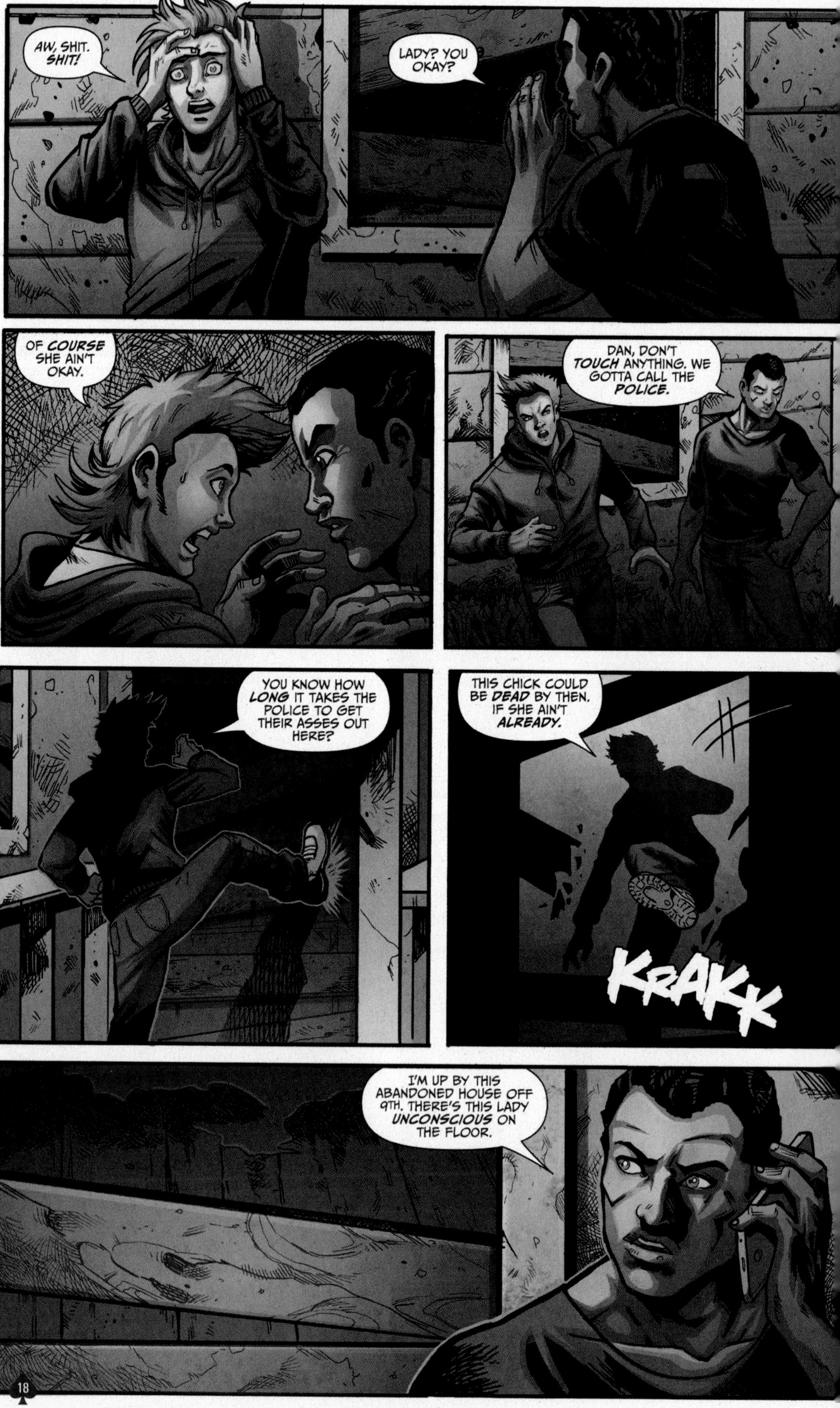
AW, SHIT. SHIT!
LADY? YOU OKAY?
OF COURSE SHE AIN'T OKAY.
DAN, DON'T TOUCH ANYTHING. WE GOTTA CALL THE POLICE.
YOU KNOW HOW LONG IT TAKES THE POLICE TO GET THEIR ASSES OUT HERE?
THIS CHICK COULD BE DEAD BY THEN. IF SHE AIN'T ALREADY.
KRAKK
I'M UP BY THIS ABANDONED HOUSE OFF 9TH. THERE'S THIS LADY UNCONSCIOUS ON THE FLOOR.

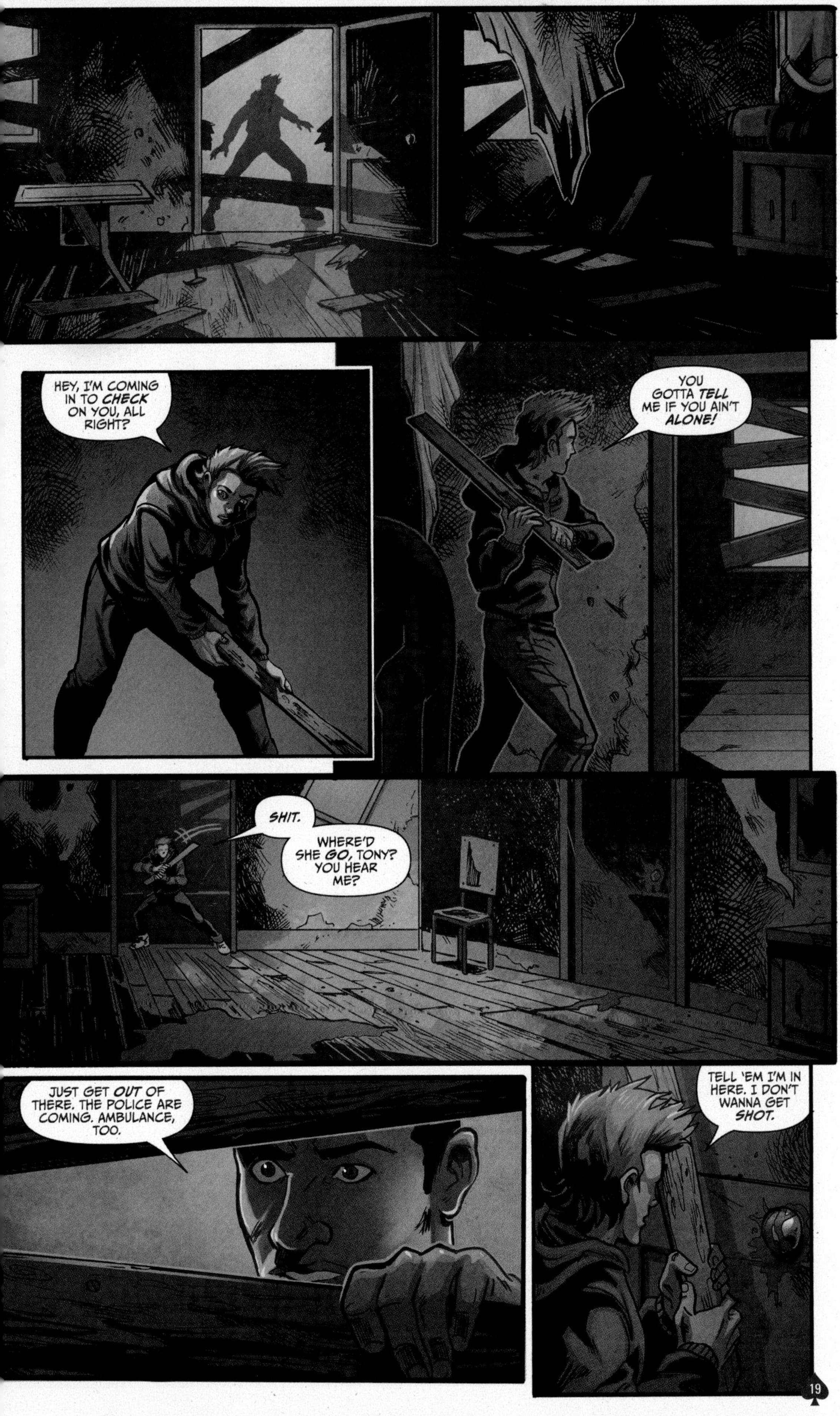
HEY, I'M COMING IN TO CHECK ON YOU, ALL RIGHT?
YOU GOTTA TELL ME IF YOU AIN'T ALONE!
SHIT.
WHERE'D SHE GO, TONY? YOU HEAR ME?
JUST GET OUT OF THERE. THE POLICE ARE COMING. AMBULANCE, TOO.
TELL 'EM I'M IN HERE. I DON'T WANNA GET SHOT.

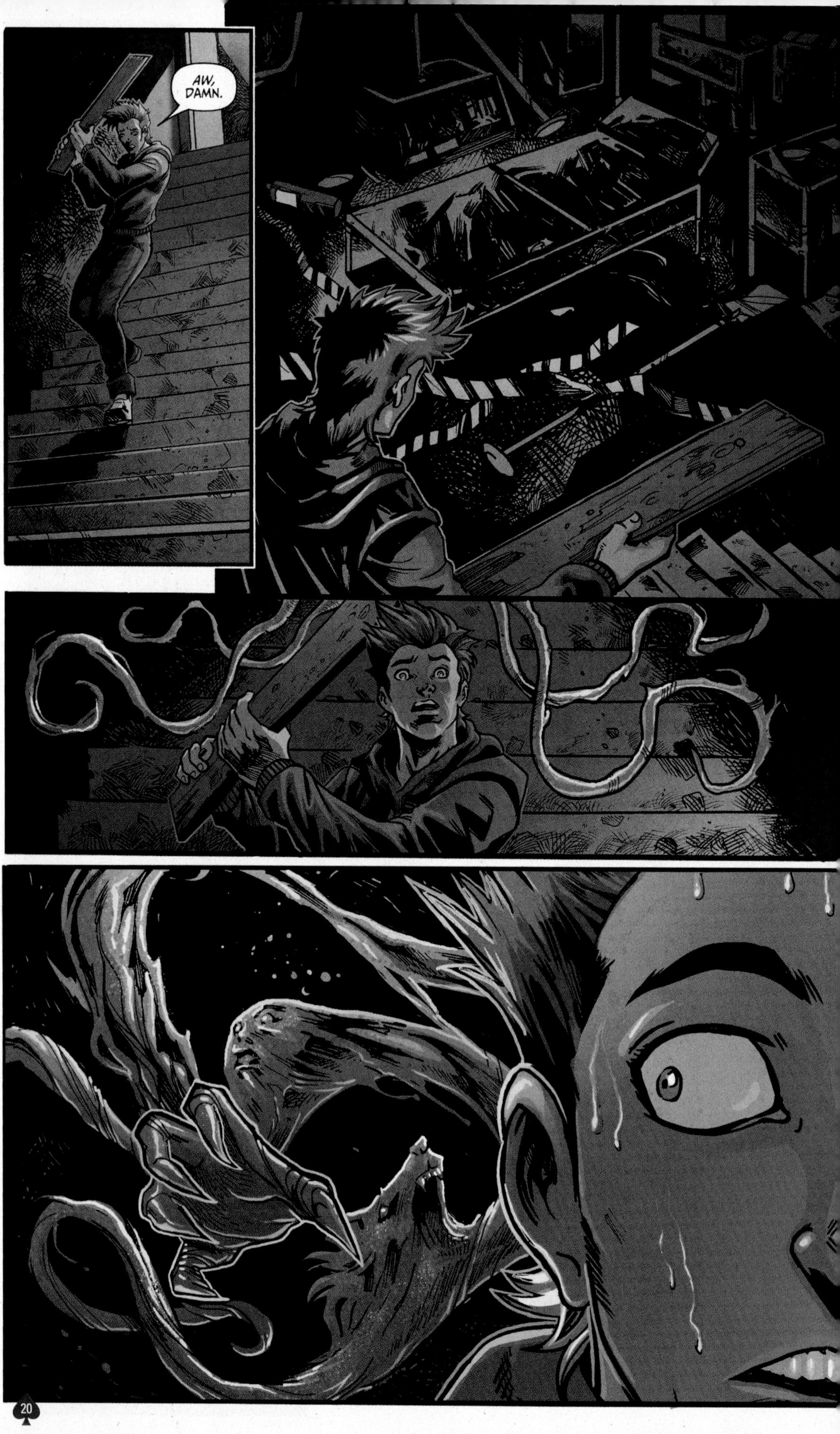
AW, DAMN.

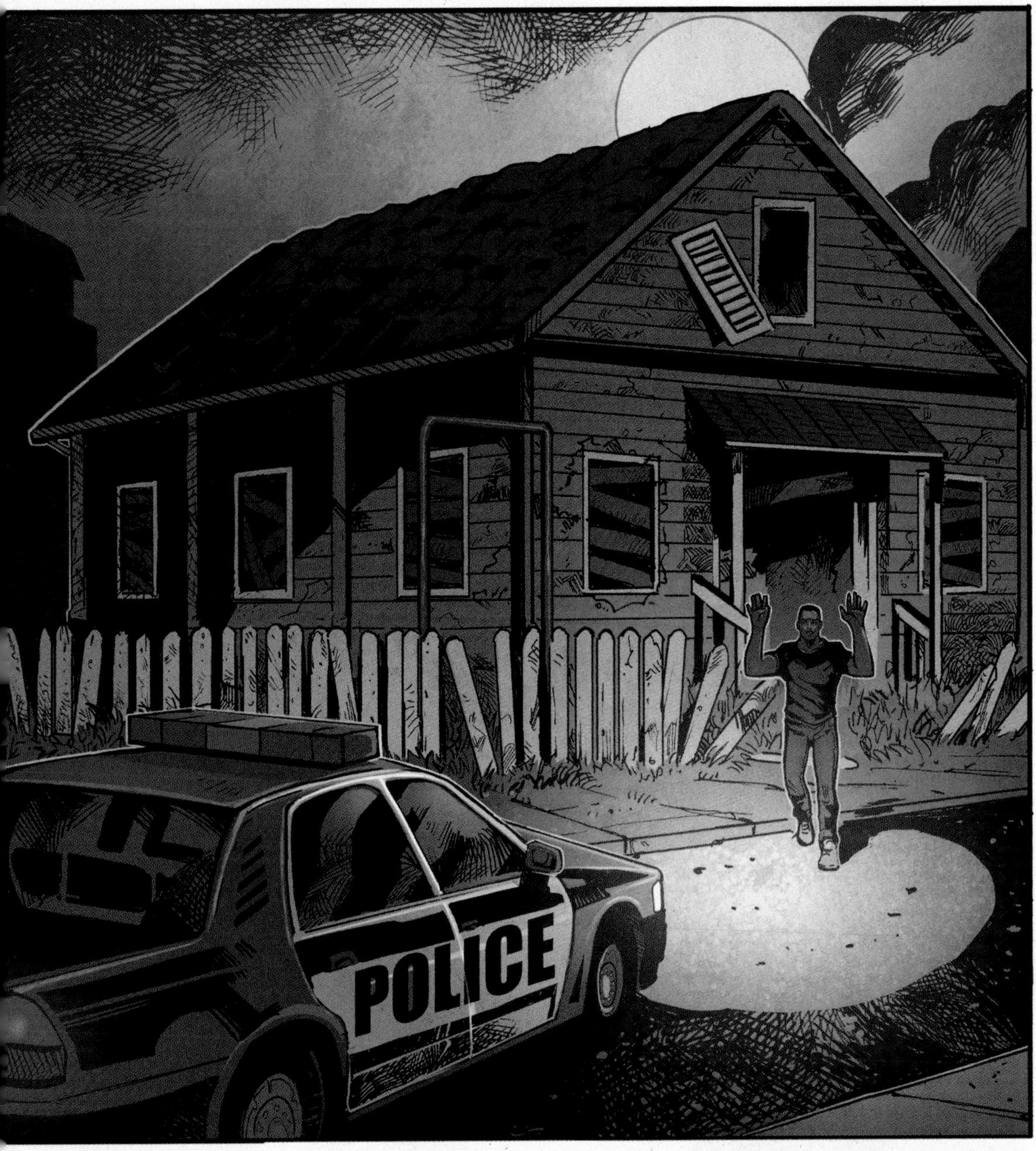
POLICE

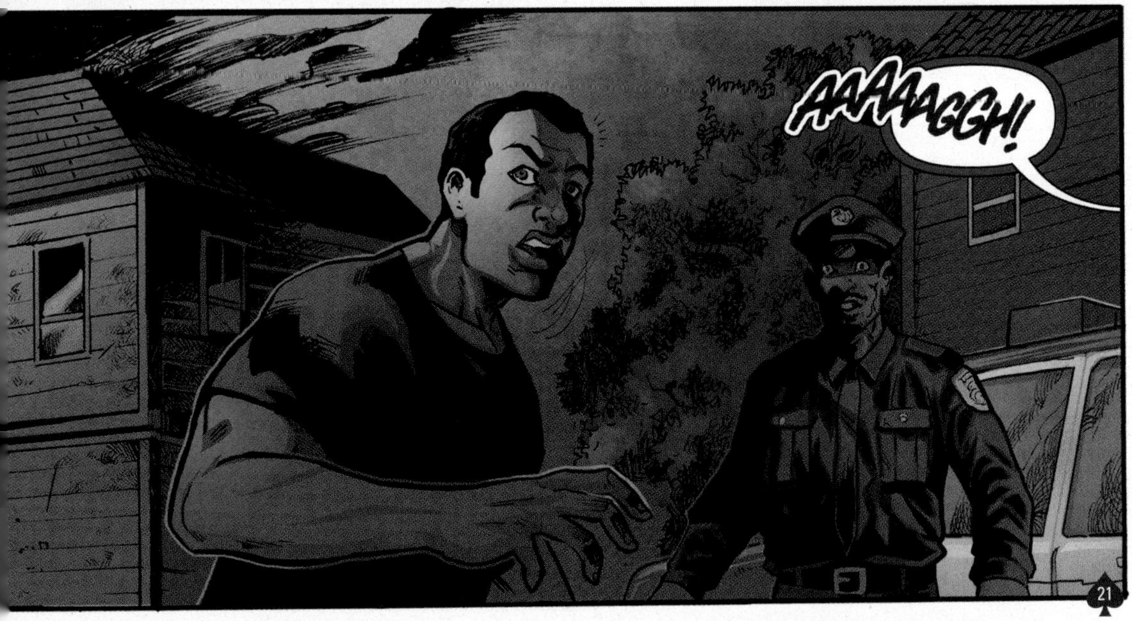
AAAAAGGH!

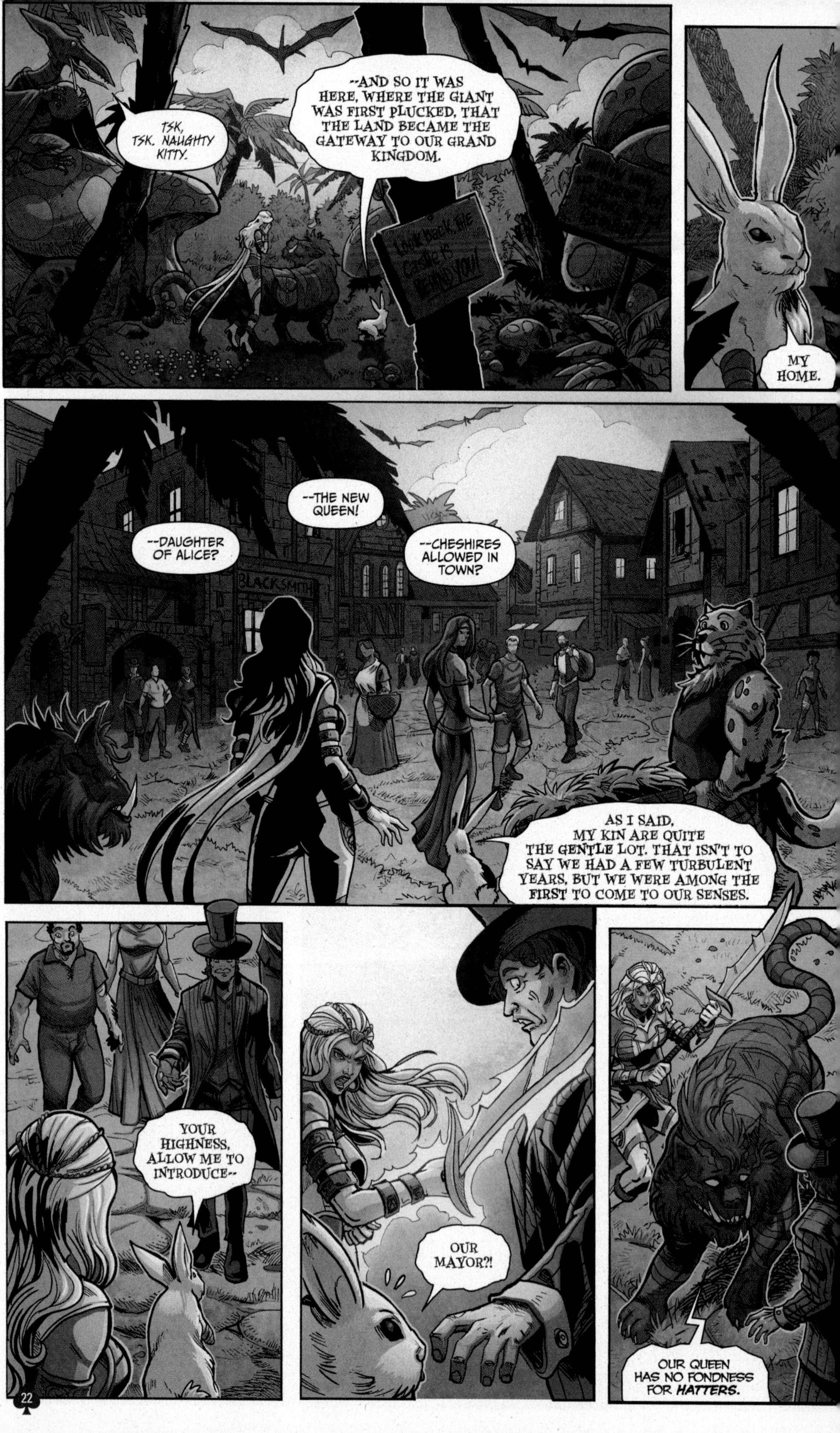
TSK, TSK. NAUGHTY KITTY.
--AND SO IT WAS HERE, WHERE THE GIANT WAS FIRST PLUCKED, THAT THE LAND BECAME THE GATEWAY TO OUR GRAND KINGDOM.
Look back, the Castle is BEHIND YOU!
MY HOME.
--DAUGHTER OF ALICE?
--THE NEW QUEEN!
--CHESHIRES ALLOWED IN TOWN?
BLACKSMITH
AS I SAID, MY KIN ARE QUITE THE GENTLE LOT. THAT ISN'T TO SAY WE HAD A FEW TURBULENT YEARS, BUT WE WERE AMONG THE FIRST TO COME TO OUR SENSES.
YOUR HIGHNESS, ALLOW ME TO INTRODUCE--
OUR MAYOR?!
OUR QUEEN HAS NO FONDNESS FOR *HATTERS*.

WITH GOOD REASON, YOUR MAJESTY. I ASSURE YOU, WORD OF YOUR DEEDS HAS SPREAD FAR AND NEAR.

AND NEAR AND FAR. CONGRATULATIONS ON YOUR GREAT VICTORY.

AND CONGRATULATIONS TO YOU AS WELL, RABBIT. THE MANTLE SUITS YOU.

I... LOOK FORWARD TO SEEING YOUR VILLAGE, MAYOR.

ENJOY! WE HAVE *MUCH* TO OFFER.

WELL, THAT WAS EXCITING.

PERHAPS, GIVEN THAT YOU CAN MANIFEST YOUR ARSENAL WITH A MERE THOUGHT, YOU COULD PUT THE WEAPON AWAY?

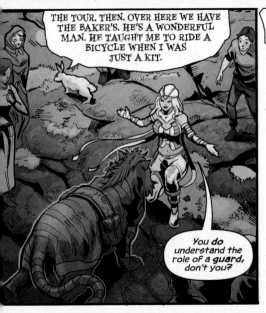

THE TOUR, THEN. OVER HERE WE HAVE THE BAKER'S. HE'S A WONDERFUL MAN. HE TAUGHT ME TO RIDE A BICYCLE WHEN I WAS JUST A KIT.

You *do* understand the role of a *guard*, don't you?

OF COURSE, BUT NEVER WERE YOU IN *DANGER*. ONE DAY YOU *WILL* BE, AND I WILL OFFER MY PROTECTION. OR I WILL LET YOU KILL FOR YOURSELF, SHOULD YOU DESIRE.

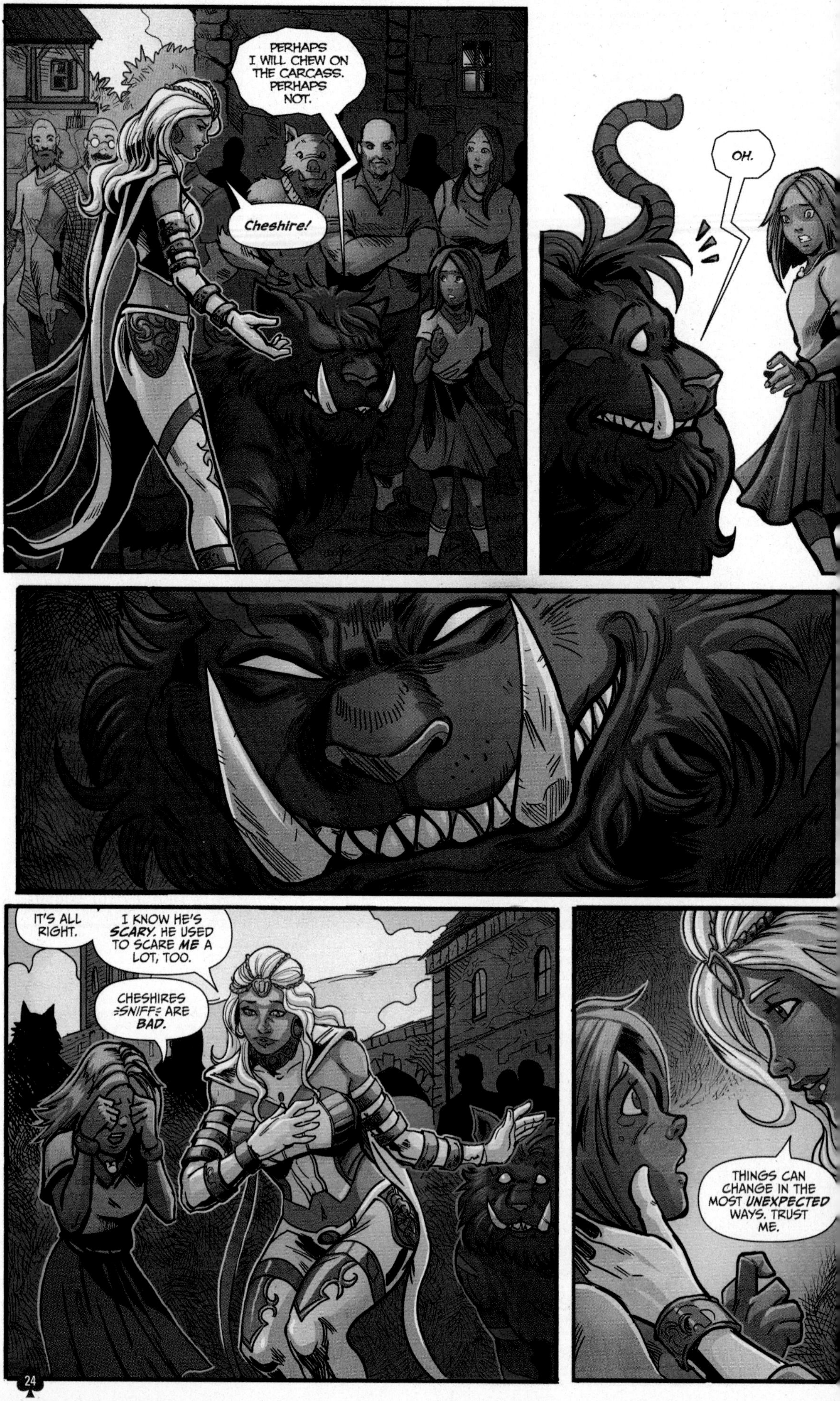
PERHAPS I WILL CHEW ON THE CARCASS. PERHAPS NOT.
Cheshire!
OH.
IT'S ALL RIGHT.
I KNOW HE'S SCARY. HE USED TO SCARE ME A LOT, TOO.
CHESHIRES =SNIFF= ARE BAD.
THINGS CAN CHANGE IN THE MOST UNEXPECTED WAYS. TRUST ME.

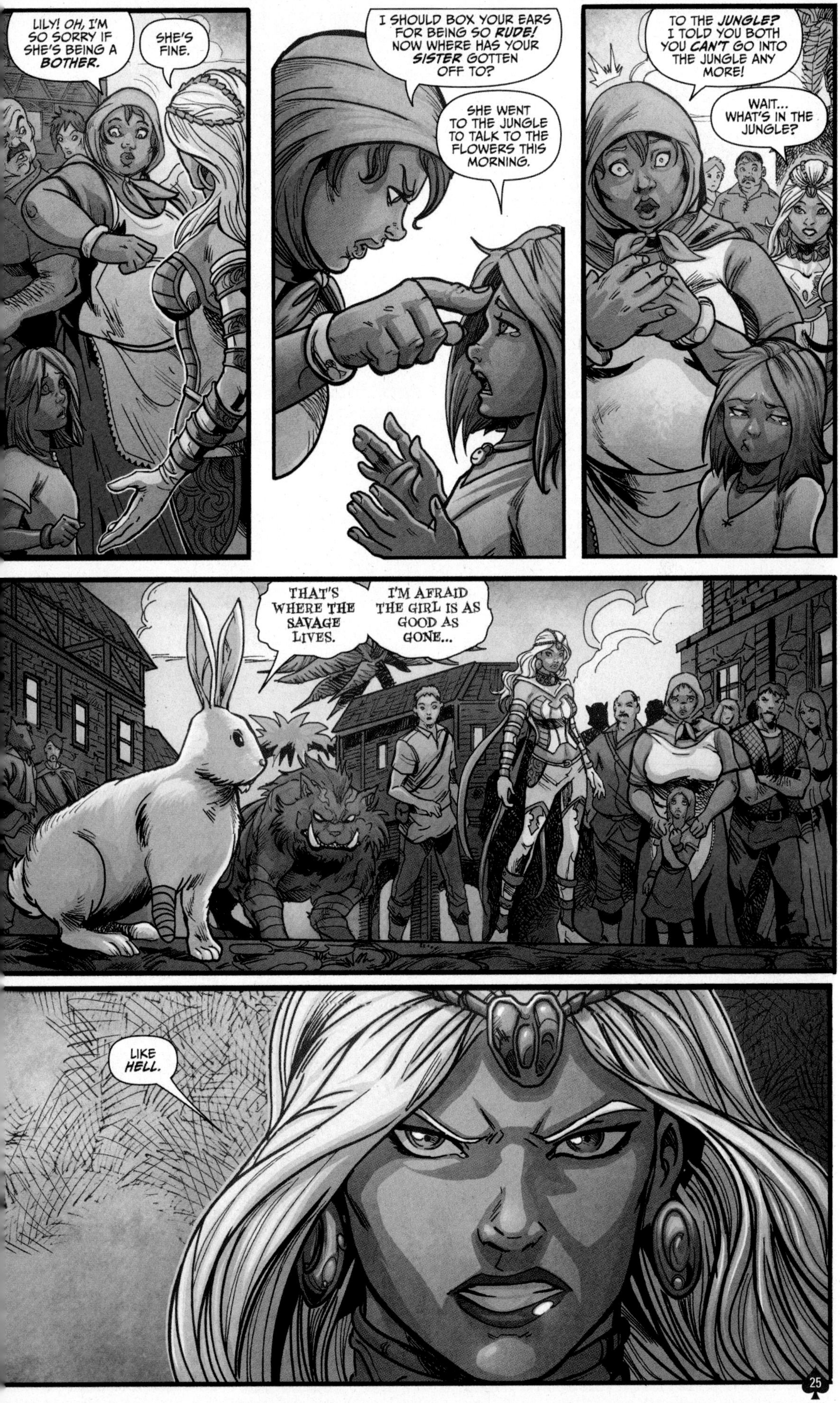
LILY! OH, I'M SO SORRY IF SHE'S BEING A BOTHER.
SHE'S FINE.
I SHOULD BOX YOUR EARS FOR BEING SO RUDE! NOW WHERE HAS YOUR SISTER GOTTEN OFF TO?
SHE WENT TO THE JUNGLE TO TALK TO THE FLOWERS THIS MORNING.
TO THE JUNGLE? I TOLD YOU BOTH YOU CAN'T GO INTO THE JUNGLE ANY MORE!
WAIT... WHAT'S IN THE JUNGLE?
THAT'S WHERE THE SAVAGE LIVES.
I'M AFRAID THE GIRL IS AS GOOD AS GONE...
LIKE HELL.

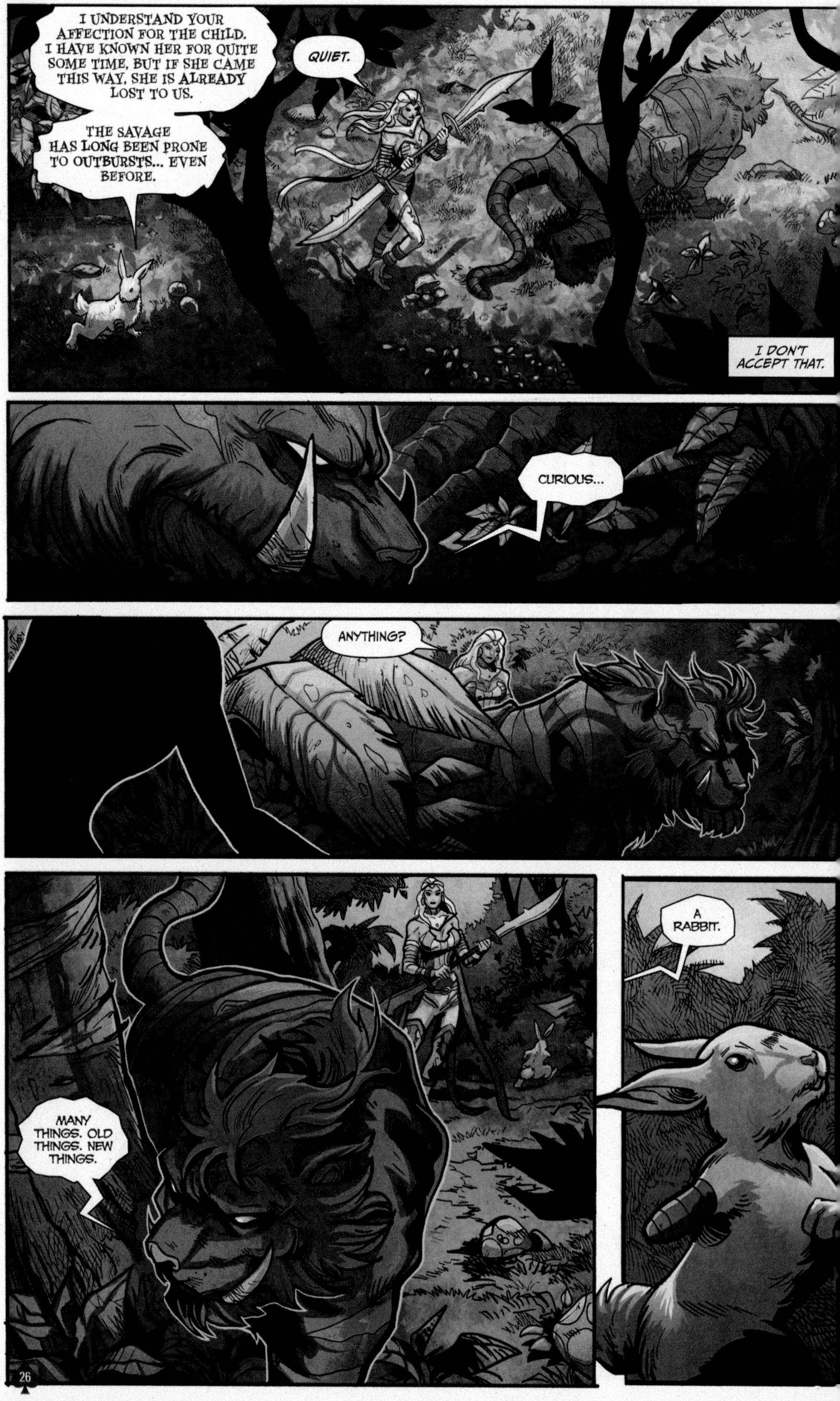
I UNDERSTAND YOUR AFFECTION FOR THE CHILD. I HAVE KNOWN HER FOR QUITE SOME TIME, BUT IF SHE CAME THIS WAY, SHE IS ALREADY LOST TO US.
THE SAVAGE HAS LONG BEEN PRONE TO OUTBURSTS... EVEN BEFORE.
QUIET.
I DON'T ACCEPT THAT.
CURIOUS...
ANYTHING?
MANY THINGS. OLD THINGS. NEW THINGS.
A RABBIT.

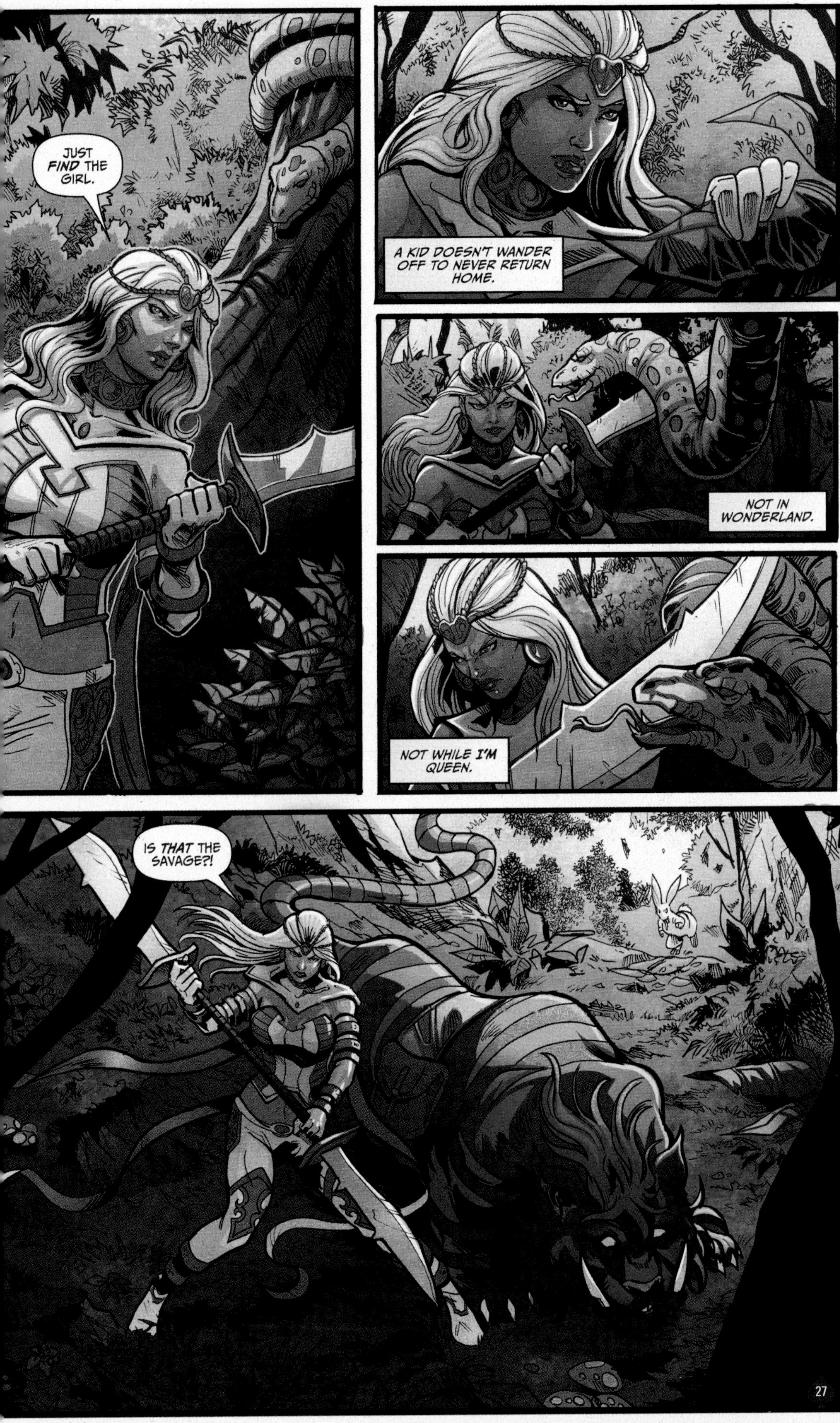
JUST FIND THE GIRL.
A KID DOESN'T WANDER OFF TO NEVER RETURN HOME.
NOT IN WONDERLAND.
NOT WHILE I'M QUEEN.
IS THAT THE SAVAGE?!

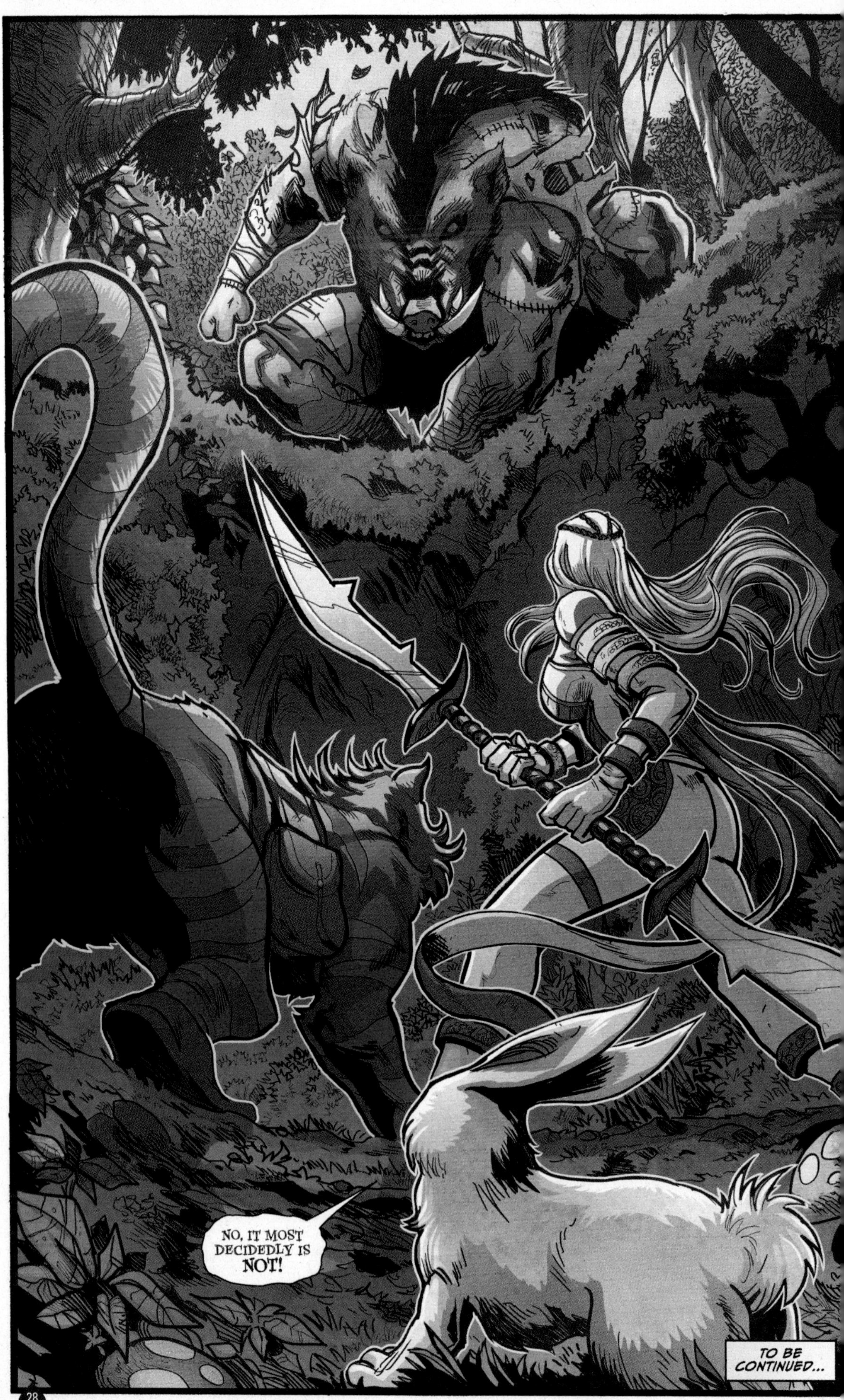
NO, IT MOST DECIDEDLY IS NOT!
TO BE CONTINUED...

END CHAPTER

RENAISSANCE

PART TWO

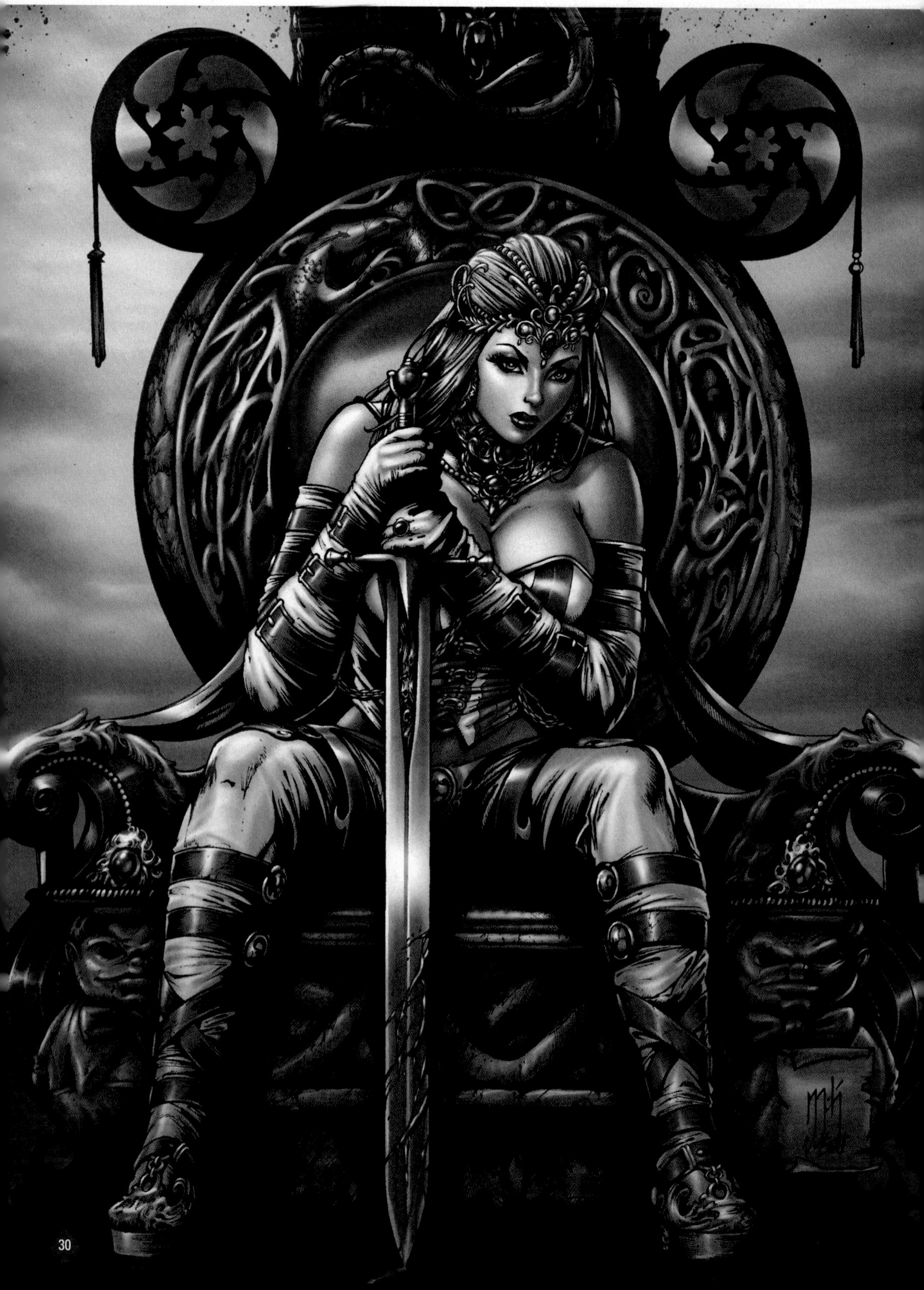

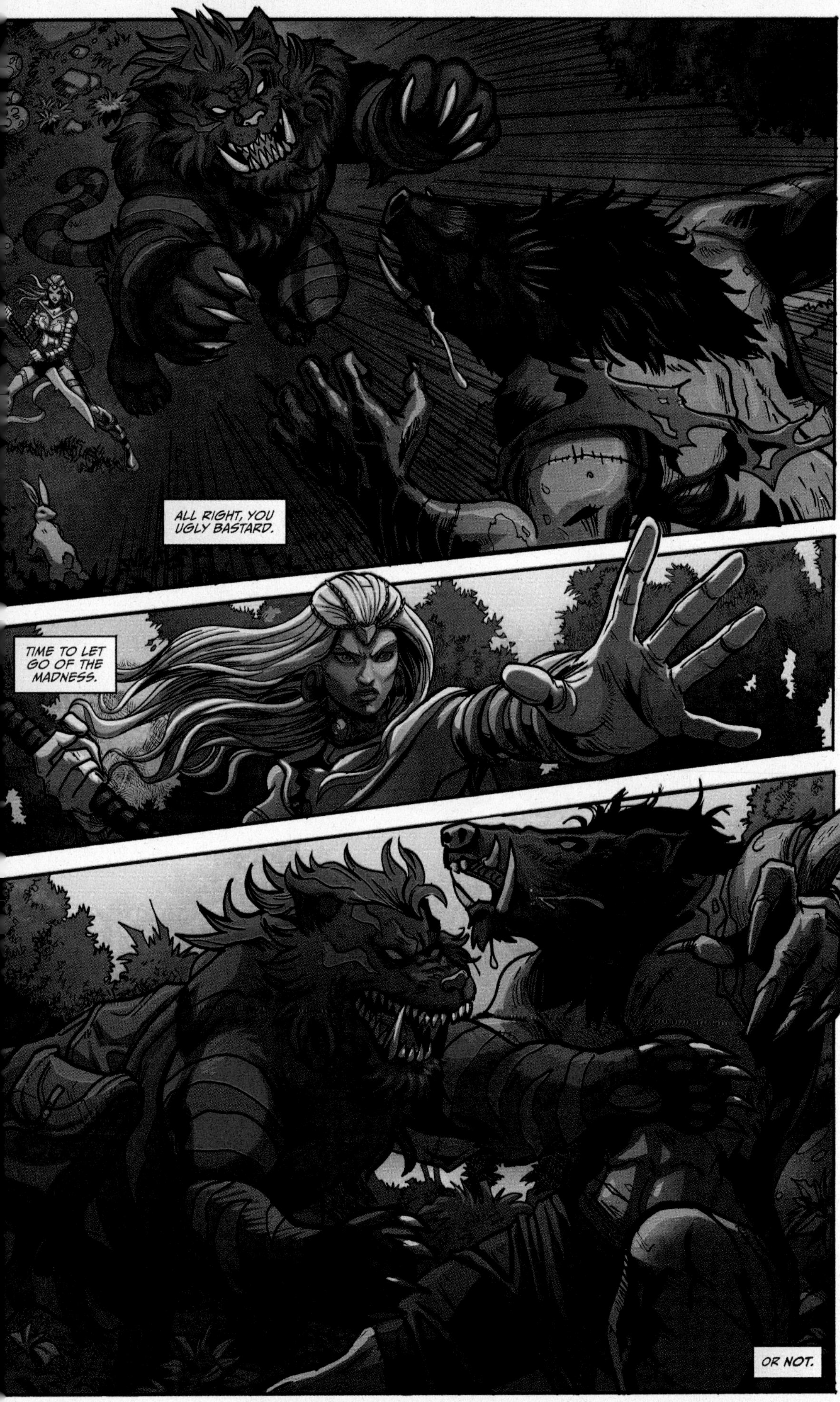
ALL RIGHT, YOU UGLY BASTARD.
TIME TO LET GO OF THE MADNESS.
OR NOT.

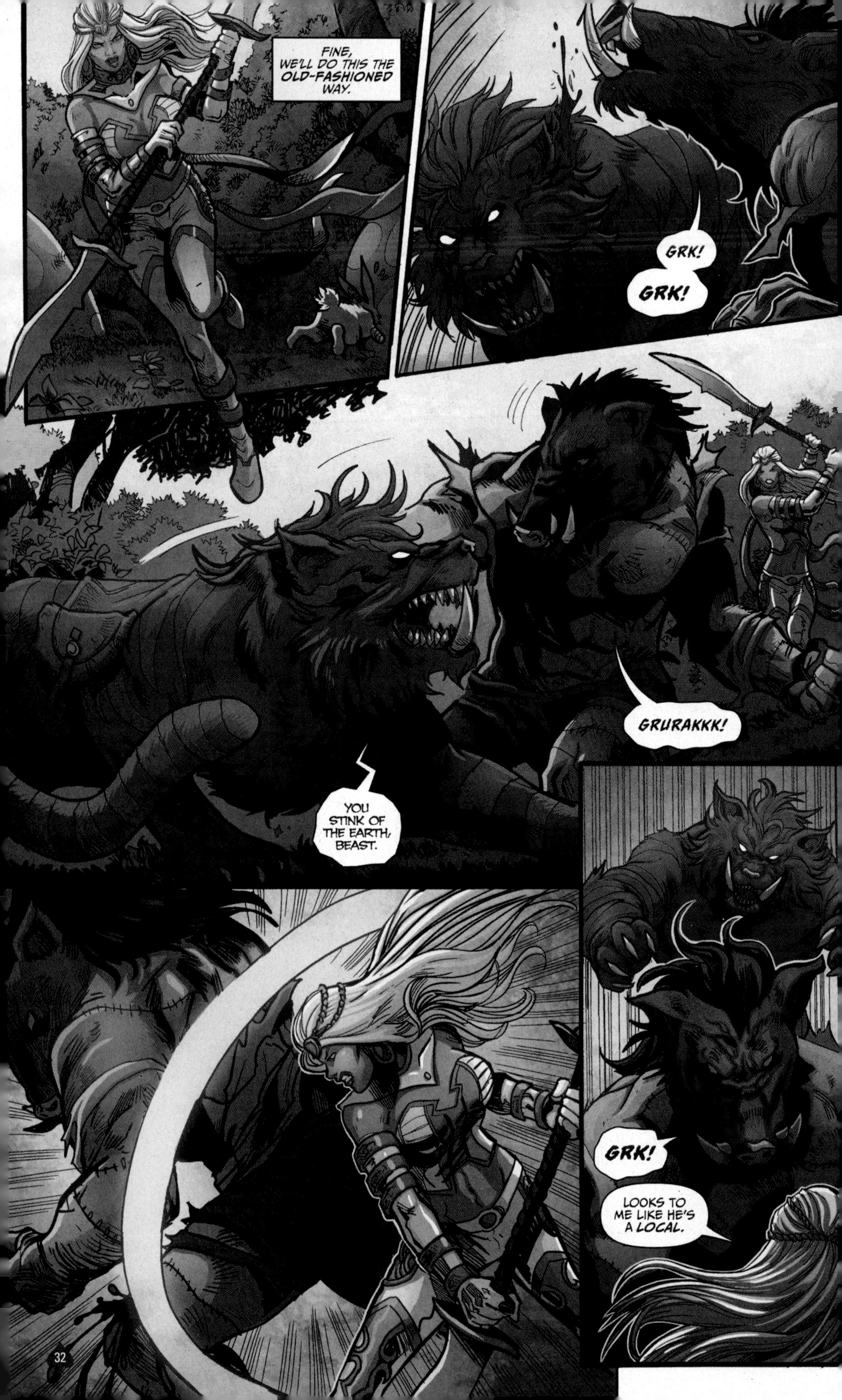
FINE, WE'LL DO THIS THE OLD-FASHIONED WAY.
GRK!
GRK!
GRURAKKK!
YOU STINK OF THE EARTH, BEAST.
GRK!
LOOKS TO ME LIKE HE'S A LOCAL.

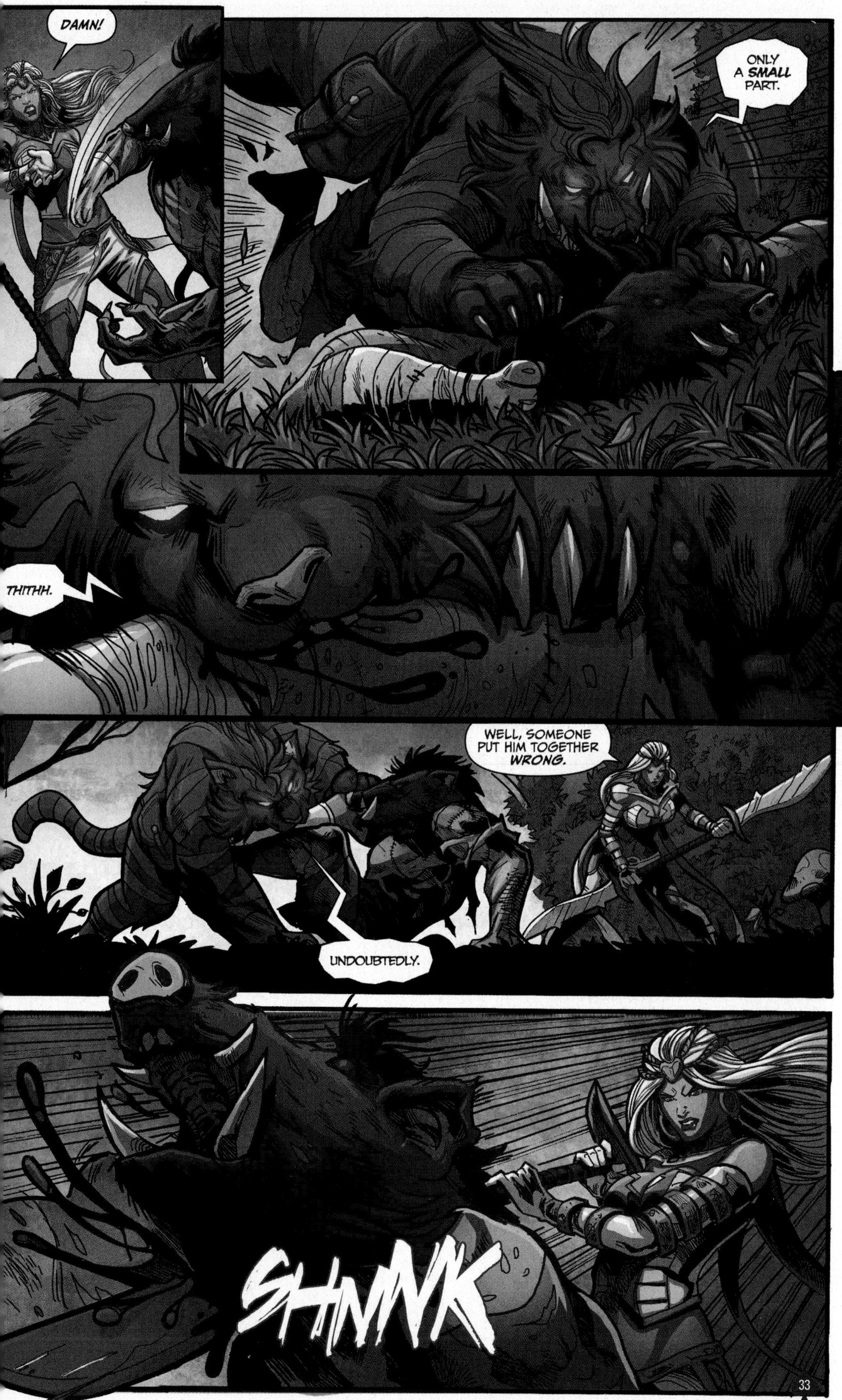
DAMN!
ONLY A SMALL PART.
THITHH.
WELL, SOMEONE PUT HIM TOGETHER WRONG.
UNDOUBTEDLY.
SHNNK

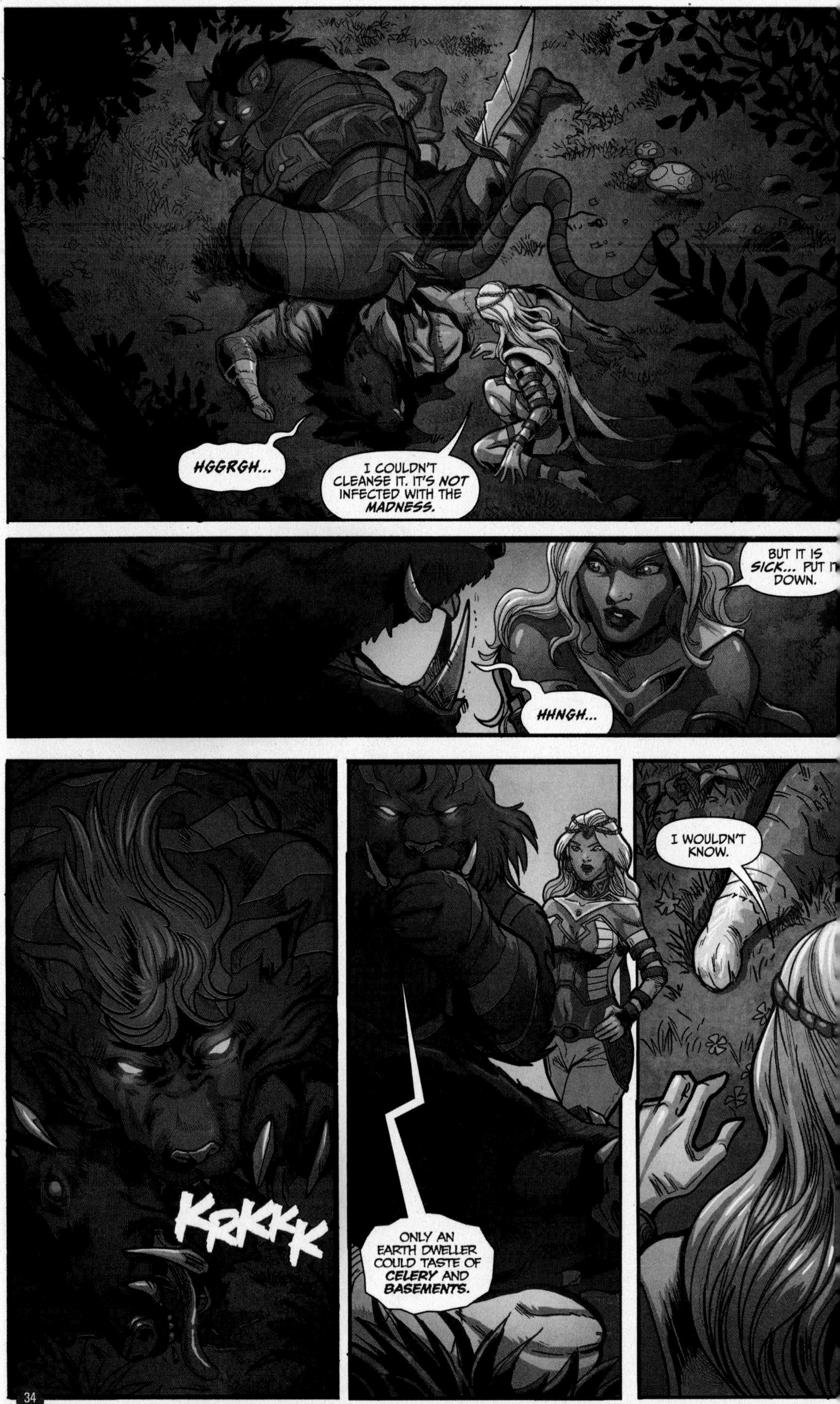
HGGRGH...
I COULDN'T CLEANSE IT. IT'S *NOT* INFECTED WITH THE *MADNESS.*
BUT IT IS *SICK...* PUT IT DOWN.
HHNGH...
KRKKK
ONLY AN EARTH DWELLER COULD TASTE OF *CELERY* AND *BASEMENTS.*
I WOULDN'T KNOW.

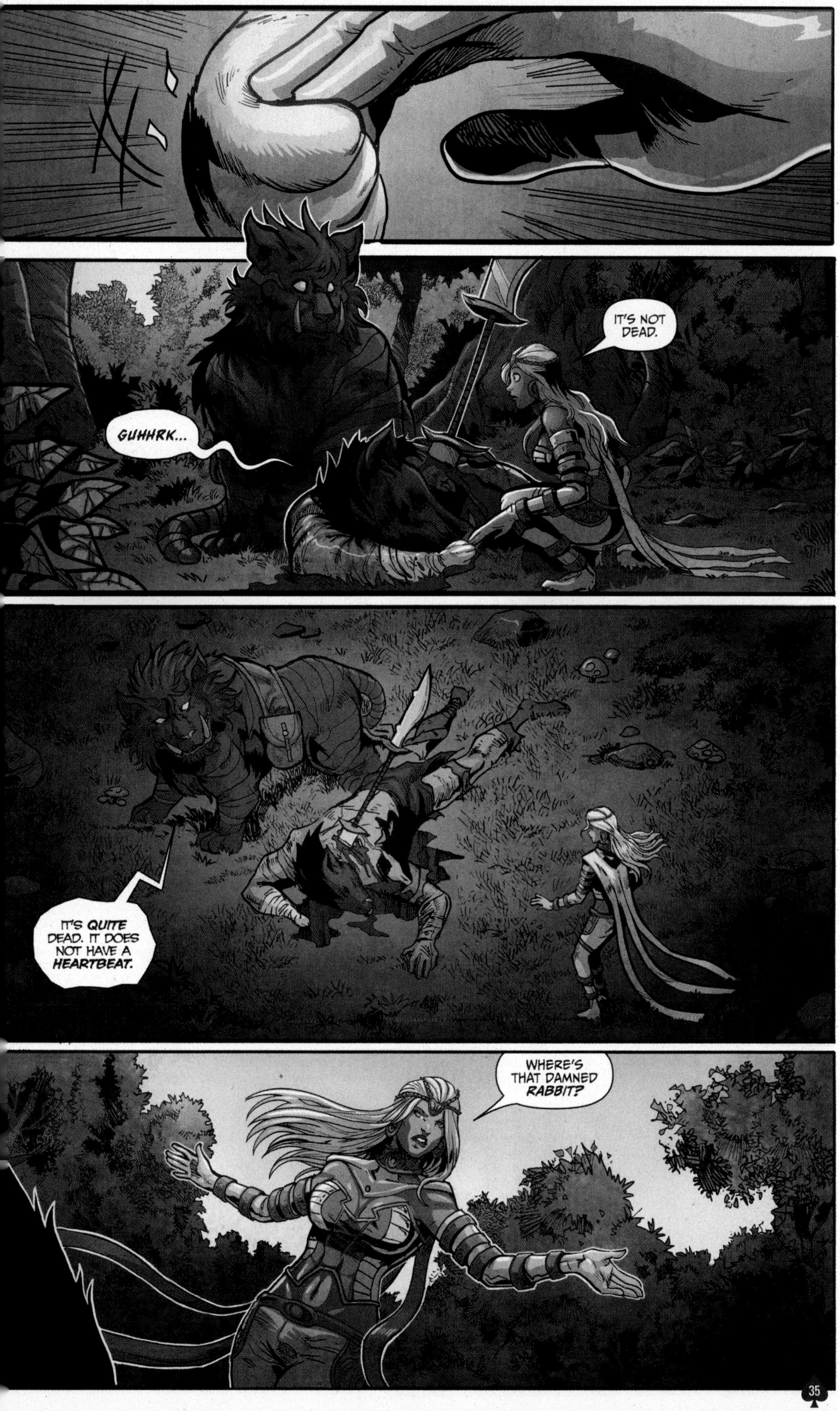
IT'S NOT DEAD.
GUHHRK...
IT'S QUITE DEAD. IT DOES NOT HAVE A HEARTBEAT.
WHERE'S THAT DAMNED RABBIT?

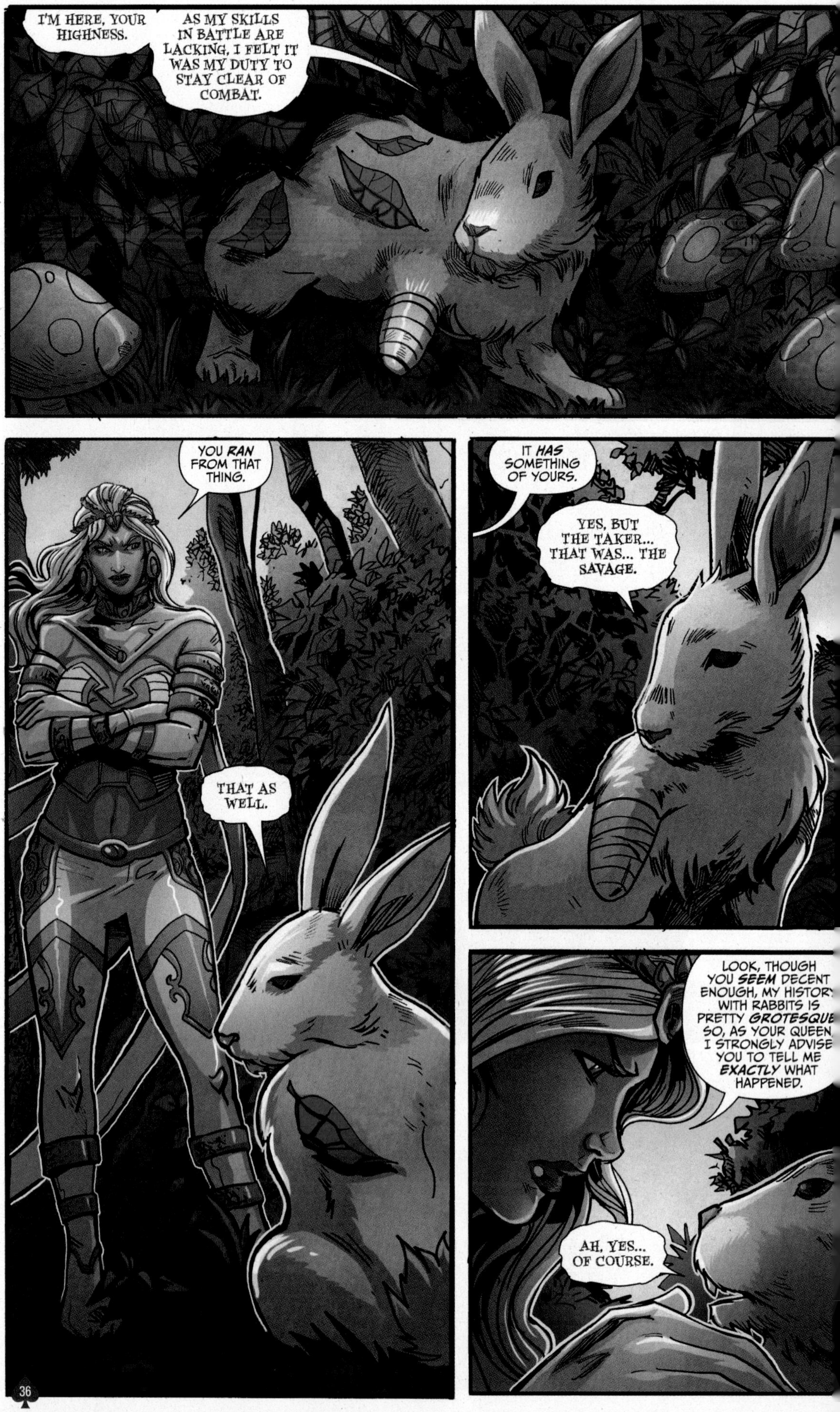
I'M HERE, YOUR HIGHNESS.
AS MY SKILLS IN BATTLE ARE LACKING, I FELT IT WAS MY DUTY TO STAY CLEAR OF COMBAT.
YOU RAN FROM THAT THING.
THAT AS WELL.
IT HAS SOMETHING OF YOURS.
YES, BUT THE TAKER... THAT WAS... THE SAVAGE.
LOOK, THOUGH YOU SEEM DECENT ENOUGH, MY HISTORY WITH RABBITS IS PRETTY GROTESQUE SO, AS YOUR QUEEN I STRONGLY ADVISE YOU TO TELL ME EXACTLY WHAT HAPPENED.
AH, YES... OF COURSE.

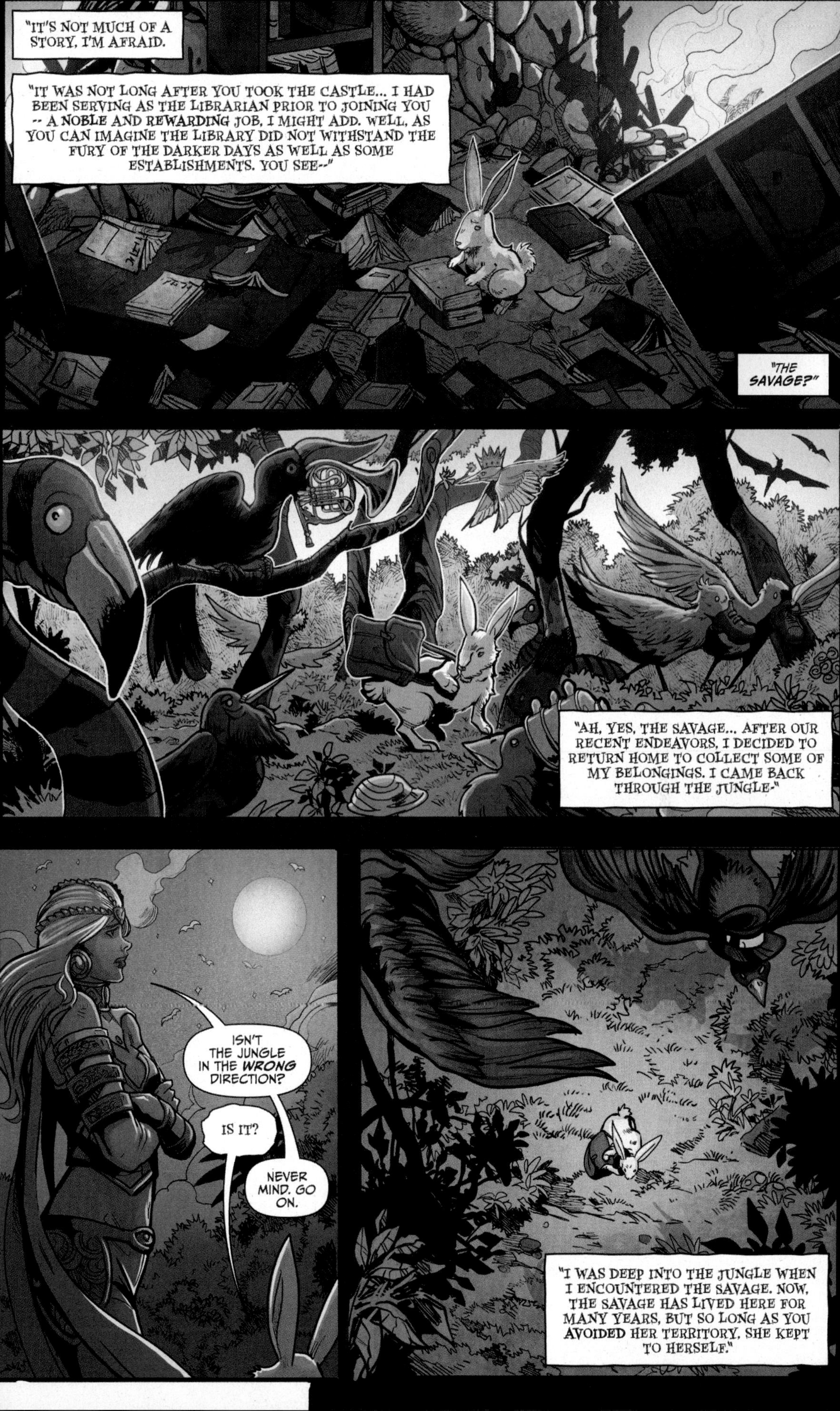
"IT'S NOT MUCH OF A STORY, I'M AFRAID.
"IT WAS NOT LONG AFTER YOU TOOK THE CASTLE... I HAD BEEN SERVING AS THE LIBRARIAN PRIOR TO JOINING YOU -- A NOBLE AND REWARDING JOB, I MIGHT ADD. WELL, AS YOU CAN IMAGINE THE LIBRARY DID NOT WITHSTAND THE FURY OF THE DARKER DAYS AS WELL AS SOME ESTABLISHMENTS. YOU SEE--"
"THE SAVAGE?"
"AH, YES, THE SAVAGE... AFTER OUR RECENT ENDEAVORS, I DECIDED TO RETURN HOME TO COLLECT SOME OF MY BELONGINGS. I CAME BACK THROUGH THE JUNGLE-"
ISN'T THE JUNGLE IN THE WRONG DIRECTION?
IS IT?
NEVER MIND. GO ON.
"I WAS DEEP INTO THE JUNGLE WHEN I ENCOUNTERED THE SAVAGE. NOW, THE SAVAGE HAS LIVED HERE FOR MANY YEARS, BUT SO LONG AS YOU AVOIDED HER TERRITORY, SHE KEPT TO HERSELF."

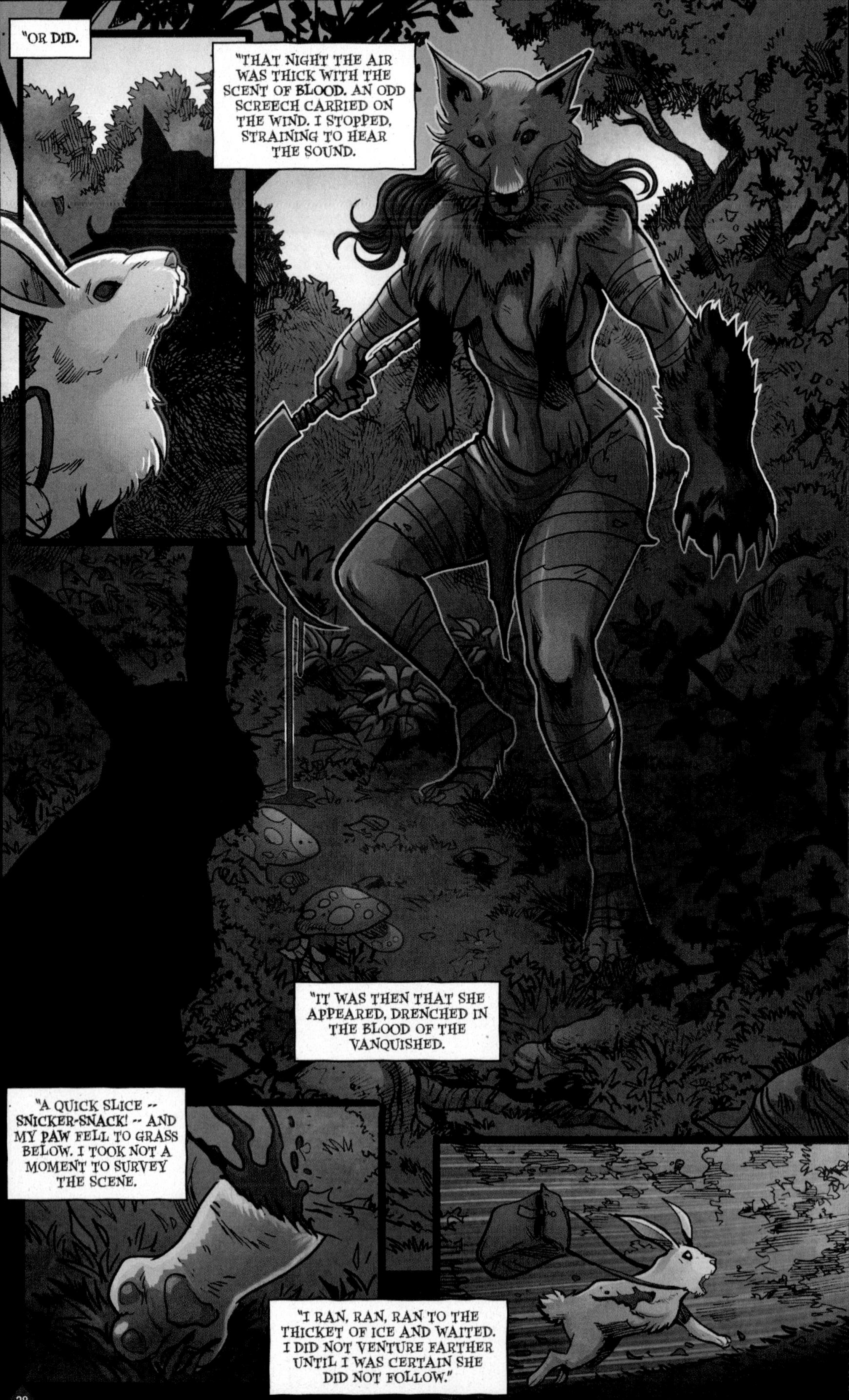
"OR DID.
"THAT NIGHT THE AIR WAS THICK WITH THE SCENT OF BLOOD. AN ODD SCREECH CARRIED ON THE WIND. I STOPPED, STRAINING TO HEAR THE SOUND.
"IT WAS THEN THAT SHE APPEARED, DRENCHED IN THE BLOOD OF THE VANQUISHED.
"A QUICK SLICE -- SNICKER-SNACK! -- AND MY PAW FELL TO GRASS BELOW. I TOOK NOT A MOMENT TO SURVEY THE SCENE.
"I RAN, RAN, RAN TO THE THICKET OF ICE AND WAITED. I DID NOT VENTURE FARTHER UNTIL I WAS CERTAIN SHE DID NOT FOLLOW."

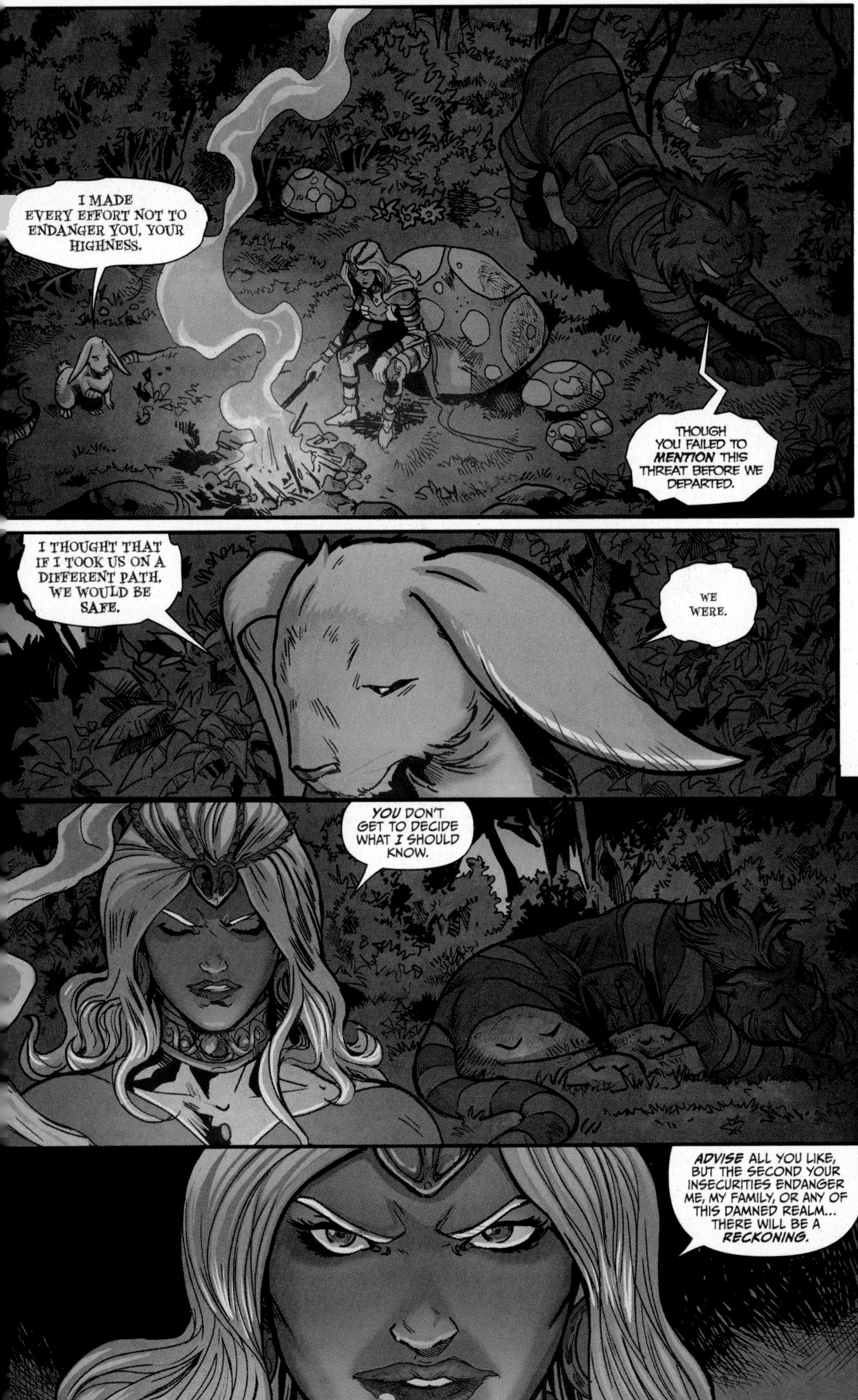
I MADE EVERY EFFORT NOT TO ENDANGER YOU, YOUR HIGHNESS.
THOUGH YOU FAILED TO MENTION THIS THREAT BEFORE WE DEPARTED.
I THOUGHT THAT IF I TOOK US ON A DIFFERENT PATH, WE WOULD BE SAFE.
WE WERE.
YOU DON'T GET TO DECIDE WHAT I SHOULD KNOW.
ADVISE ALL YOU LIKE, BUT THE SECOND YOUR INSECURITIES ENDANGER ME, MY FAMILY, OR ANY OF THIS DAMNED REALM... THERE WILL BE A RECKONING.

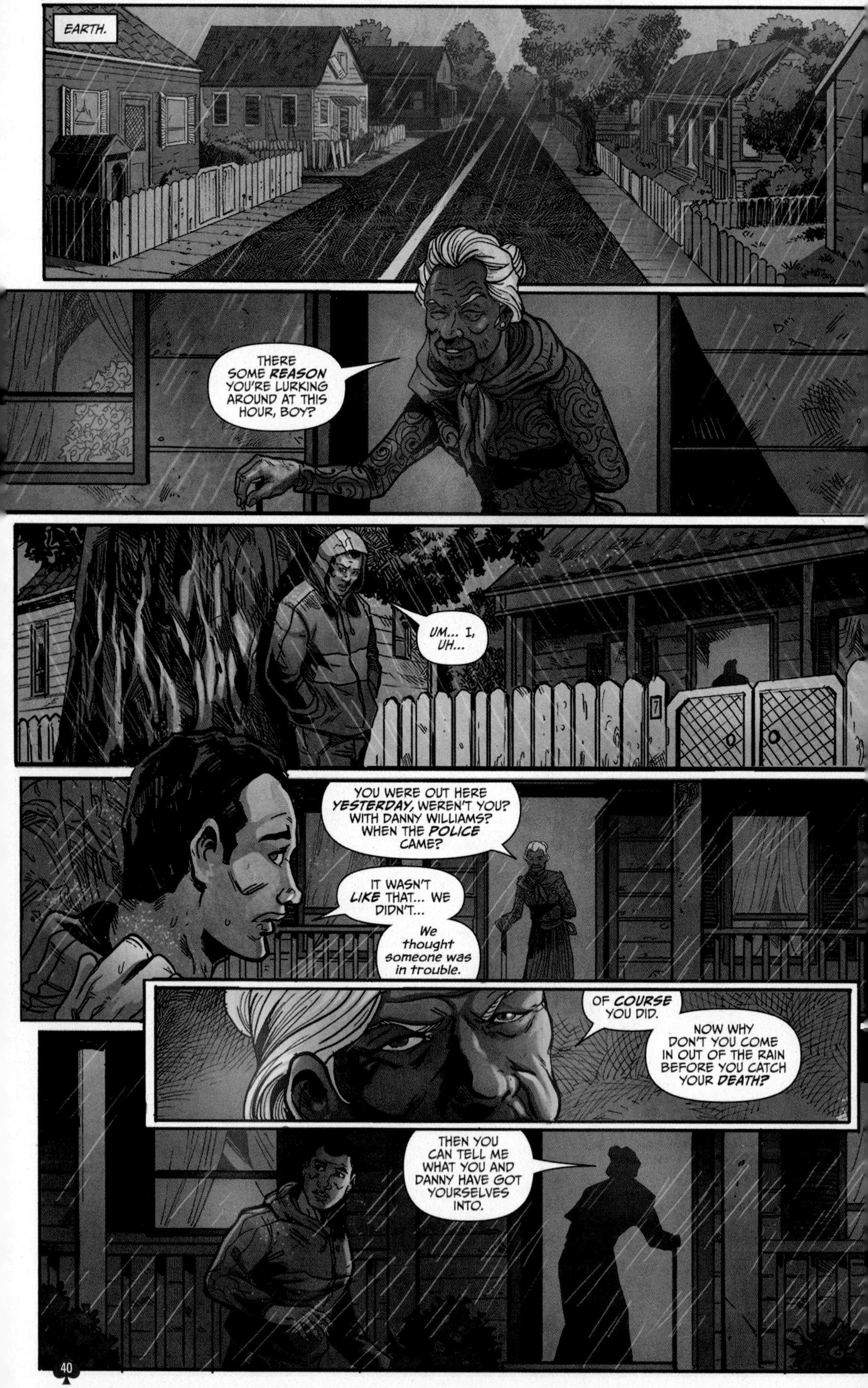
EARTH.
THERE SOME REASON YOU'RE LURKING AROUND AT THIS HOUR, BOY?
UM... I, UH...
YOU WERE OUT HERE YESTERDAY, WEREN'T YOU? WITH DANNY WILLIAMS? WHEN THE POLICE CAME?
IT WASN'T LIKE THAT... WE DIDN'T...
We thought someone was in trouble.
OF COURSE YOU DID.
NOW WHY DON'T YOU COME IN OUT OF THE RAIN BEFORE YOU CATCH YOUR DEATH?
THEN YOU CAN TELL ME WHAT YOU AND DANNY HAVE GOT YOURSELVES INTO.

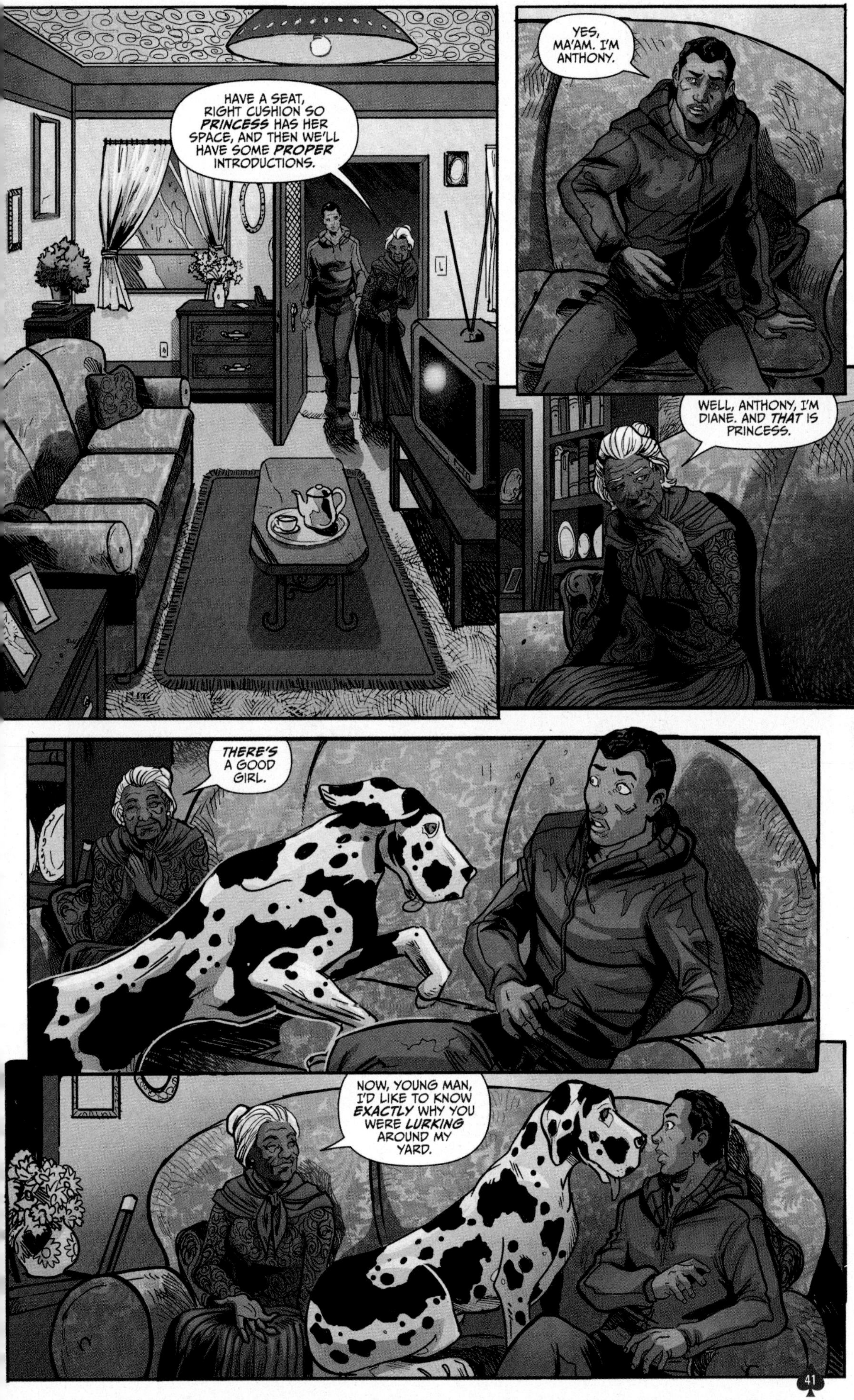
HAVE A SEAT, RIGHT CUSHION SO PRINCESS HAS HER SPACE, AND THEN WE'LL HAVE SOME PROPER INTRODUCTIONS.
YES, MA'AM. I'M ANTHONY.
WELL, ANTHONY, I'M DIANE. AND THAT IS PRINCESS.
THERE'S A GOOD GIRL.
NOW, YOUNG MAN, I'D LIKE TO KNOW EXACTLY WHY YOU WERE LURKING AROUND MY YARD.

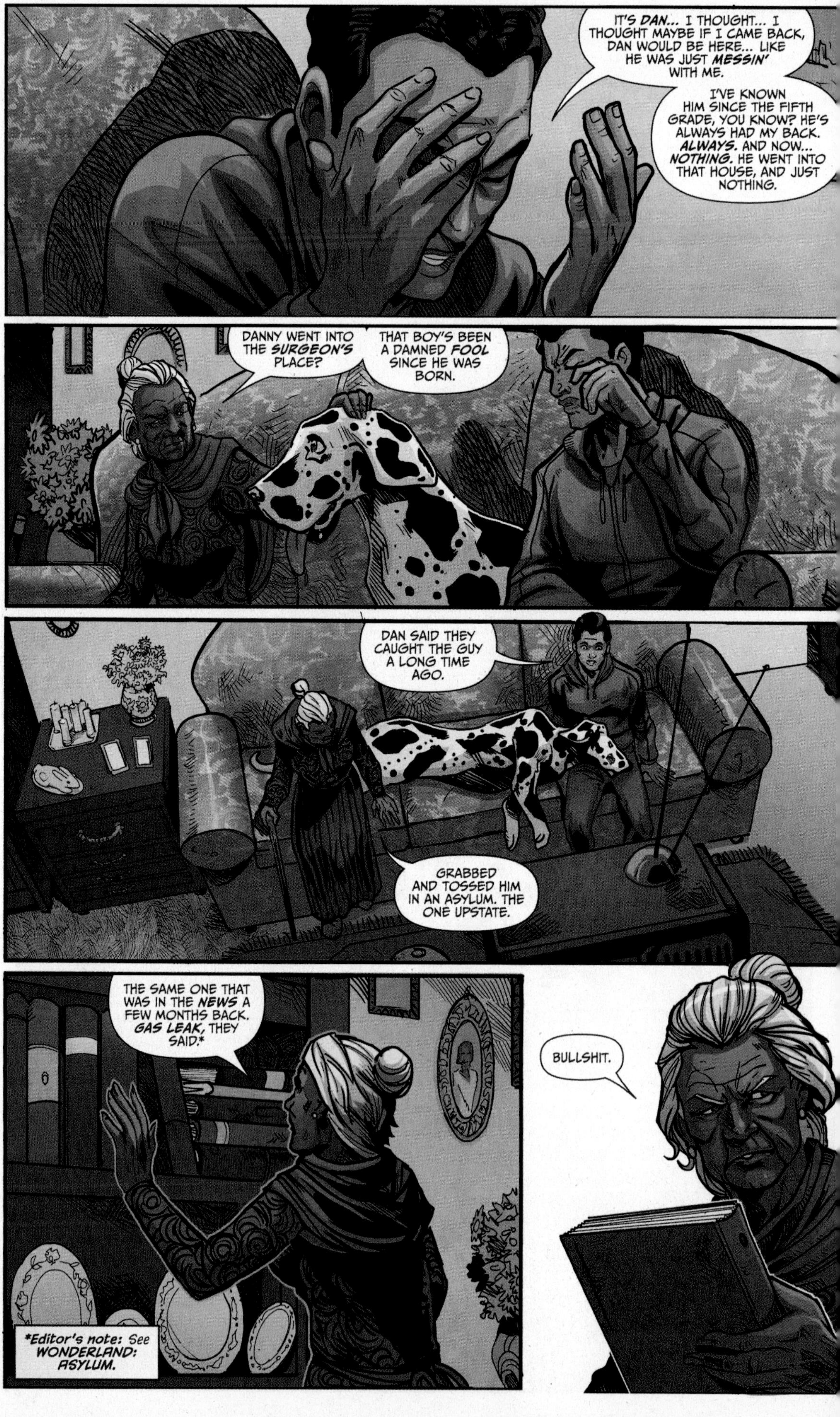
IT'S DAN... I THOUGHT... I THOUGHT MAYBE IF I CAME BACK, DAN WOULD BE HERE... LIKE HE WAS JUST MESSIN' WITH ME.
I'VE KNOWN HIM SINCE THE FIFTH GRADE, YOU KNOW? HE'S ALWAYS HAD MY BACK. ALWAYS. AND NOW... NOTHING. HE WENT INTO THAT HOUSE, AND JUST NOTHING.
DANNY WENT INTO THE SURGEON'S PLACE?
THAT BOY'S BEEN A DAMNED FOOL SINCE HE WAS BORN.
DAN SAID THEY CAUGHT THE GUY A LONG TIME AGO.
GRABBED AND TOSSED HIM IN AN ASYLUM. THE ONE UPSTATE.
THE SAME ONE THAT WAS IN THE NEWS A FEW MONTHS BACK. GAS LEAK, THEY SAID.*
*Editor's note: See WONDERLAND: ASYLUM.
BULLSHIT.

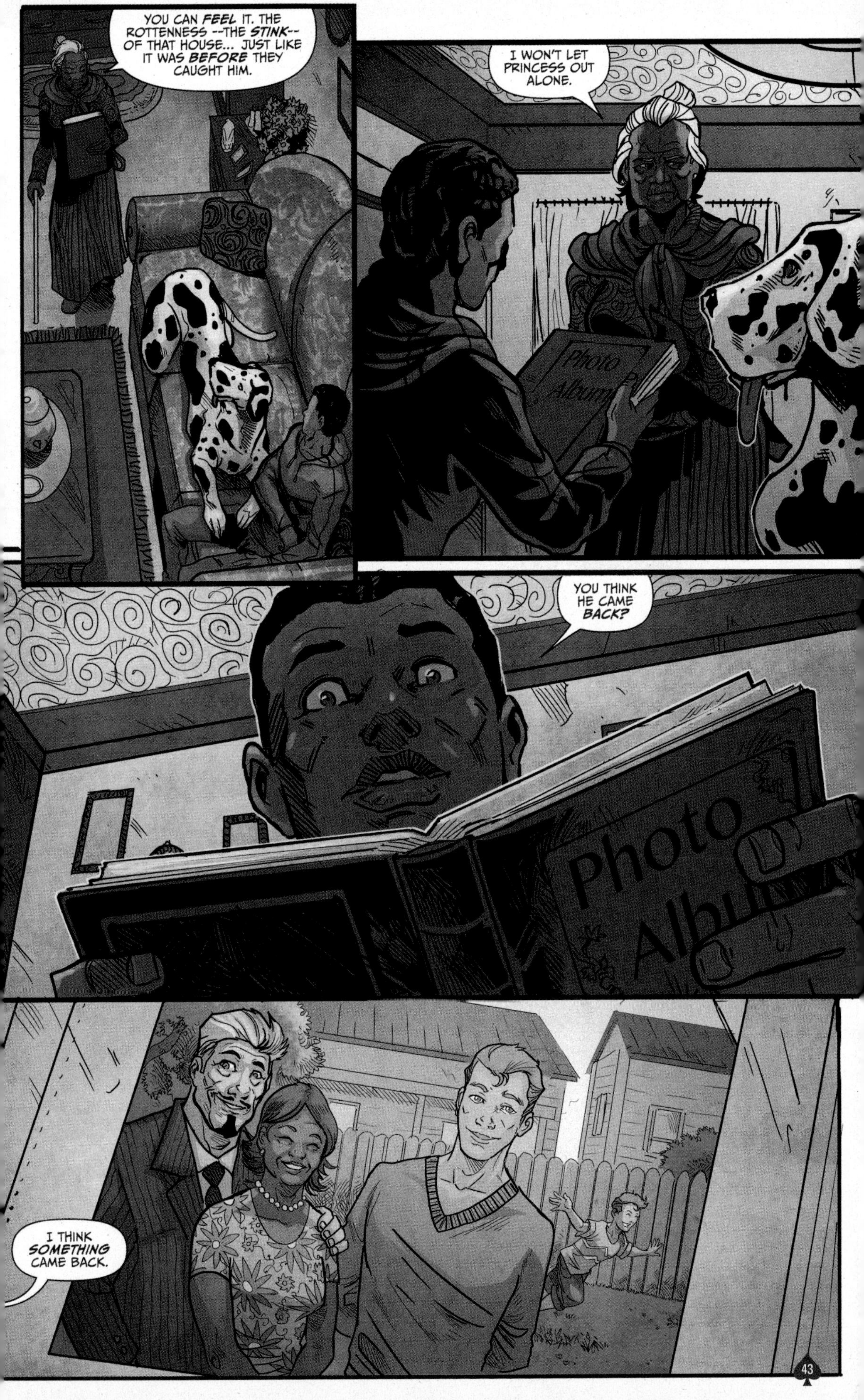
YOU CAN FEEL IT. THE ROTTENNESS --THE STINK-- OF THAT HOUSE... JUST LIKE IT WAS BEFORE THEY CAUGHT HIM.
I WON'T LET PRINCESS OUT ALONE.
Photo Album
YOU THINK HE CAME BACK?
Photo Album
I THINK SOMETHING CAME BACK.
43

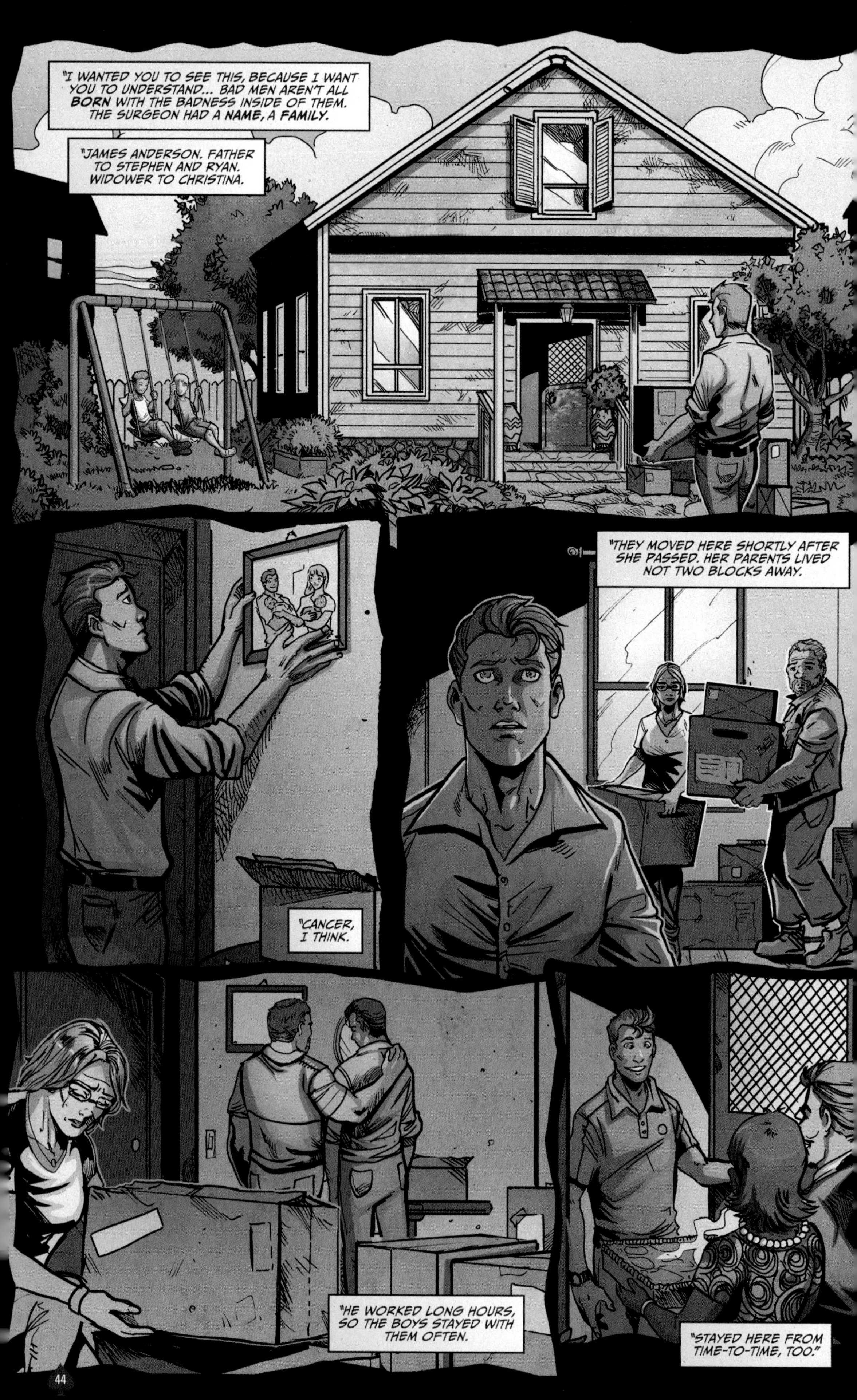
"I WANTED YOU TO SEE THIS, BECAUSE I WANT YOU TO UNDERSTAND... BAD MEN AREN'T ALL BORN WITH THE BADNESS INSIDE OF THEM. THE SURGEON HAD A NAME, A FAMILY.
"JAMES ANDERSON. FATHER TO STEPHEN AND RYAN. WIDOWER TO CHRISTINA.
"CANCER, I THINK.
"THEY MOVED HERE SHORTLY AFTER SHE PASSED. HER PARENTS LIVED NOT TWO BLOCKS AWAY.
"HE WORKED LONG HOURS, SO THE BOYS STAYED WITH THEM OFTEN.
"STAYED HERE FROM TIME-TO-TIME, TOO."

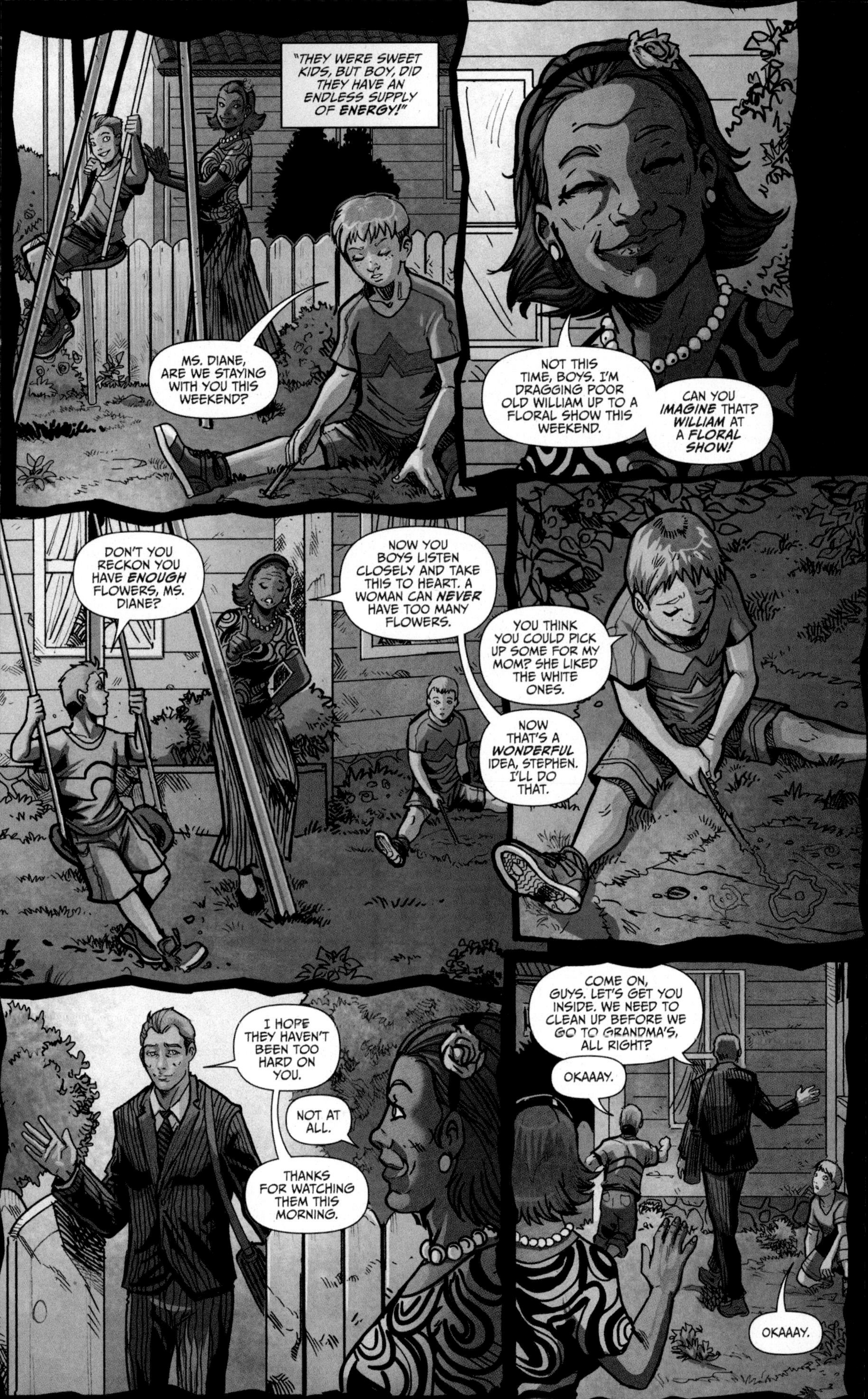
"THEY WERE SWEET KIDS, BUT BOY, DID THEY HAVE AN ENDLESS SUPPLY OF ENERGY!"
MS. DIANE, ARE WE STAYING WITH YOU THIS WEEKEND?
NOT THIS TIME, BOYS. I'M DRAGGING POOR OLD WILLIAM UP TO A FLORAL SHOW THIS WEEKEND.
CAN YOU IMAGINE THAT? WILLIAM AT A FLORAL SHOW!
DON'T YOU RECKON YOU HAVE ENOUGH FLOWERS, MS. DIANE?
NOW YOU BOYS LISTEN CLOSELY AND TAKE THIS TO HEART. A WOMAN CAN NEVER HAVE TOO MANY FLOWERS.
YOU THINK YOU COULD PICK UP SOME FOR MY MOM? SHE LIKED THE WHITE ONES.
NOW THAT'S A WONDERFUL IDEA, STEPHEN. I'LL DO THAT.
I HOPE THEY HAVEN'T BEEN TOO HARD ON YOU.
NOT AT ALL.
THANKS FOR WATCHING THEM THIS MORNING.
COME ON, GUYS. LET'S GET YOU INSIDE. WE NEED TO CLEAN UP BEFORE WE GO TO GRANDMA'S, ALL RIGHT?
OKAAAY.
OKAAAY.

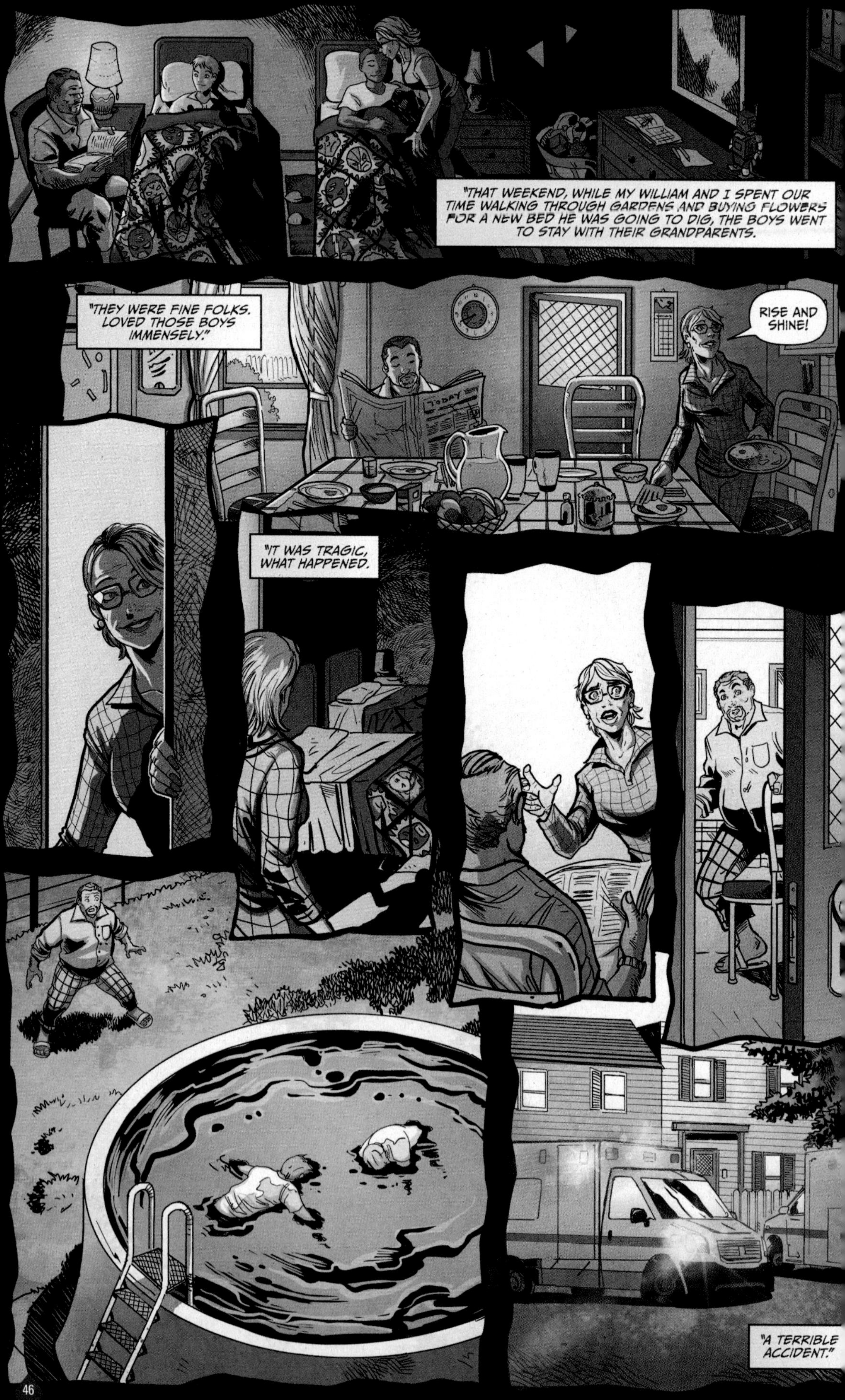
"THAT WEEKEND, WHILE MY WILLIAM AND I SPENT OUR TIME WALKING THROUGH GARDENS AND BUYING FLOWERS FOR A NEW BED HE WAS GOING TO DIG, THE BOYS WENT TO STAY WITH THEIR GRANDPARENTS.
"THEY WERE FINE FOLKS. LOVED THOSE BOYS IMMENSELY."
TODAY
RISE AND SHINE!
"IT WAS TRAGIC, WHAT HAPPENED.
"A TERRIBLE ACCIDENT."

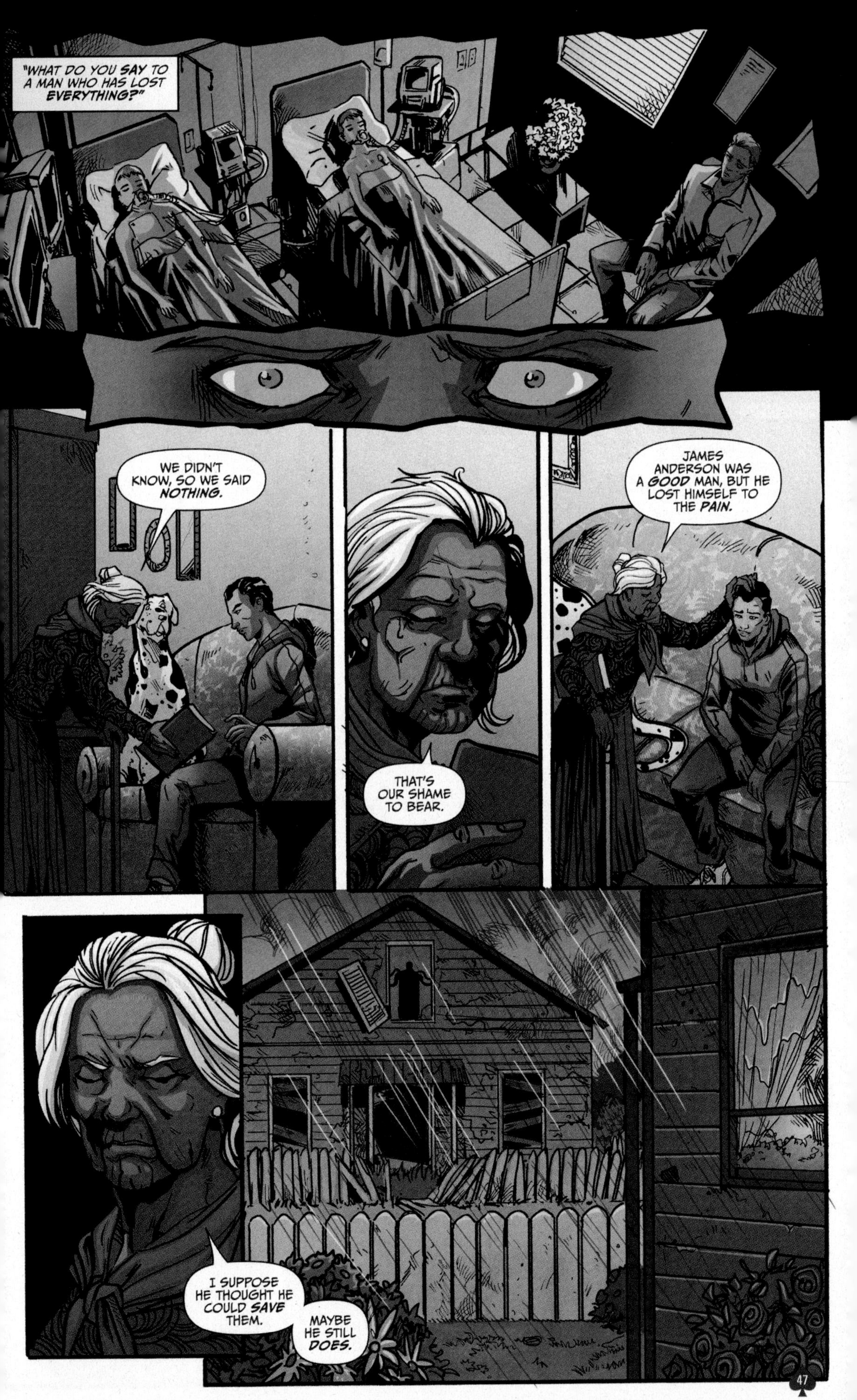
"WHAT DO YOU SAY TO A MAN WHO HAS LOST EVERYTHING?"
WE DIDN'T KNOW, SO WE SAID NOTHING.
THAT'S OUR SHAME TO BEAR.
JAMES ANDERSON WAS A GOOD MAN, BUT HE LOST HIMSELF TO THE PAIN.
I SUPPOSE HE THOUGHT HE COULD SAVE THEM.
MAYBE HE STILL DOES.

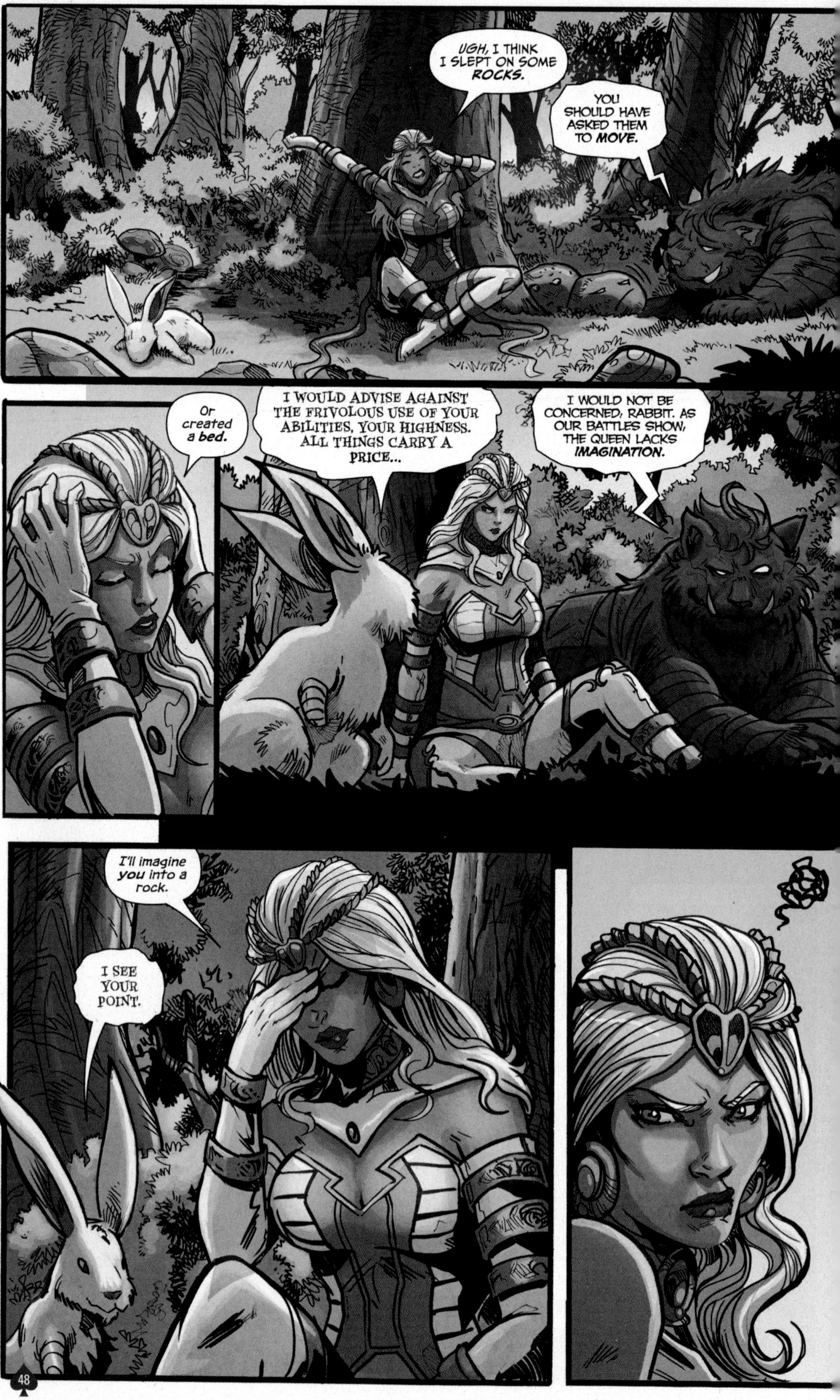
UGH, I THINK I SLEPT ON SOME ROCKS.
YOU SHOULD HAVE ASKED THEM TO MOVE.
Or created a bed.
I WOULD ADVISE AGAINST THE FRIVOLOUS USE OF YOUR ABILITIES, YOUR HIGHNESS. ALL THINGS CARRY A PRICE...
I WOULD NOT BE CONCERNED, RABBIT. AS OUR BATTLES SHOW, THE QUEEN LACKS IMAGINATION.
I'll imagine you into a rock.
I SEE YOUR POINT.

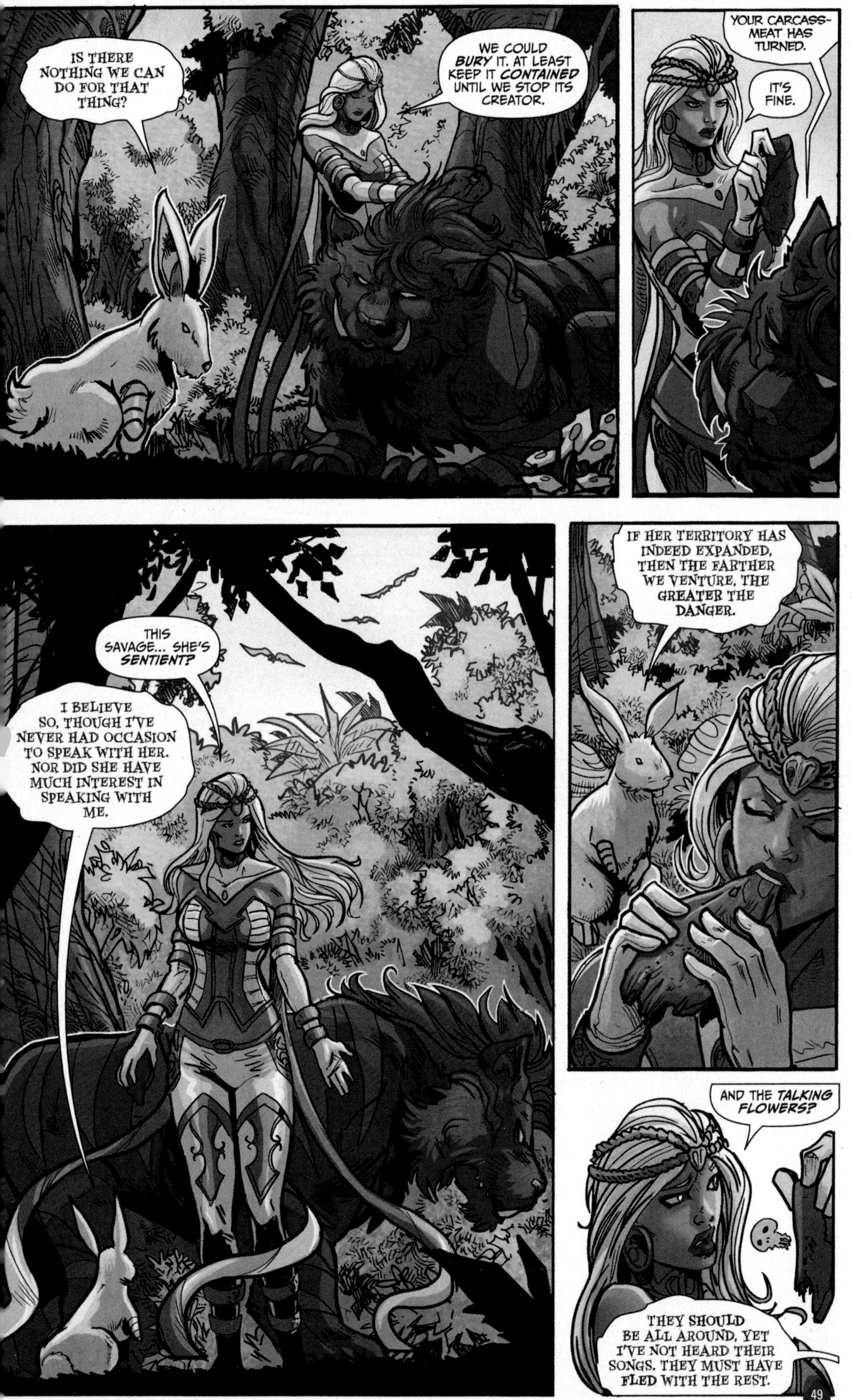
IS THERE NOTHING WE CAN DO FOR THAT THING?
WE COULD BURY IT. AT LEAST KEEP IT CONTAINED UNTIL WE STOP ITS CREATOR.
YOUR CARCASS-MEAT HAS TURNED.
IT'S FINE.
THIS SAVAGE... SHE'S SENTIENT?
I BELIEVE SO, THOUGH I'VE NEVER HAD OCCASION TO SPEAK WITH HER. NOR DID SHE HAVE MUCH INTEREST IN SPEAKING WITH ME.
IF HER TERRITORY HAS INDEED EXPANDED, THEN THE FARTHER WE VENTURE, THE GREATER THE DANGER.
AND THE TALKING FLOWERS?
THEY SHOULD BE ALL AROUND, YET I'VE NOT HEARD THEIR SONGS. THEY MUST HAVE FLED WITH THE REST.

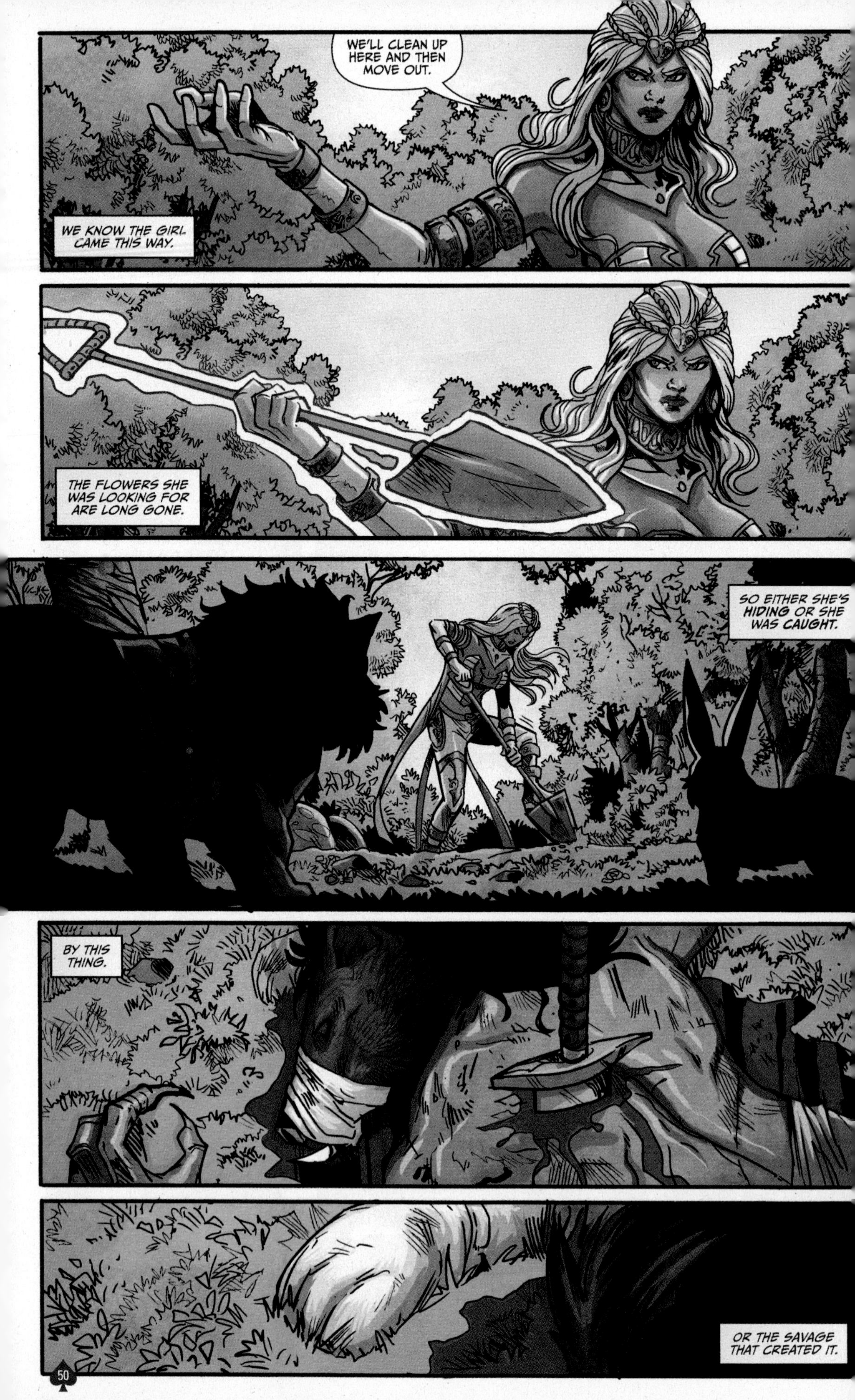
WE'LL CLEAN UP HERE AND THEN MOVE OUT.
WE KNOW THE GIRL CAME THIS WAY.
THE FLOWERS SHE WAS LOOKING FOR ARE LONG GONE.
SO EITHER SHE'S HIDING OR SHE WAS CAUGHT.
BY THIS THING.
OR THE SAVAGE THAT CREATED IT.

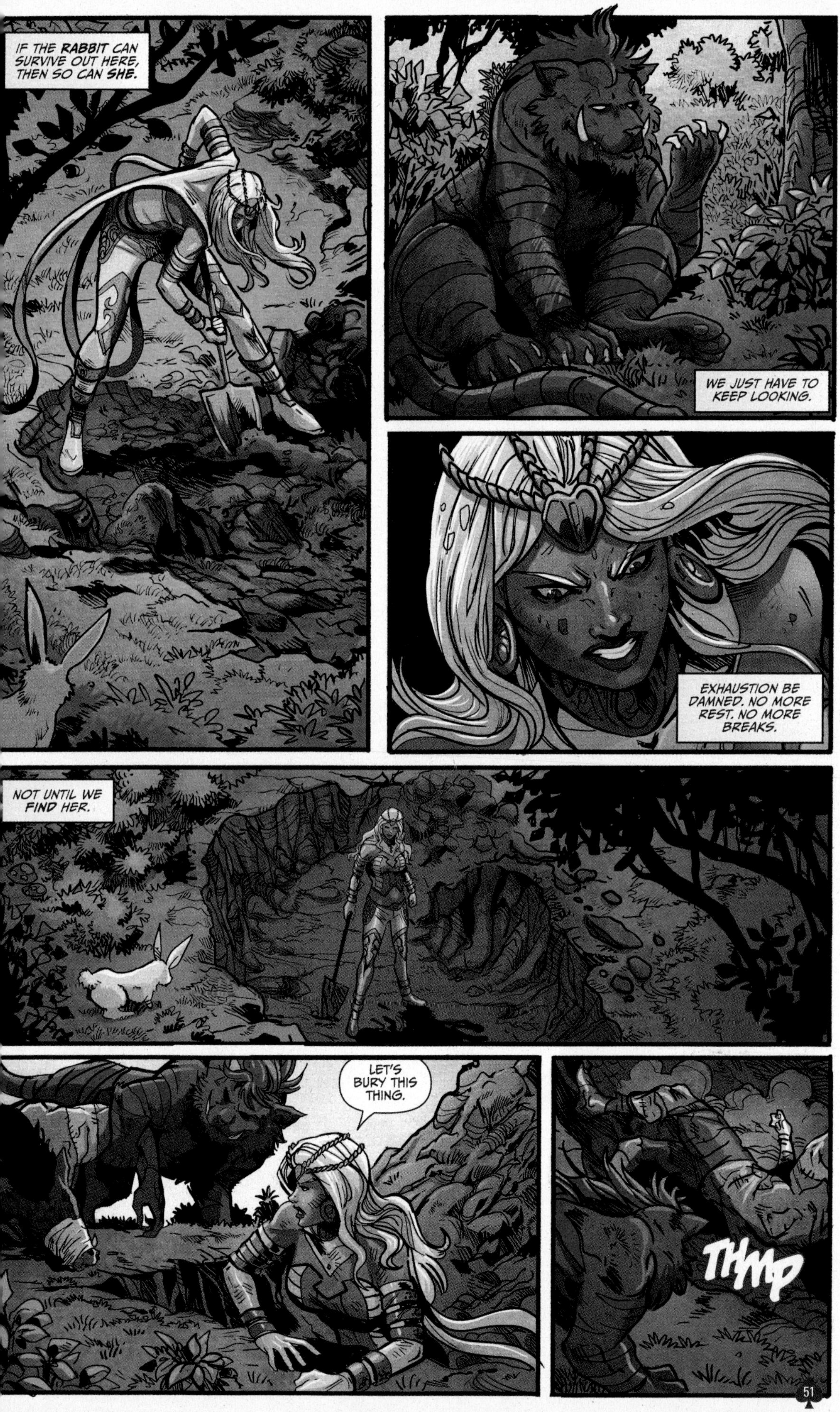
IF THE RABBIT CAN SURVIVE OUT HERE, THEN SO CAN SHE.
WE JUST HAVE TO KEEP LOOKING.
EXHAUSTION BE DAMNED. NO MORE REST. NO MORE BREAKS.
NOT UNTIL WE FIND HER.
LET'S BURY THIS THING.
THMP

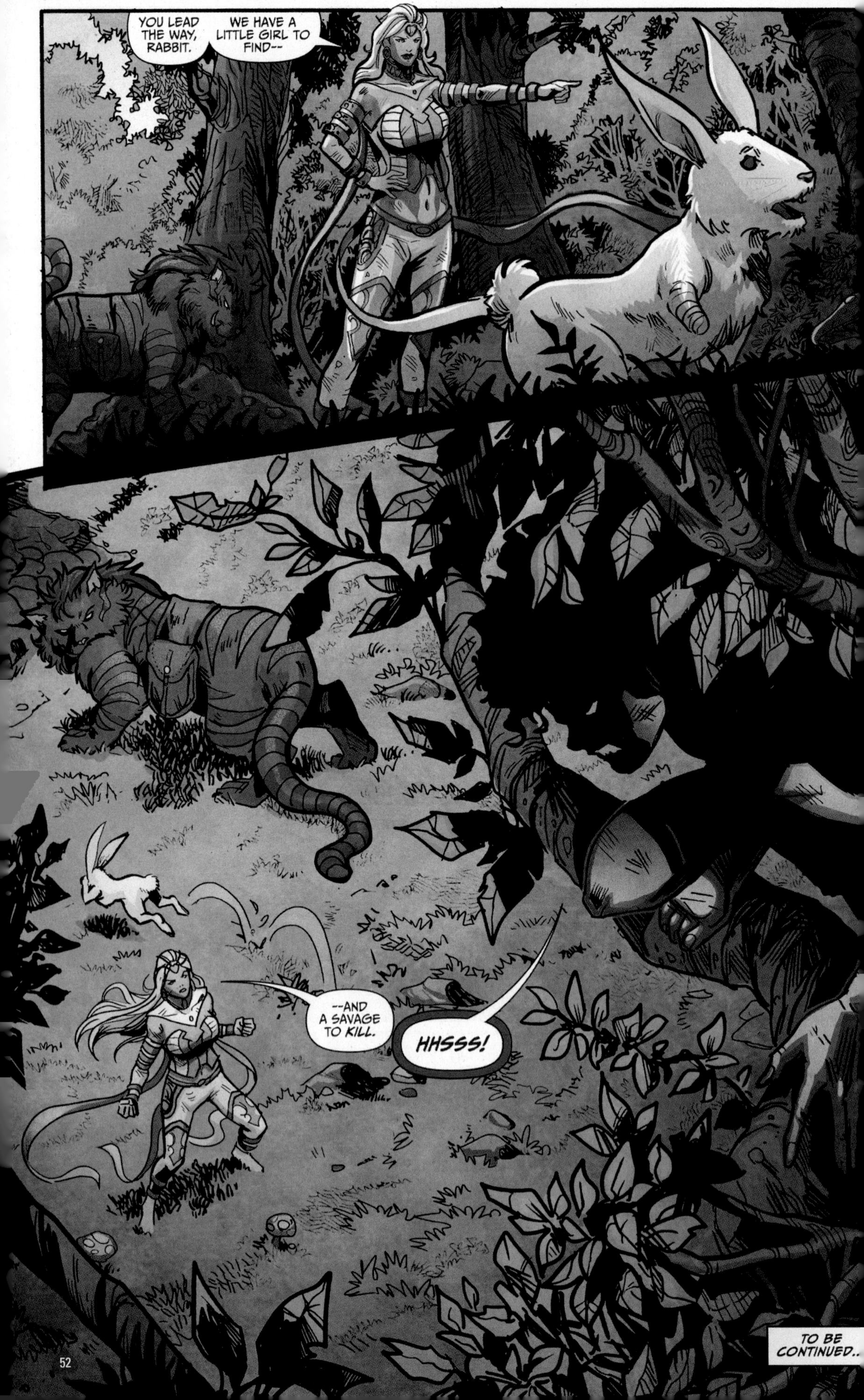
YOU LEAD THE WAY, RABBIT.
WE HAVE A LITTLE GIRL TO FIND--
--AND A SAVAGE TO KILL.
HHSSS!
TO BE CONTINUED..

END CHAPTER

RENAISSANCE

PART THREE

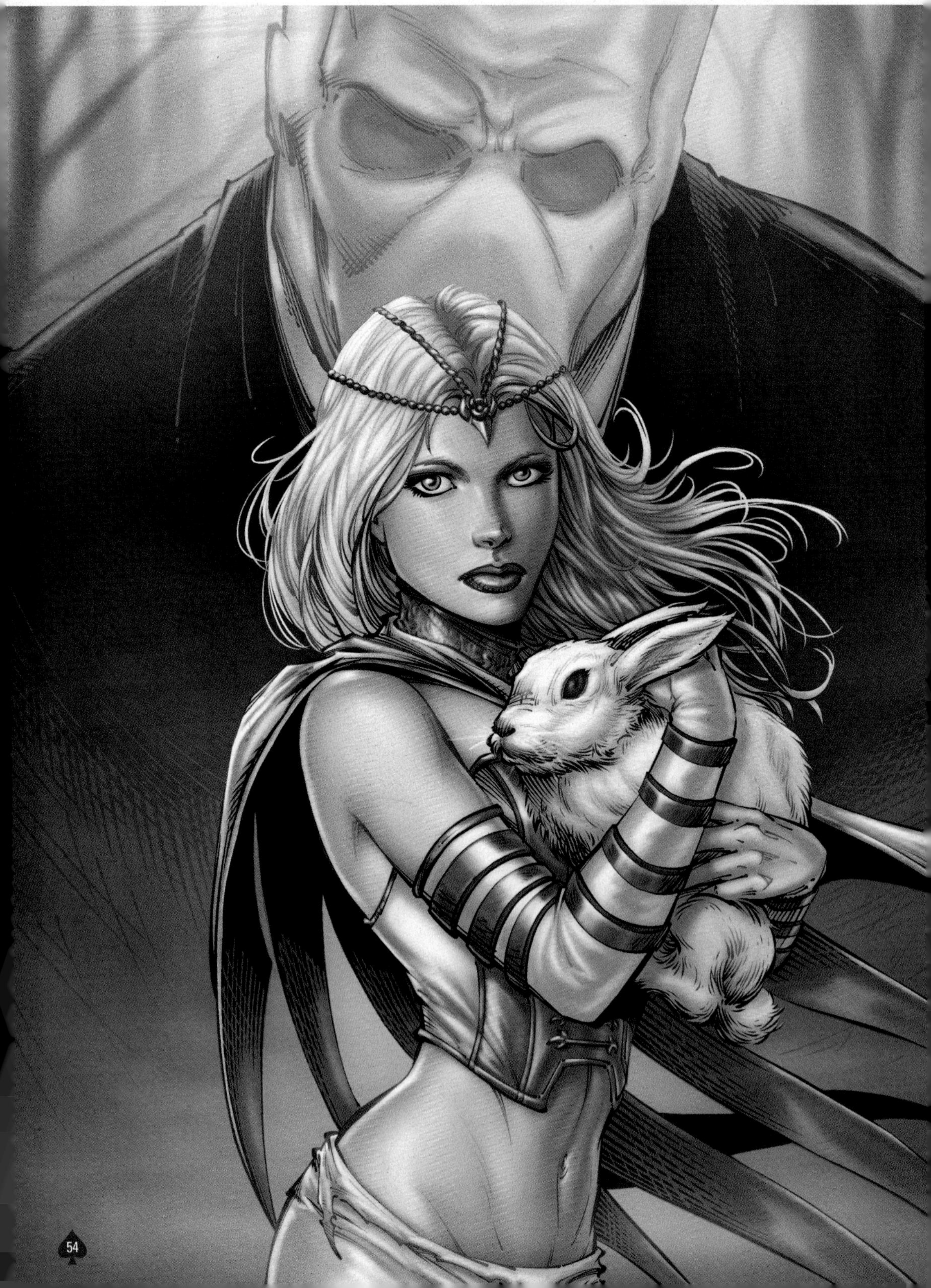

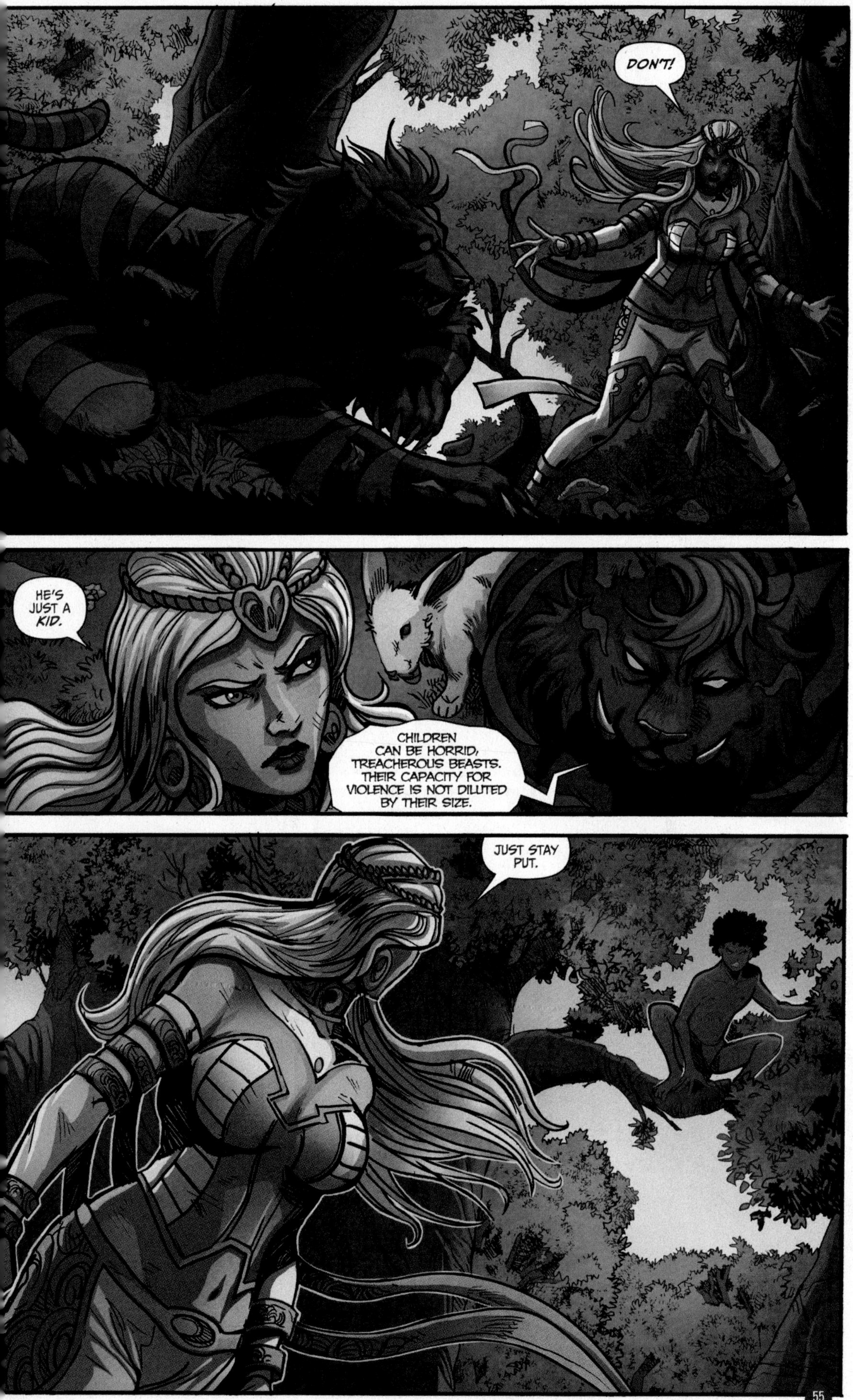

DON'T!
HE'S JUST A KID.
CHILDREN CAN BE HORRID, TREACHEROUS BEASTS. THEIR CAPACITY FOR VIOLENCE IS NOT DILUTED BY THEIR SIZE.
JUST STAY PUT.

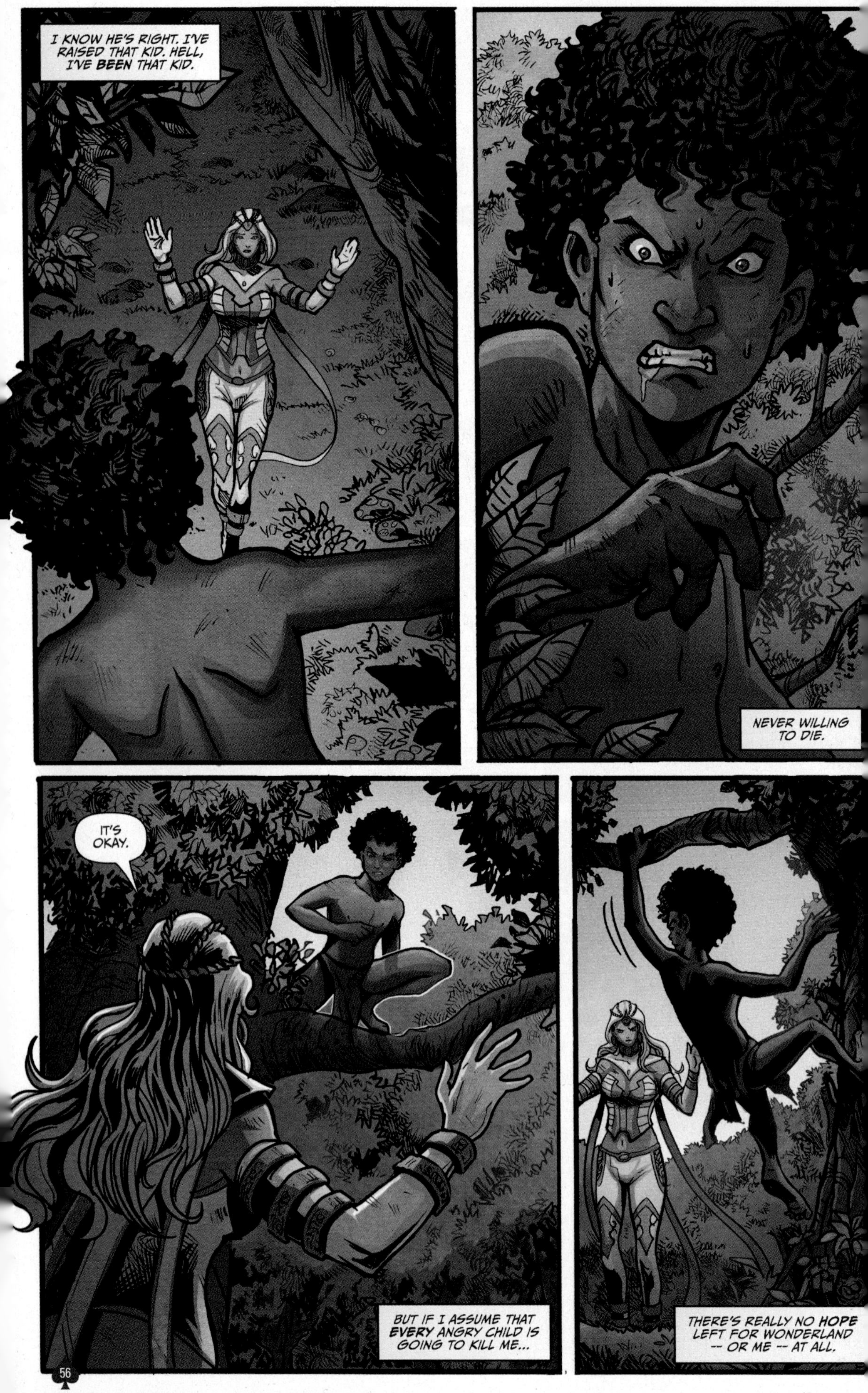

I KNOW HE'S RIGHT. I'VE RAISED THAT KID. HELL, I'VE BEEN THAT KID.
NEVER WILLING TO DIE.
IT'S OKAY.
BUT IF I ASSUME THAT EVERY ANGRY CHILD IS GOING TO KILL ME...
THERE'S REALLY NO HOPE LEFT FOR WONDERLAND -- OR ME -- AT ALL.

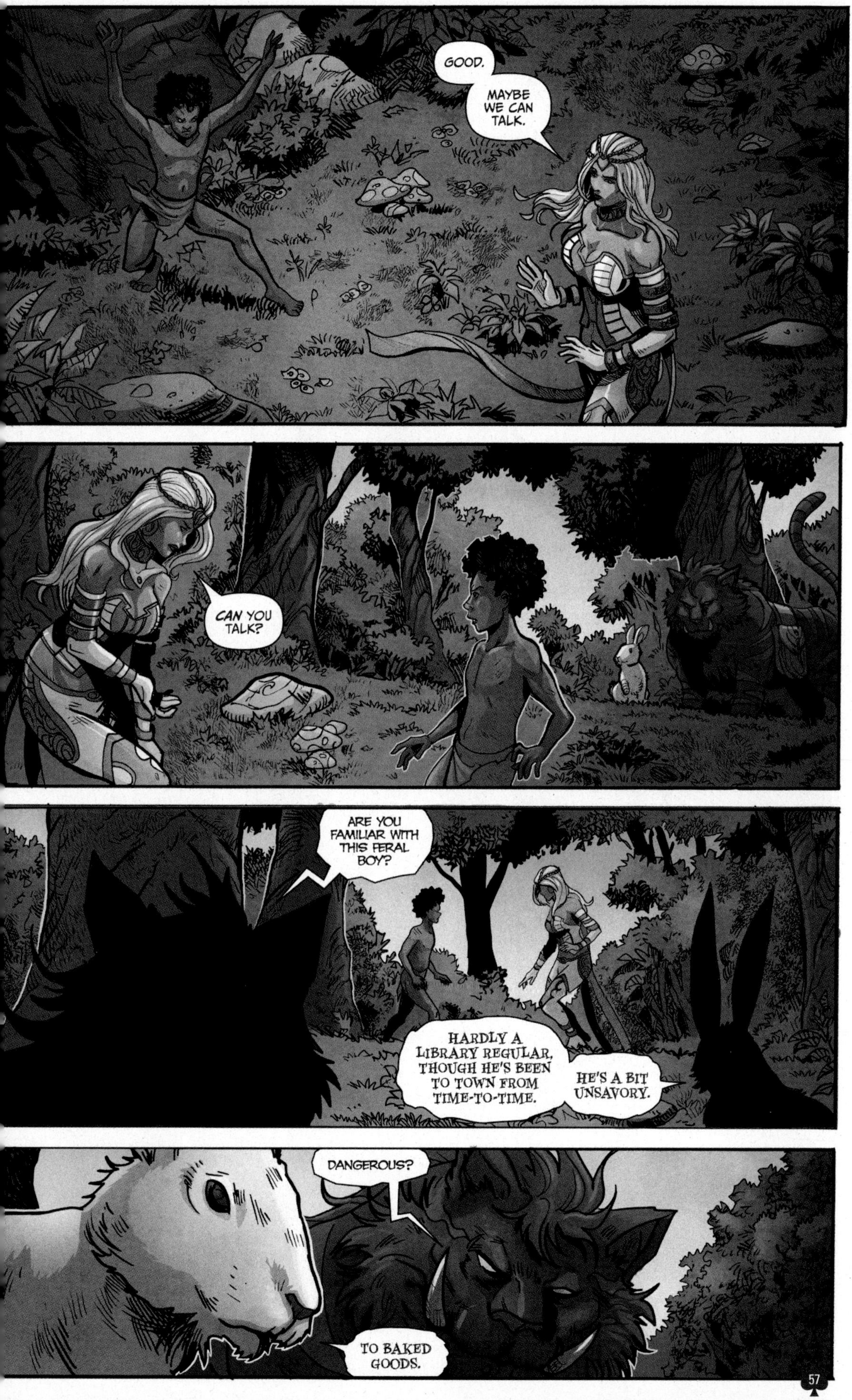
GOOD.
MAYBE WE CAN TALK.
CAN YOU TALK?
ARE YOU FAMILIAR WITH THIS FERAL BOY?
HARDLY A LIBRARY REGULAR, THOUGH HE'S BEEN TO TOWN FROM TIME-TO-TIME.
HE'S A BIT UNSAVORY.
DANGEROUS?
TO BAKED GOODS.

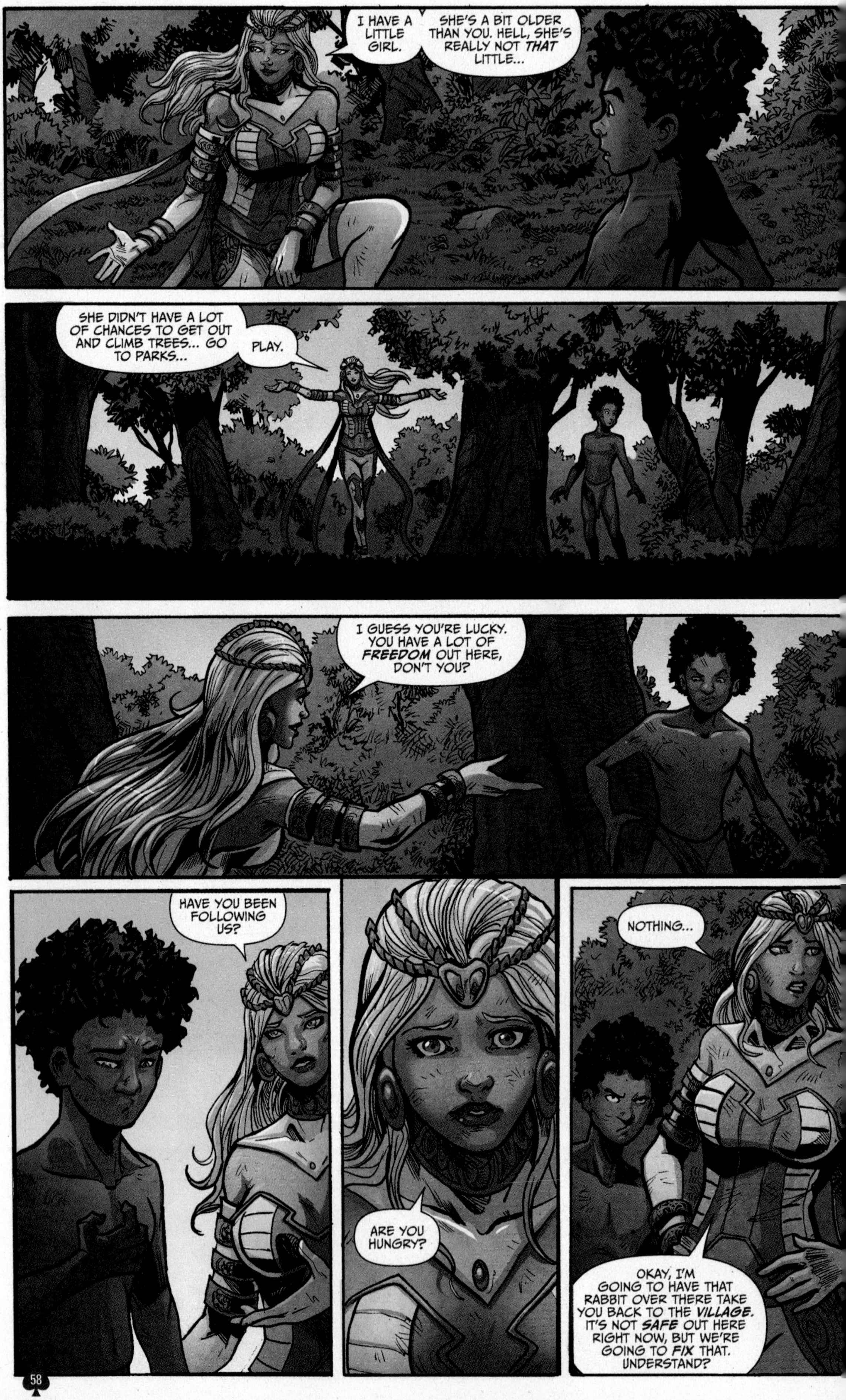
I HAVE A LITTLE GIRL.
SHE'S A BIT OLDER THAN YOU. HELL, SHE'S REALLY NOT THAT LITTLE...
SHE DIDN'T HAVE A LOT OF CHANCES TO GET OUT AND CLIMB TREES... GO TO PARKS...
PLAY.
I GUESS YOU'RE LUCKY. YOU HAVE A LOT OF FREEDOM OUT HERE, DON'T YOU?
HAVE YOU BEEN FOLLOWING US?
ARE YOU HUNGRY?
NOTHING...
OKAY, I'M GOING TO HAVE THAT RABBIT OVER THERE TAKE YOU BACK TO THE VILLAGE. IT'S NOT SAFE OUT HERE RIGHT NOW, BUT WE'RE GOING TO FIX THAT. UNDERSTAND?

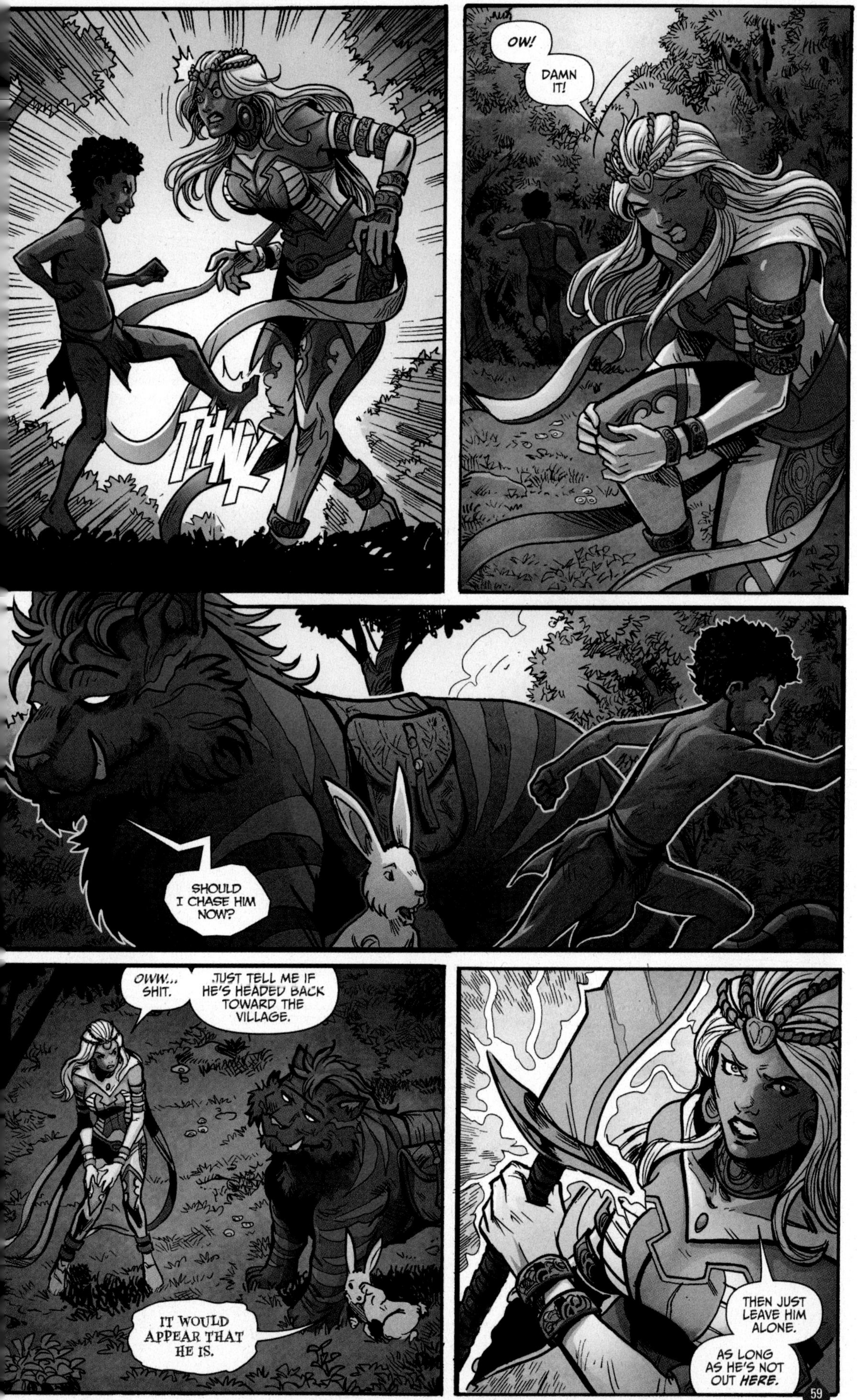
THNK
OW!
DAMN IT!
SHOULD I CHASE HIM NOW?
OWW... SHIT.
JUST TELL ME IF HE'S HEADED BACK TOWARD THE VILLAGE.
IT WOULD APPEAR THAT HE IS.
THEN JUST LEAVE HIM ALONE.
AS LONG AS HE'S NOT OUT *HERE*.

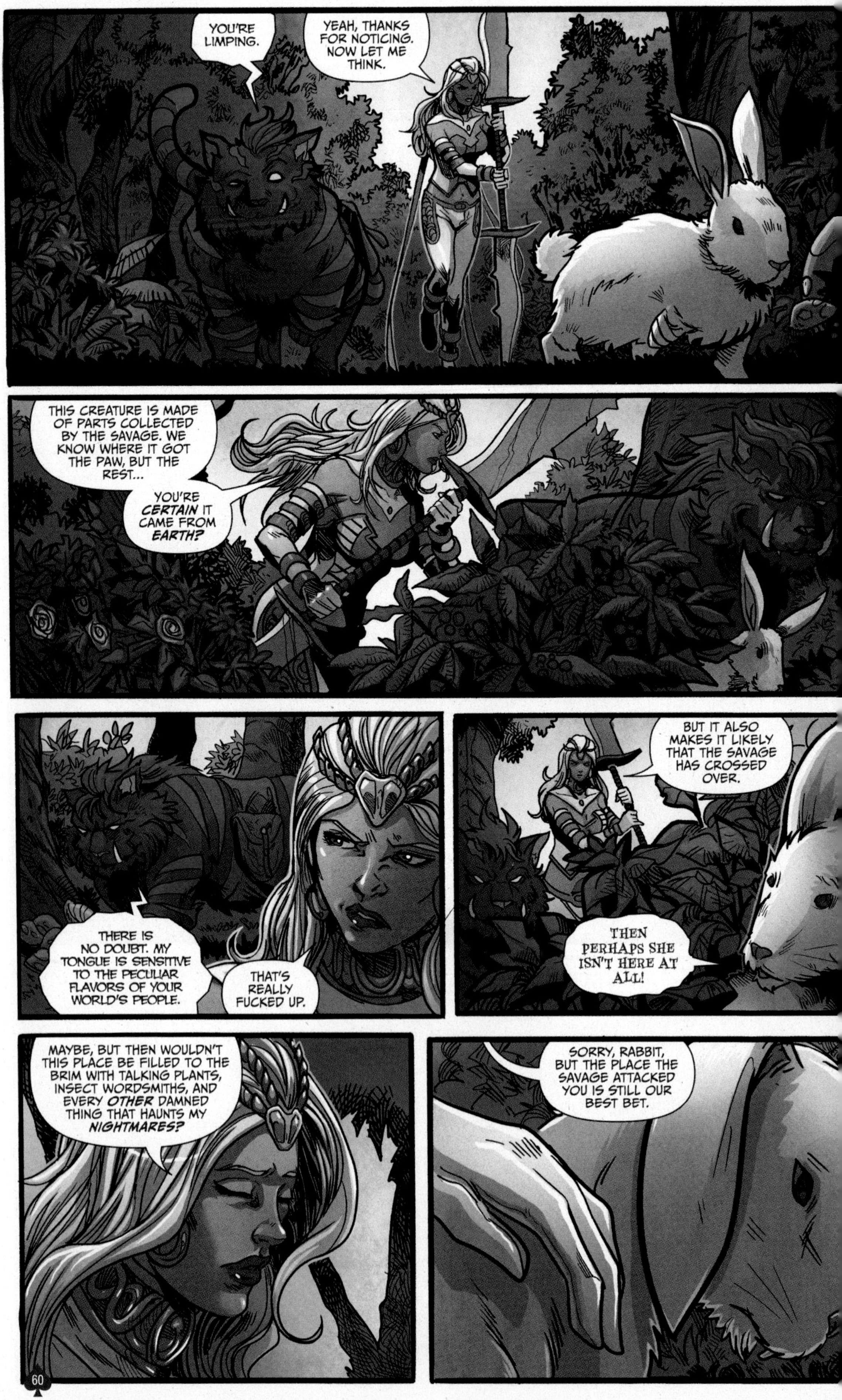
YOU'RE LIMPING.
YEAH, THANKS FOR NOTICING. NOW LET ME THINK.
THIS CREATURE IS MADE OF PARTS COLLECTED BY THE SAVAGE. WE KNOW WHERE IT GOT THE PAW, BUT THE REST...
YOU'RE CERTAIN IT CAME FROM EARTH?
THERE IS NO DOUBT. MY TONGUE IS SENSITIVE TO THE PECULIAR FLAVORS OF YOUR WORLD'S PEOPLE.
THAT'S REALLY FUCKED UP.
BUT IT ALSO MAKES IT LIKELY THAT THE SAVAGE HAS CROSSED OVER.
THEN PERHAPS SHE ISN'T HERE AT ALL!
MAYBE, BUT THEN WOULDN'T THIS PLACE BE FILLED TO THE BRIM WITH TALKING PLANTS, INSECT WORDSMITHS, AND EVERY OTHER DAMNED THING THAT HAUNTS MY NIGHTMARES?
SORRY, RABBIT, BUT THE PLACE THE SAVAGE ATTACKED YOU IS STILL OUR BEST BET.

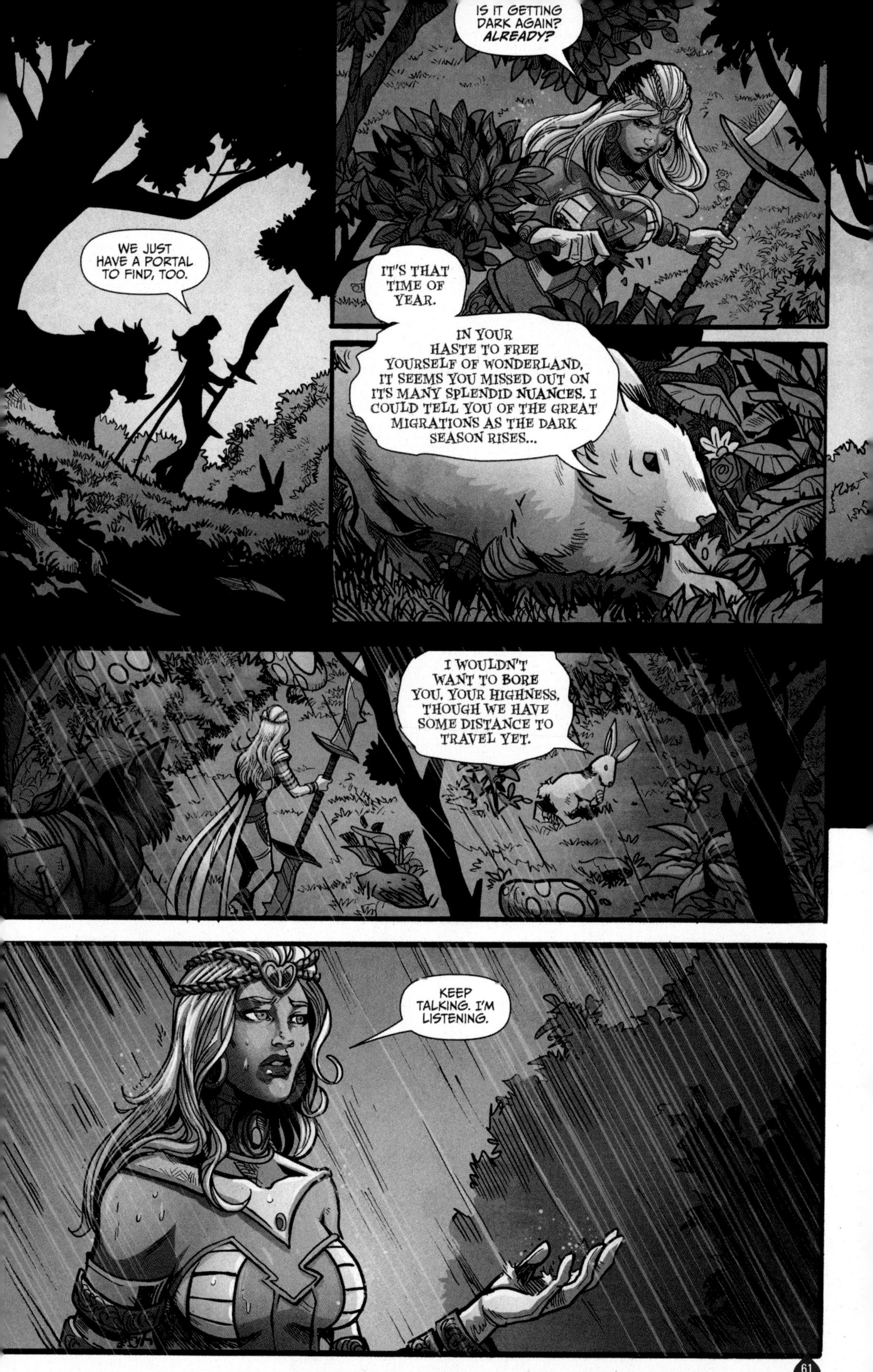
WE JUST HAVE A PORTAL TO FIND, TOO.
IS IT GETTING DARK AGAIN? *ALREADY?*
IT'S THAT TIME OF YEAR.
IN YOUR HASTE TO FREE YOURSELF OF WONDERLAND, IT SEEMS YOU MISSED OUT ON IT'S MANY SPLENDID NUANCES. I COULD TELL YOU OF THE GREAT MIGRATIONS AS THE DARK SEASON RISES...
I WOULDN'T WANT TO BORE YOU, YOUR HIGHNESS, THOUGH WE HAVE SOME DISTANCE TO TRAVEL YET.
KEEP TALKING. I'M LISTENING.

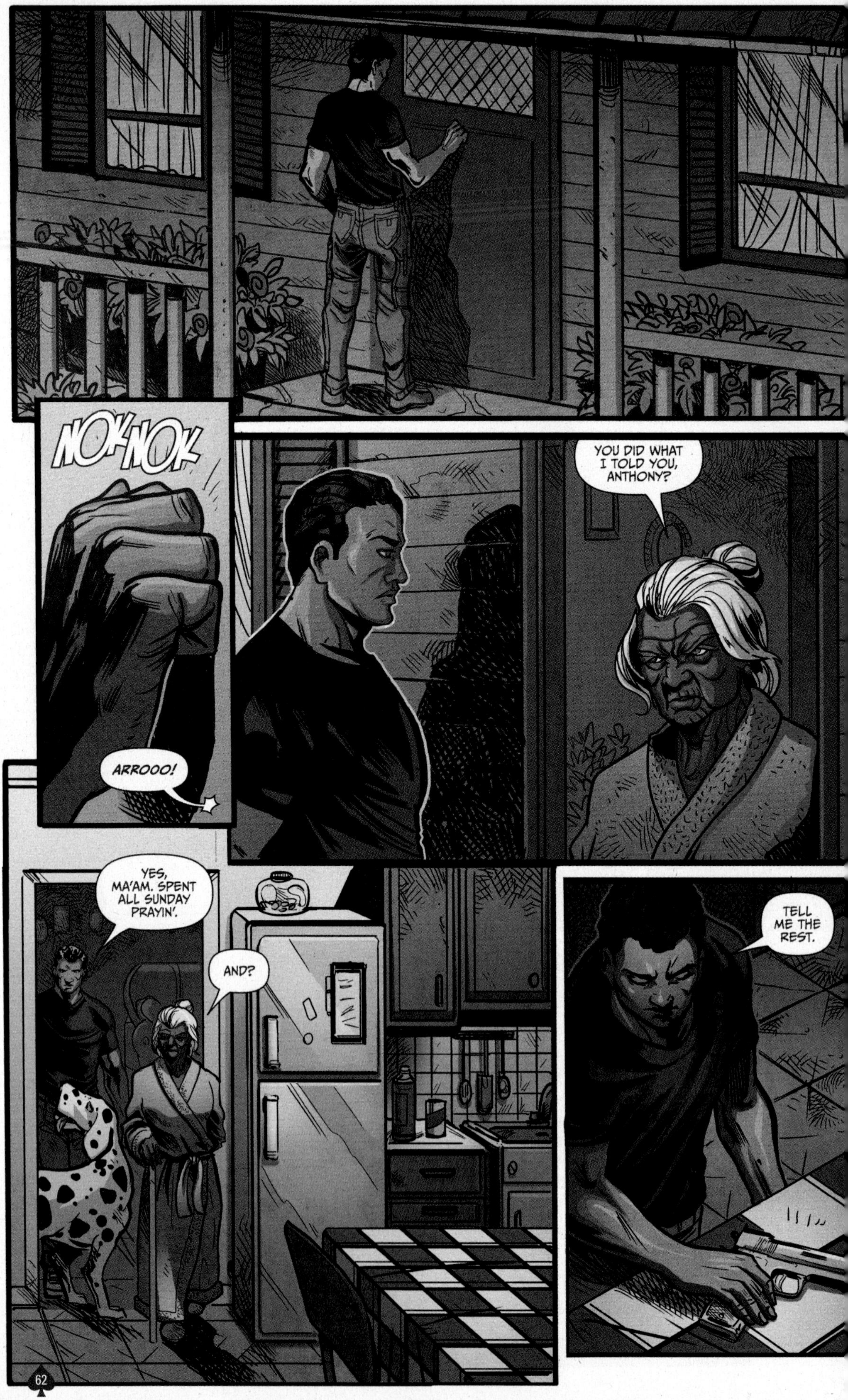
NOK-NOK
ARROOO!
YOU DID WHAT I TOLD YOU, ANTHONY?
YES, MA'AM. SPENT ALL SUNDAY PRAYIN'.
AND?
TELL ME THE REST.

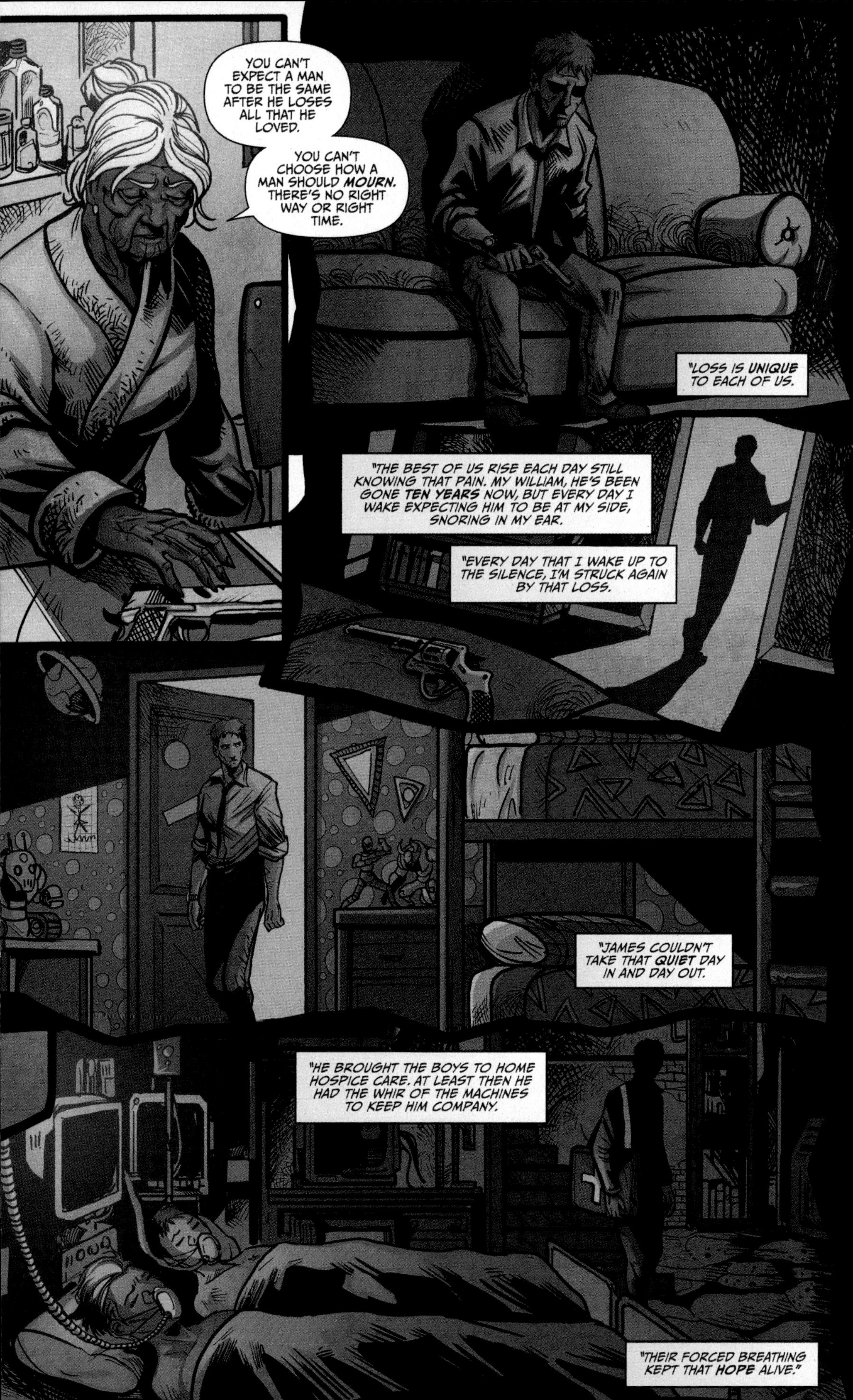
YOU CAN'T EXPECT A MAN TO BE THE SAME AFTER HE LOSES ALL THAT HE LOVED.
YOU CAN'T CHOOSE HOW A MAN SHOULD MOURN. THERE'S NO RIGHT WAY OR RIGHT TIME.
"LOSS IS UNIQUE TO EACH OF US.
"THE BEST OF US RISE EACH DAY STILL KNOWING THAT PAIN. MY WILLIAM, HE'S BEEN GONE TEN YEARS NOW, BUT EVERY DAY I WAKE EXPECTING HIM TO BE AT MY SIDE, SNORING IN MY EAR.
"EVERY DAY THAT I WAKE UP TO THE SILENCE, I'M STRUCK AGAIN BY THAT LOSS.
"JAMES COULDN'T TAKE THAT QUIET DAY IN AND DAY OUT.
"HE BROUGHT THE BOYS TO HOME HOSPICE CARE. AT LEAST THEN HE HAD THE WHIR OF THE MACHINES TO KEEP HIM COMPANY.
"THEIR FORCED BREATHING KEPT THAT HOPE ALIVE."

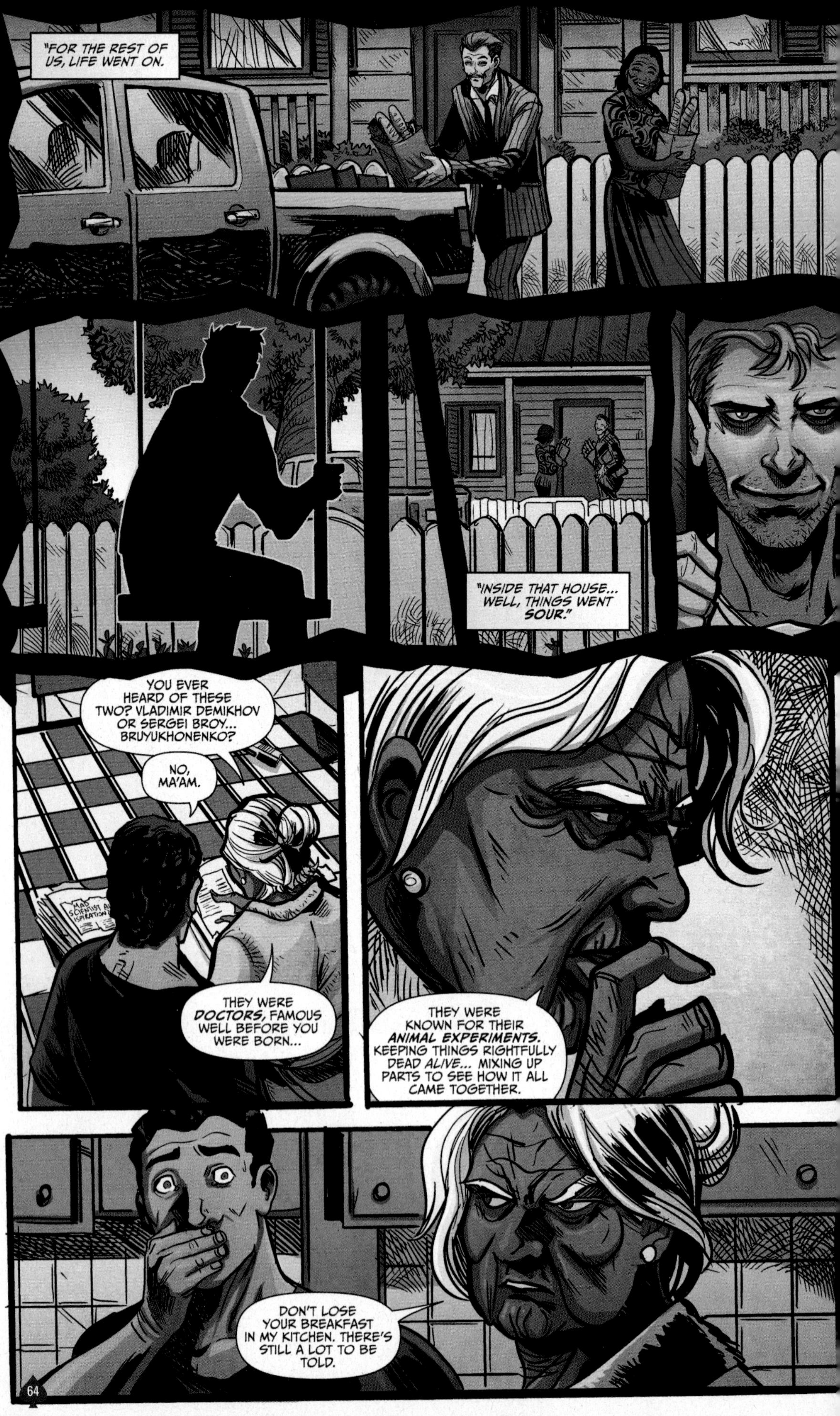
"FOR THE REST OF US, LIFE WENT ON.
"INSIDE THAT HOUSE... WELL, THINGS WENT SOUR."
YOU EVER HEARD OF THESE TWO? VLADIMIR DEMIKHOV OR SERGEI BROY... BRUYUKHONENKO?
NO, MA'AM.
THEY WERE DOCTORS, FAMOUS WELL BEFORE YOU WERE BORN...
THEY WERE KNOWN FOR THEIR ANIMAL EXPERIMENTS. KEEPING THINGS RIGHTFULLY DEAD ALIVE... MIXING UP PARTS TO SEE HOW IT ALL CAME TOGETHER.
DON'T LOSE YOUR BREAKFAST IN MY KITCHEN. THERE'S STILL A LOT TO BE TOLD.

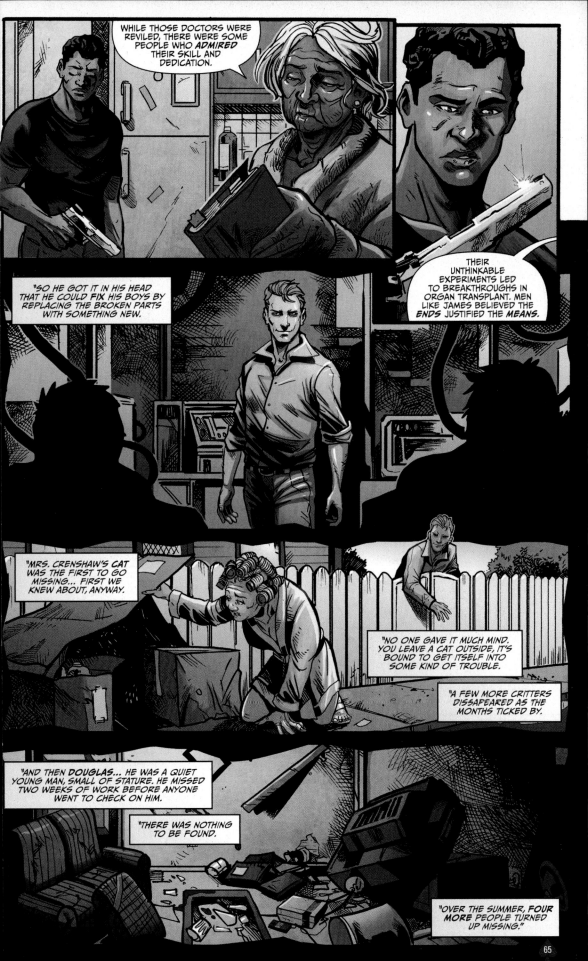

WHILE THOSE DOCTORS WERE REVILED, THERE WERE SOME PEOPLE WHO *ADMIRED* THEIR SKILL AND DEDICATION.

THEIR UNTHINKABLE EXPERIMENTS LED TO BREAKTHROUGHS IN ORGAN TRANSPLANT. MEN LIKE JAMES BELIEVED THE *ENDS* JUSTIFIED THE *MEANS*.

"SO HE GOT IT IN HIS HEAD THAT HE COULD *FIX* HIS BOYS BY REPLACING THE BROKEN PARTS WITH SOMETHING NEW.

"MRS. CRENSHAW'S *CAT* WAS THE FIRST TO GO MISSING... FIRST WE KNEW ABOUT, ANYWAY.

"NO ONE GAVE IT MUCH MIND. YOU LEAVE A CAT OUTSIDE, IT'S BOUND TO GET ITSELF INTO SOME KIND OF TROUBLE.

"A FEW MORE CRITTERS DISSAPEARED AS THE MONTHS TICKED BY.

"AND THEN *DOUGLAS*... HE WAS A QUIET YOUNG MAN, SMALL OF STATURE. HE MISSED TWO WEEKS OF WORK BEFORE ANYONE WENT TO CHECK ON HIM.

"THERE WAS NOTHING TO BE FOUND.

"OVER THE SUMMER, *FOUR* MORE PEOPLE TURNED UP MISSING."

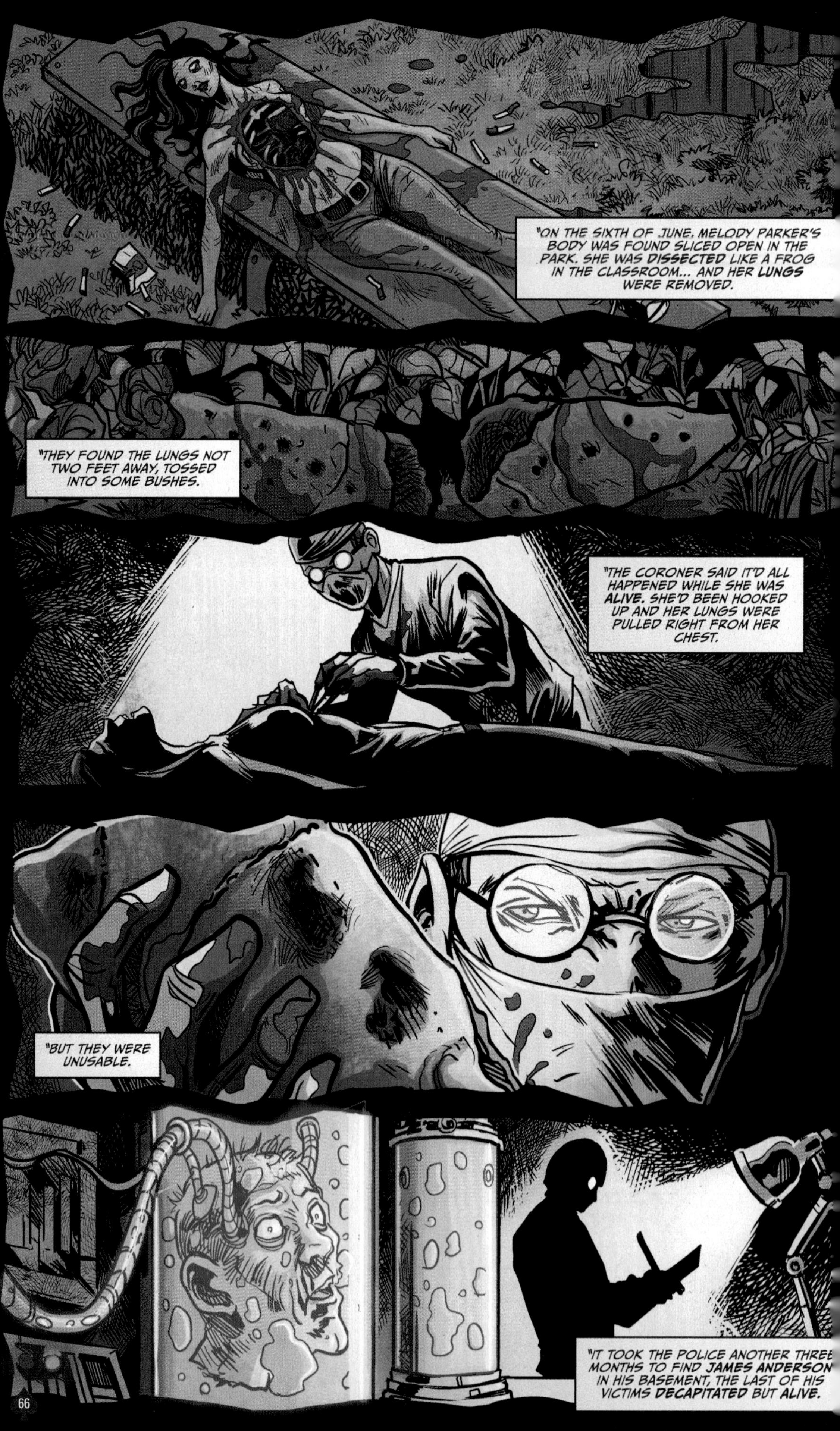
"ON THE SIXTH OF JUNE, MELODY PARKER'S BODY WAS FOUND SLICED OPEN IN THE PARK. SHE WAS DISSECTED LIKE A FROG IN THE CLASSROOM... AND HER LUNGS WERE REMOVED.
"THEY FOUND THE LUNGS NOT TWO FEET AWAY, TOSSED INTO SOME BUSHES.
"THE CORONER SAID IT'D ALL HAPPENED WHILE SHE WAS ALIVE. SHE'D BEEN HOOKED UP AND HER LUNGS WERE PULLED RIGHT FROM HER CHEST.
"BUT THEY WERE UNUSABLE.
"IT TOOK THE POLICE ANOTHER THREE MONTHS TO FIND JAMES ANDERSON IN HIS BASEMENT, THE LAST OF HIS VICTIMS DECAPITATED BUT ALIVE.

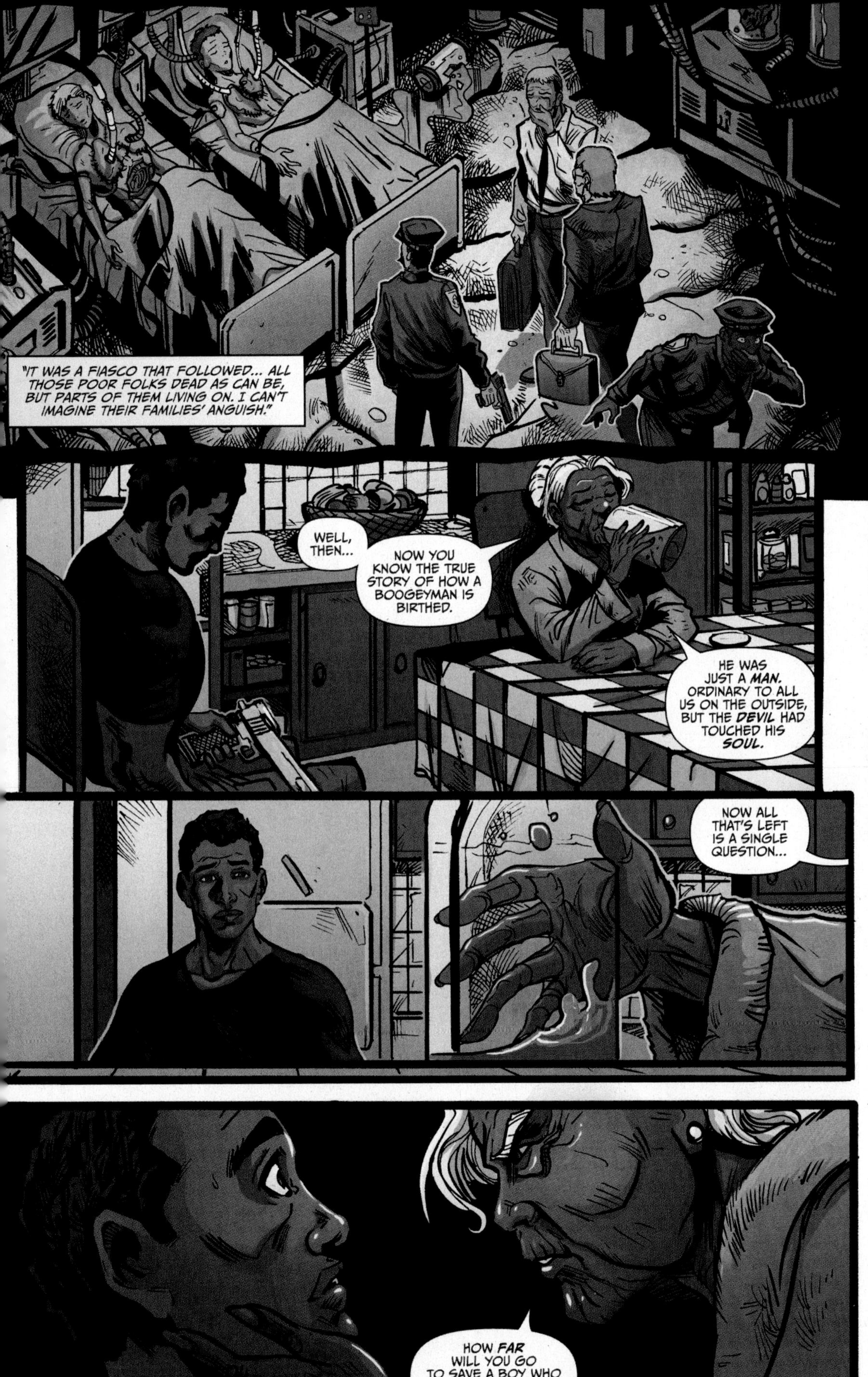
"IT WAS A FIASCO THAT FOLLOWED... ALL THOSE POOR FOLKS DEAD AS CAN BE, BUT PARTS OF THEM LIVING ON. I CAN'T IMAGINE THEIR FAMILIES' ANGUISH."
WELL, THEN...
NOW YOU KNOW THE TRUE STORY OF HOW A BOOGEYMAN IS BIRTHED.
HE WAS JUST A MAN. ORDINARY TO ALL US ON THE OUTSIDE, BUT THE DEVIL HAD TOUCHED HIS SOUL.
NOW ALL THAT'S LEFT IS A SINGLE QUESTION...
HOW FAR WILL YOU GO TO SAVE A BOY WHO MAY WELL BE DEAD?

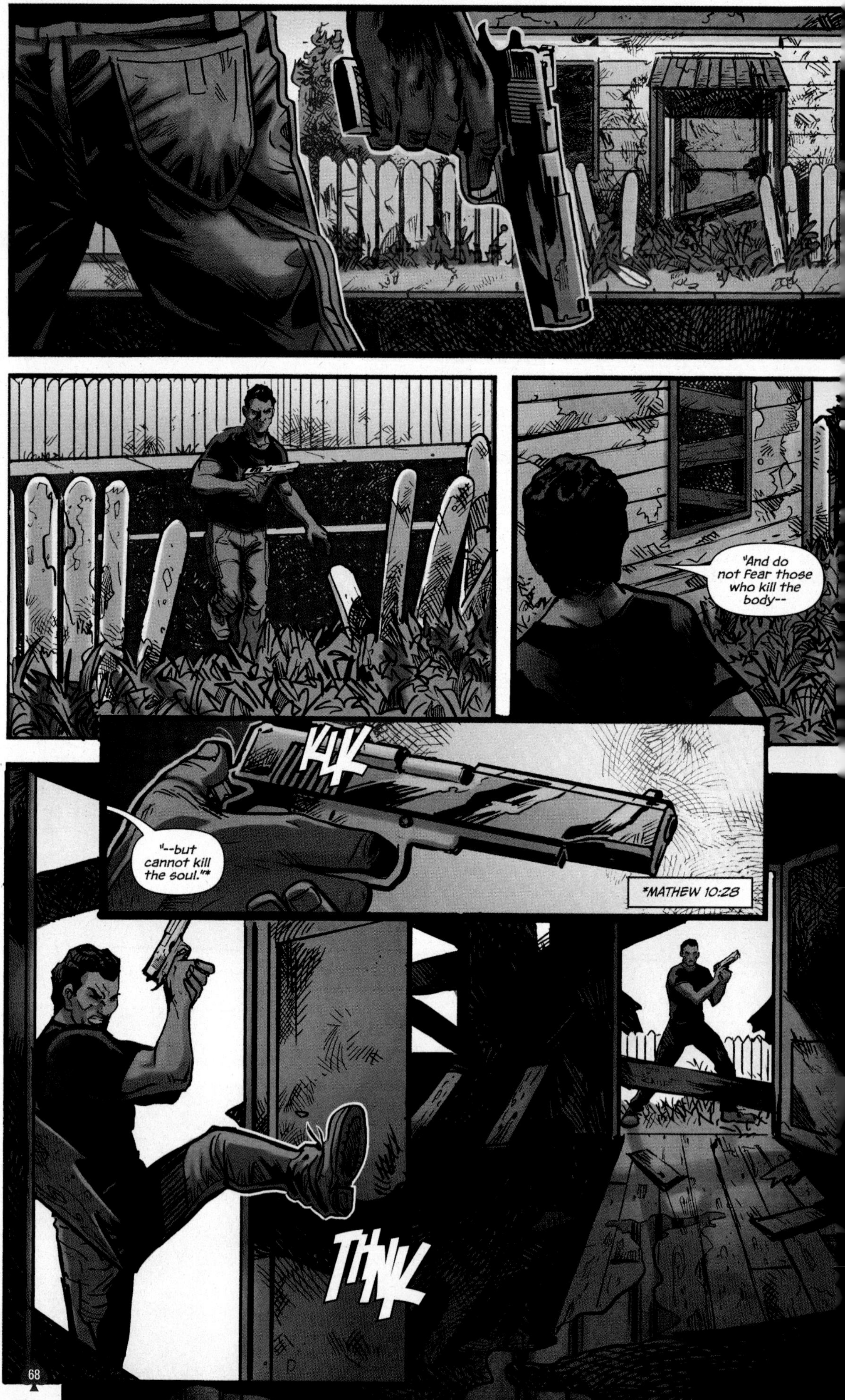
"And do not fear those who kill the body--
KLIK
"--but cannot kill the soul."*
*MATHEW 10:28
THNK

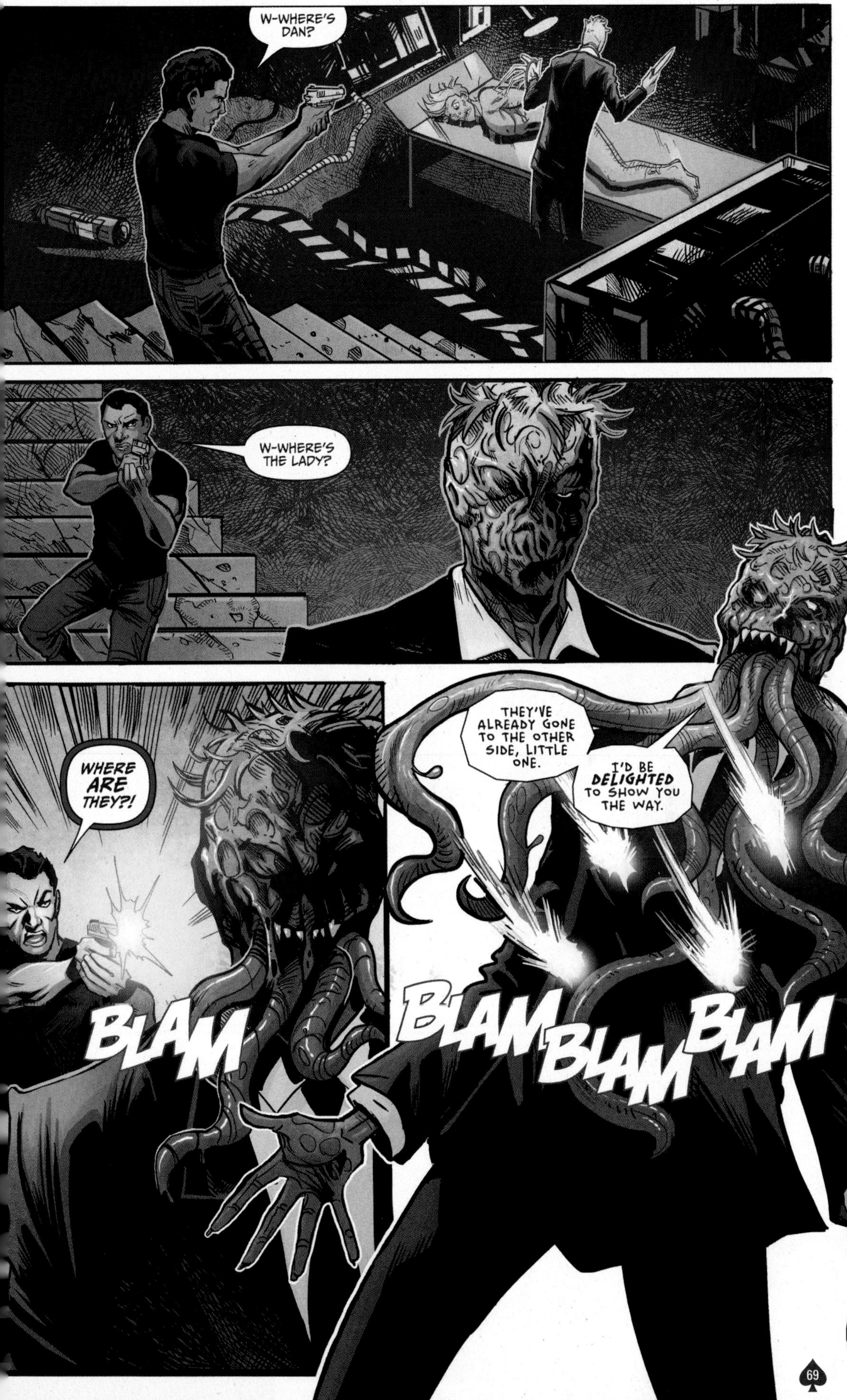

W-WHERE'S DAN?
W-WHERE'S THE LADY?
WHERE ARE THEY?!
THEY'VE ALREADY GONE TO THE OTHER SIDE, LITTLE ONE.
I'D BE DELIGHTED TO SHOW YOU THE WAY.
BLAM
BLAM BLAM BLAM

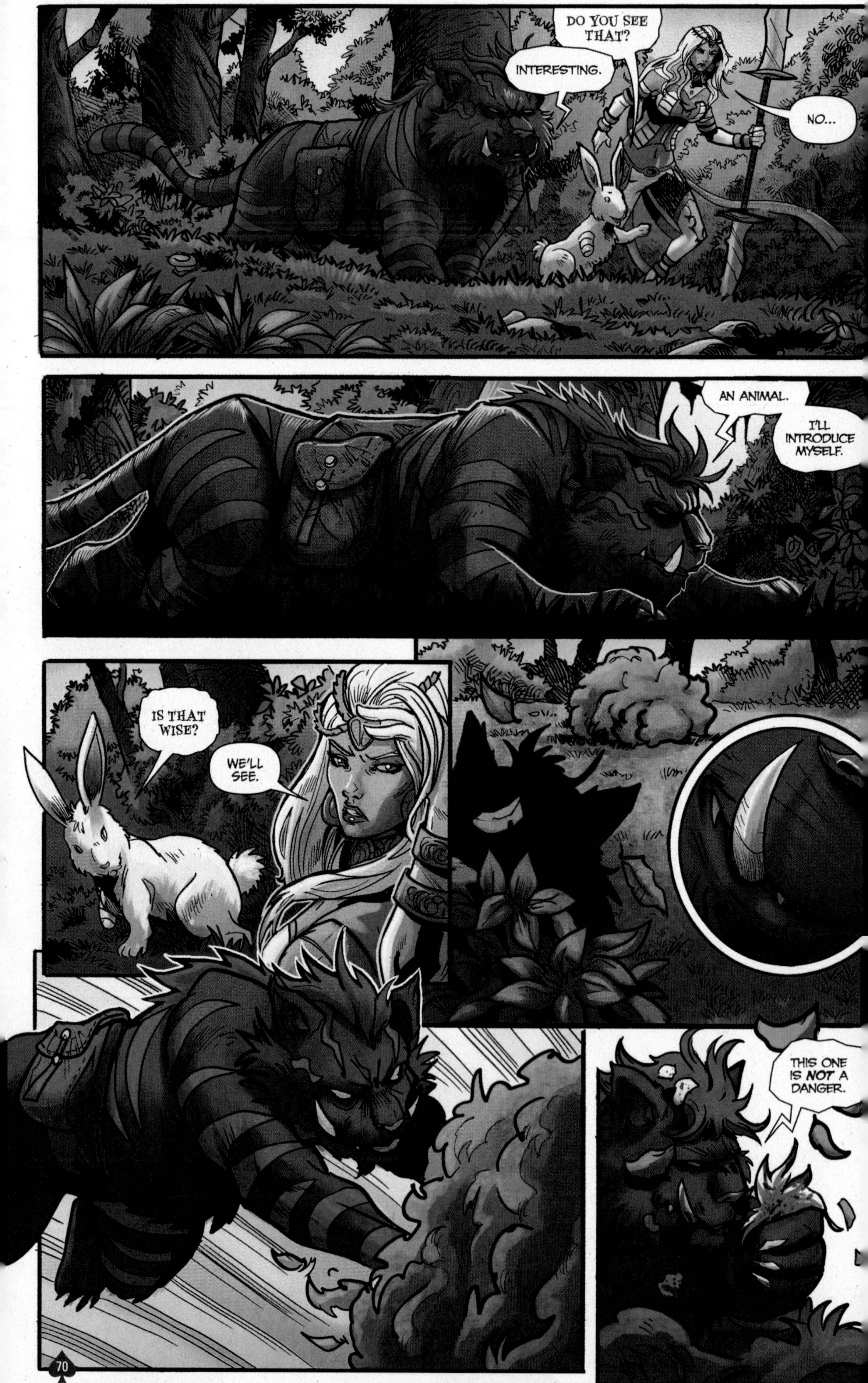
DO YOU SEE THAT?
INTERESTING.
NO...
AN ANIMAL.
I'LL INTRODUCE MYSELF.
IS THAT WISE?
WE'LL SEE.
THIS ONE IS **NOT** A DANGER.

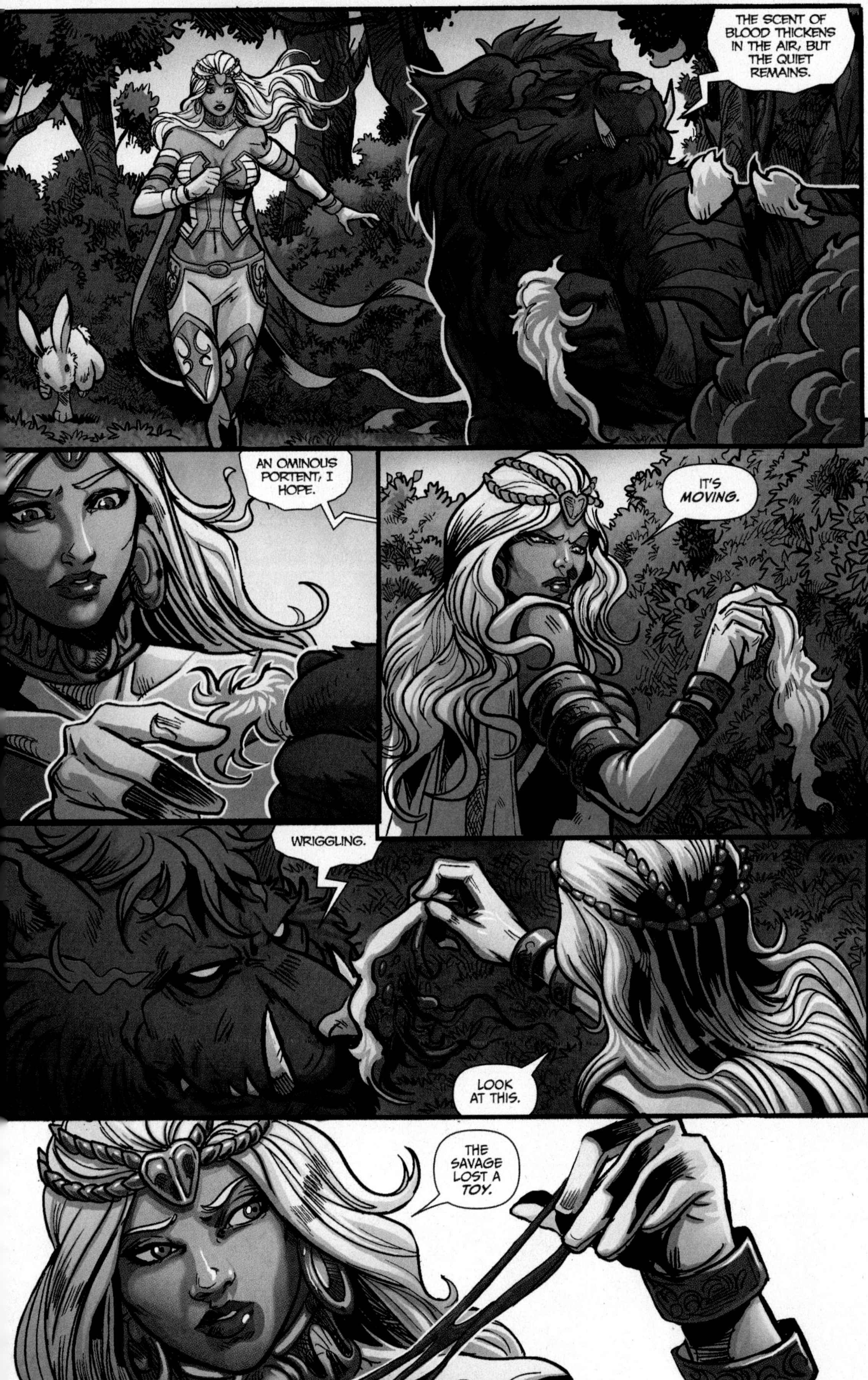
THE SCENT OF BLOOD THICKENS IN THE AIR, BUT THE QUIET REMAINS.
AN OMINOUS PORTENT, I HOPE.
IT'S *MOVING.*
WRIGGLING.
LOOK AT THIS.
THE SAVAGE LOST A *TOY.*

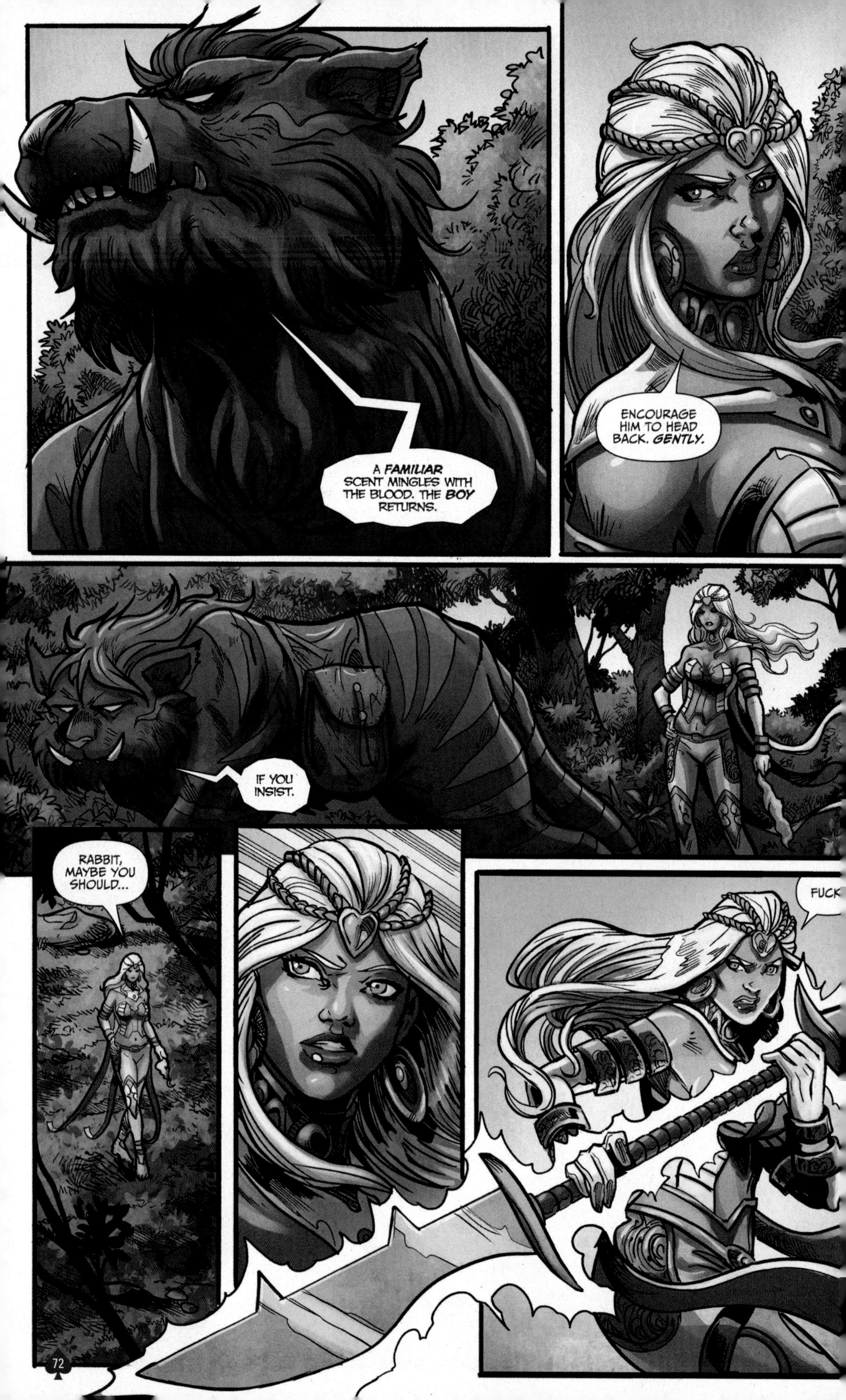
A FAMILIAR SCENT MINGLES WITH THE BLOOD. THE BOY RETURNS.
ENCOURAGE HIM TO HEAD BACK. GENTLY.
IF YOU INSIST.
RABBIT, MAYBE YOU SHOULD...
FUCK

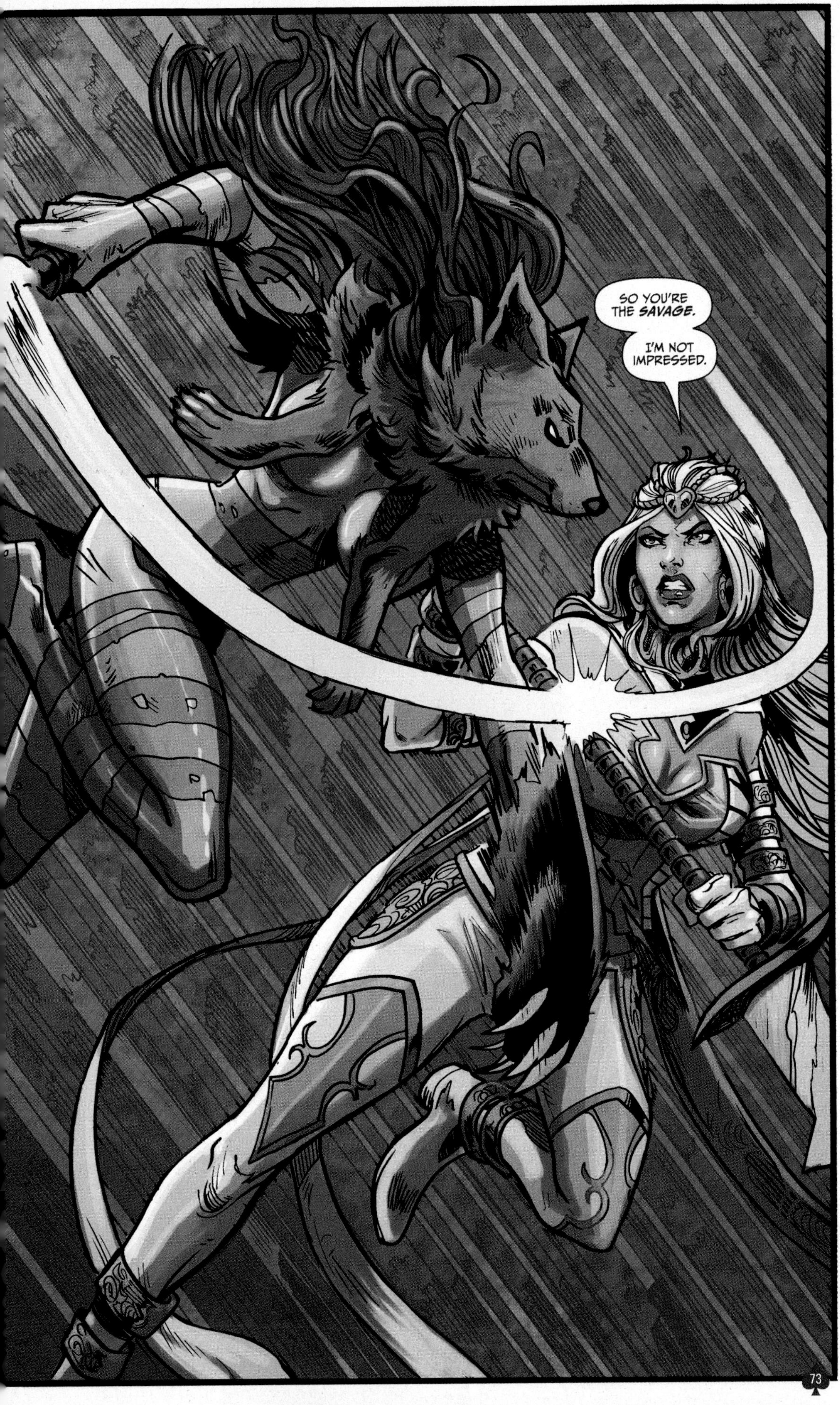
SO YOU'RE THE *SAVAGE.*
I'M NOT IMPRESSED.

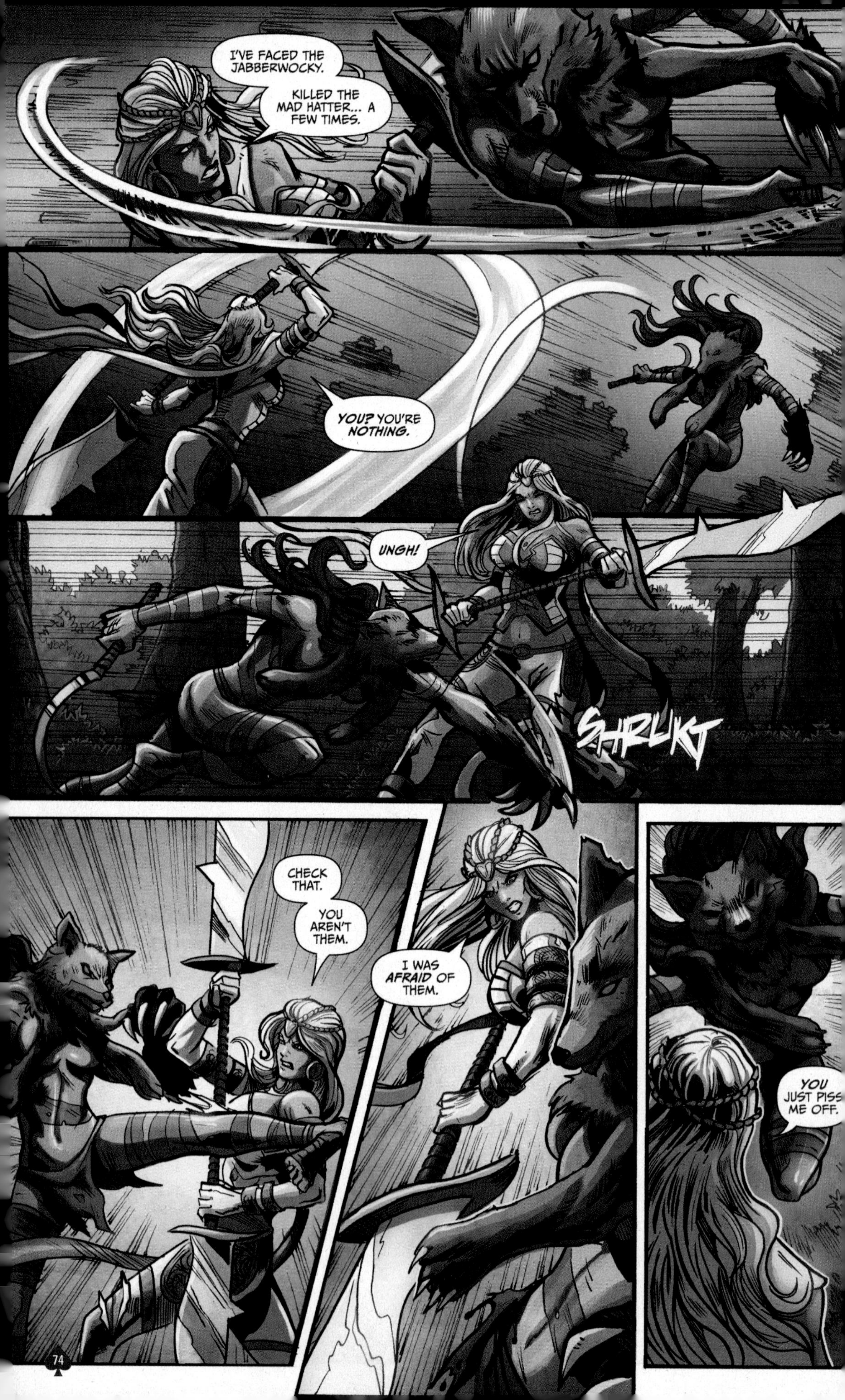
I'VE FACED THE JABBERWOCKY.
KILLED THE MAD HATTER... A FEW TIMES.
YOU? YOU'RE NOTHING.
UNGH!
SHRUKT
CHECK THAT.
YOU AREN'T THEM.
I WAS AFRAID OF THEM.
YOU JUST PISS ME OFF.

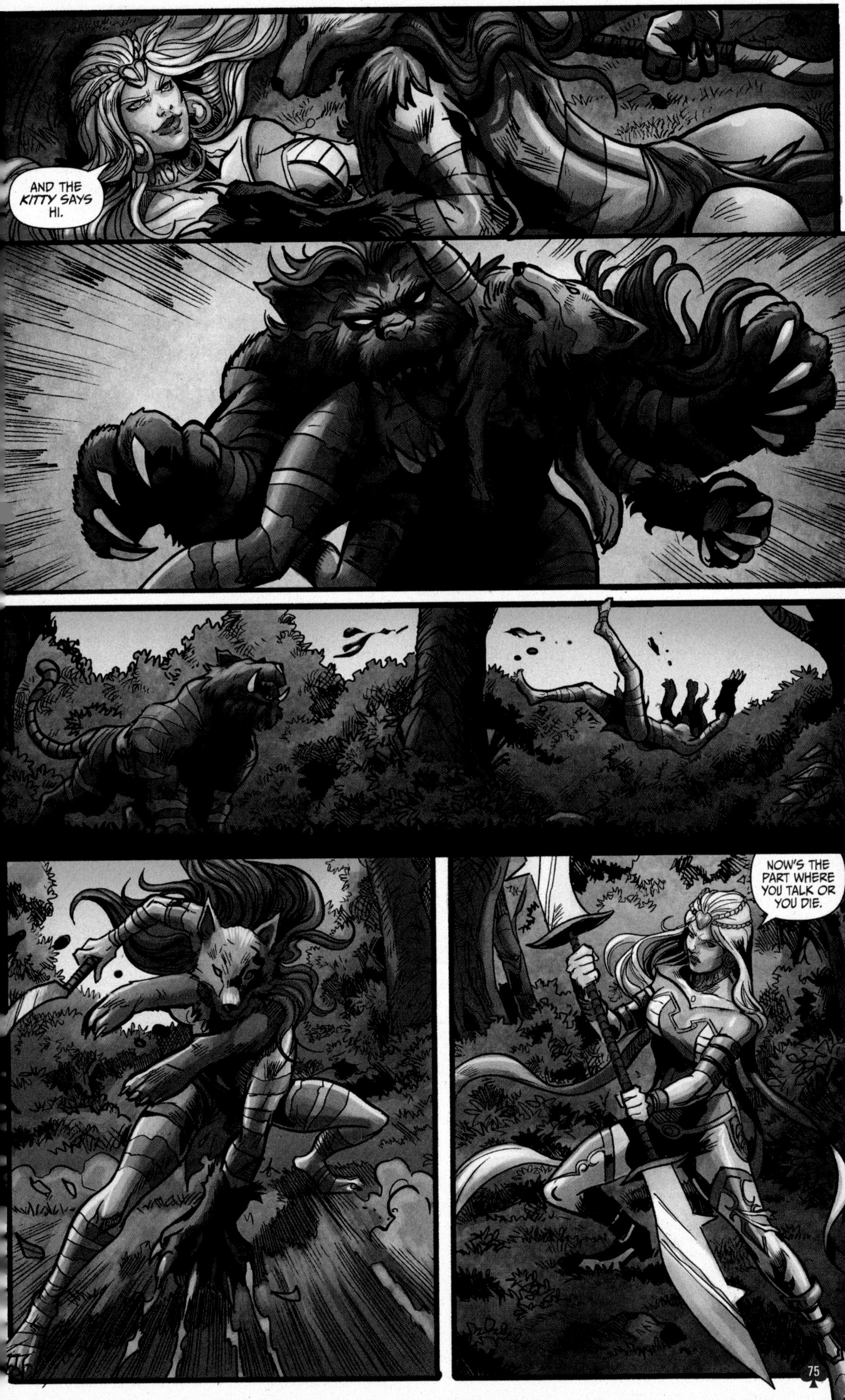
AND THE KITTY SAYS HI.
NOW'S THE PART WHERE YOU TALK OR YOU DIE.

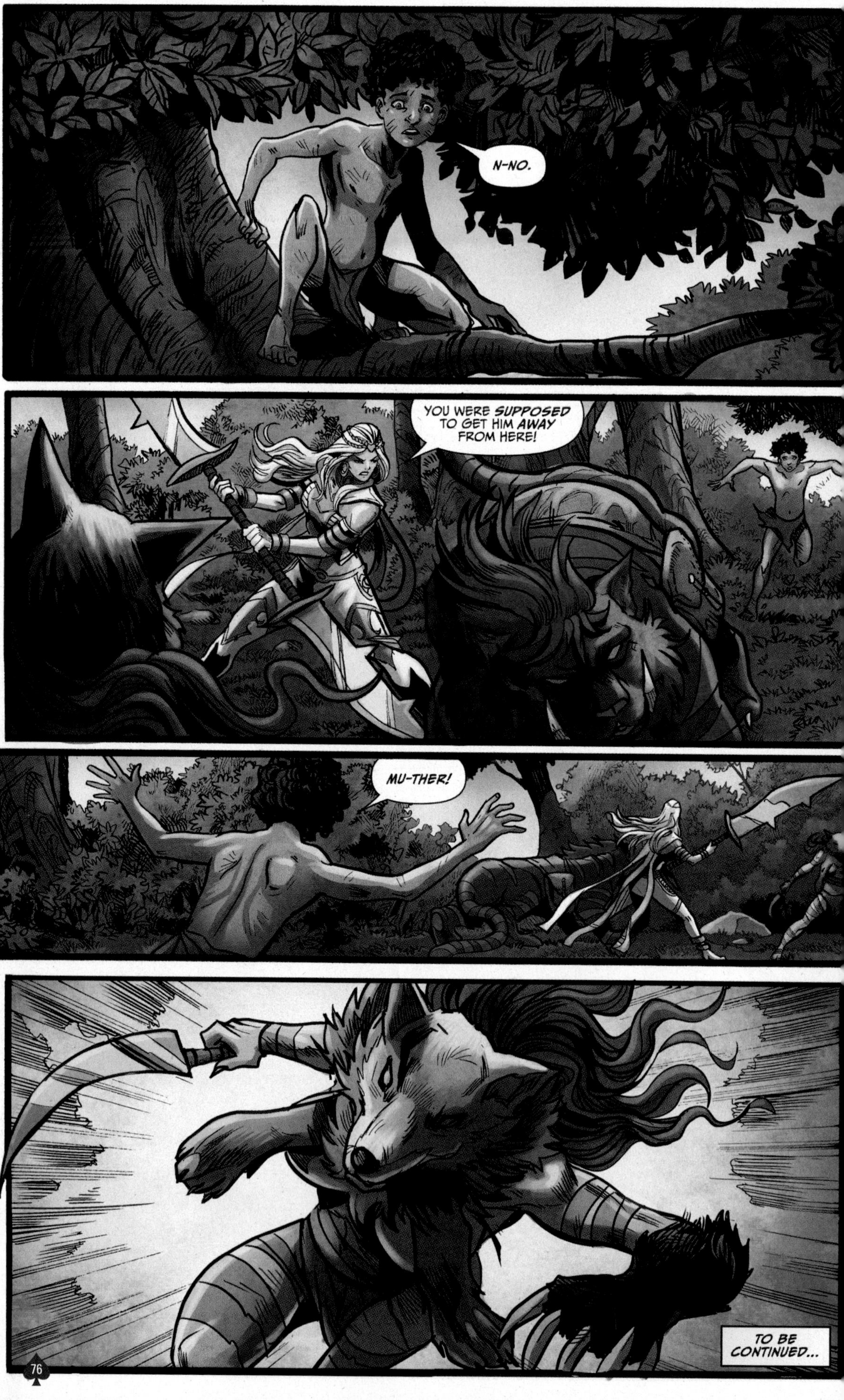
N-NO.
YOU WERE SUPPOSED TO GET HIM AWAY FROM HERE!
MU-THER!
TO BE CONTINUED...

END CHAPTER

RENAISSANCE

PART FOUR

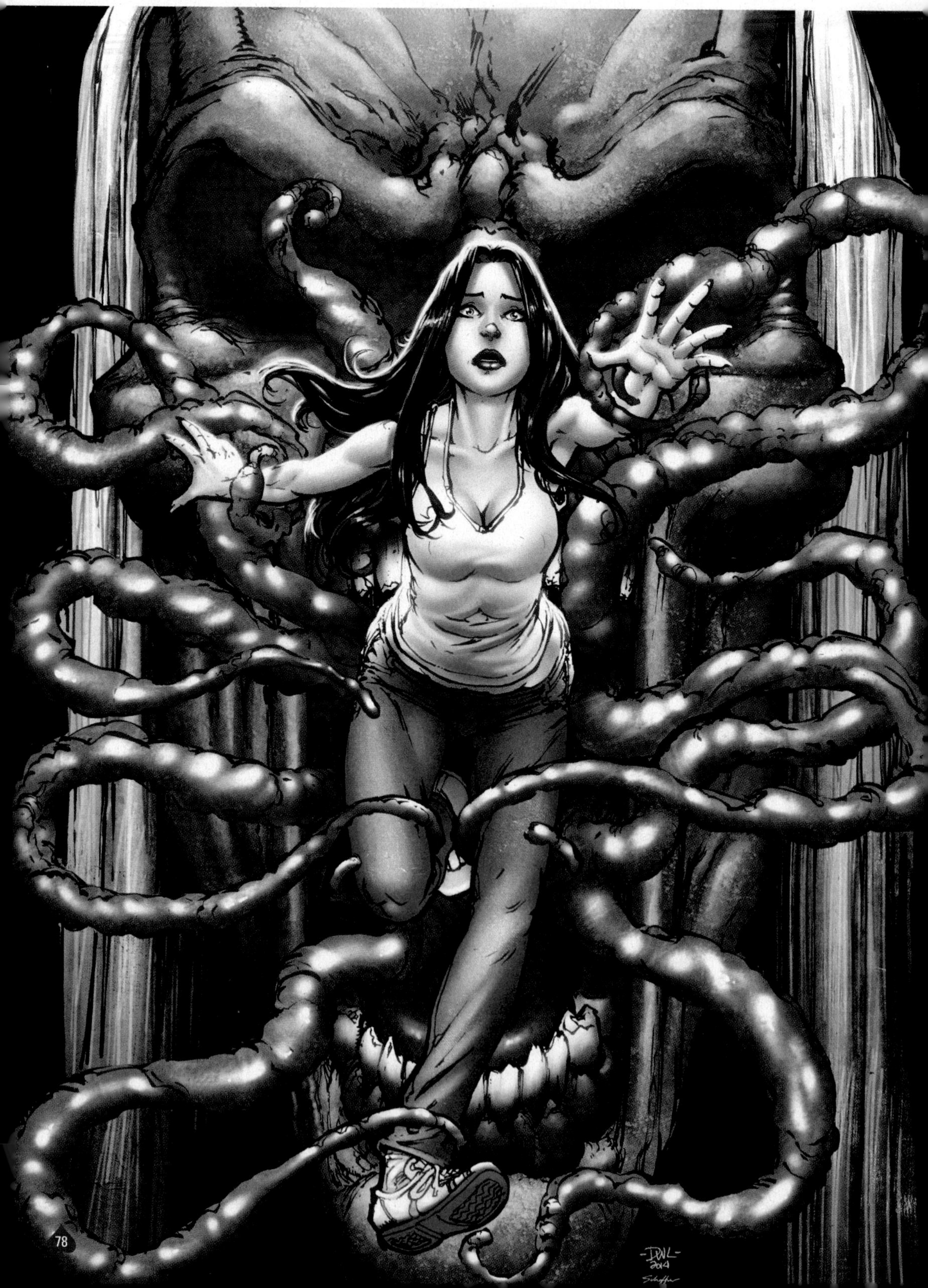

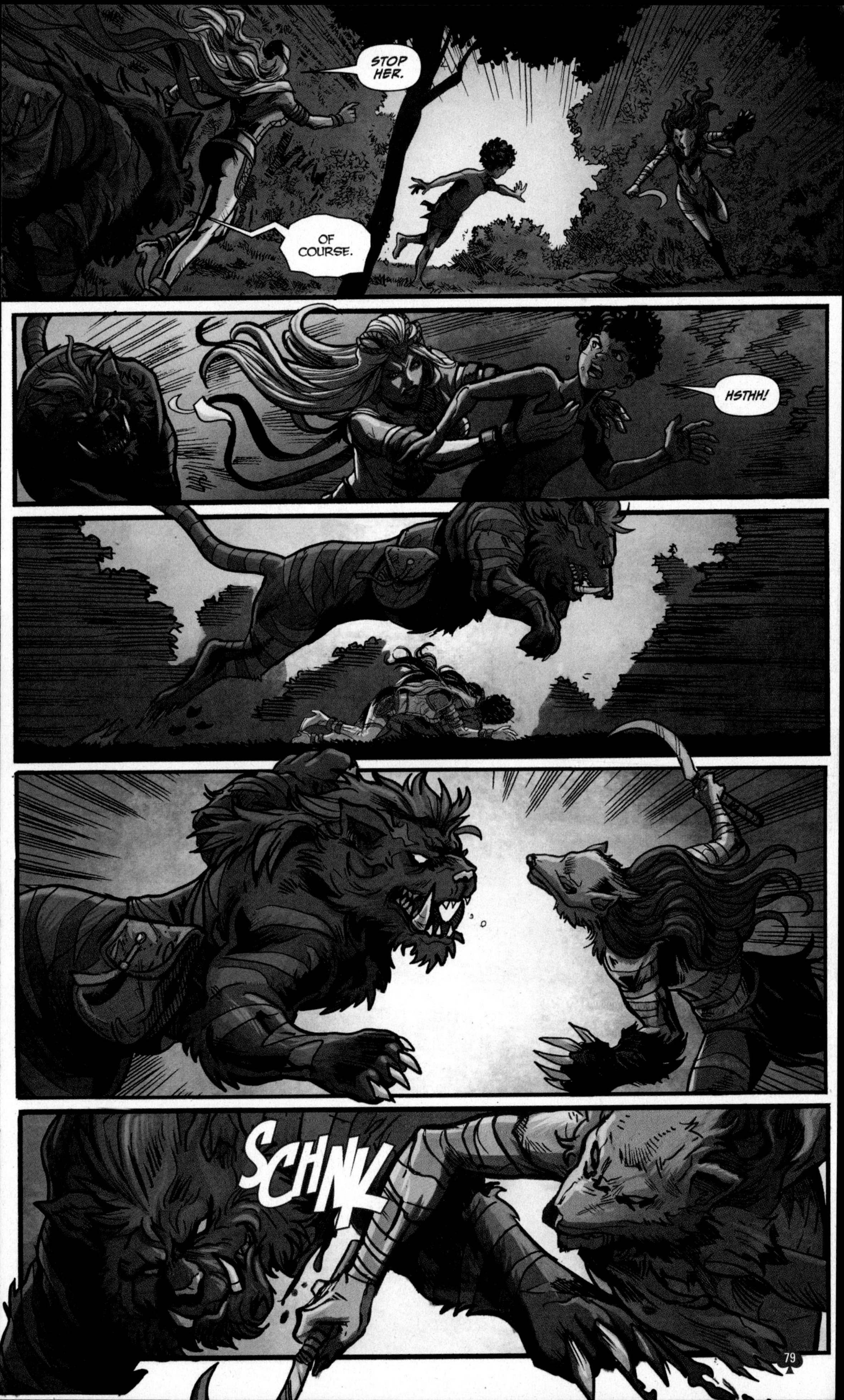
STOP HER.
OF COURSE.
HSTHH!
SCHNK

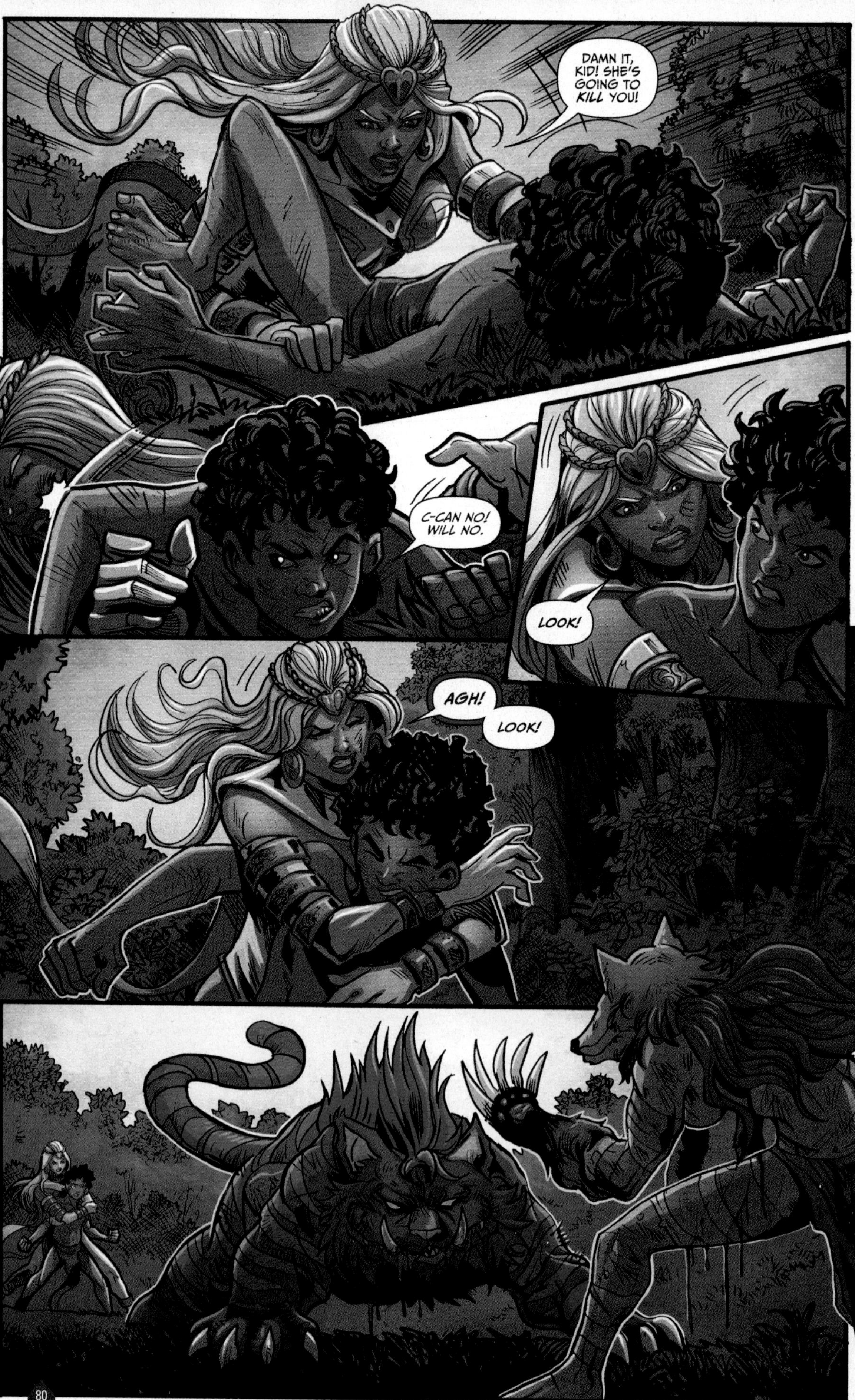
DAMN IT, KID! SHE'S GOING TO KILL YOU!
C-CAN NO! WILL NO.
LOOK!
AGH!
LOOK!

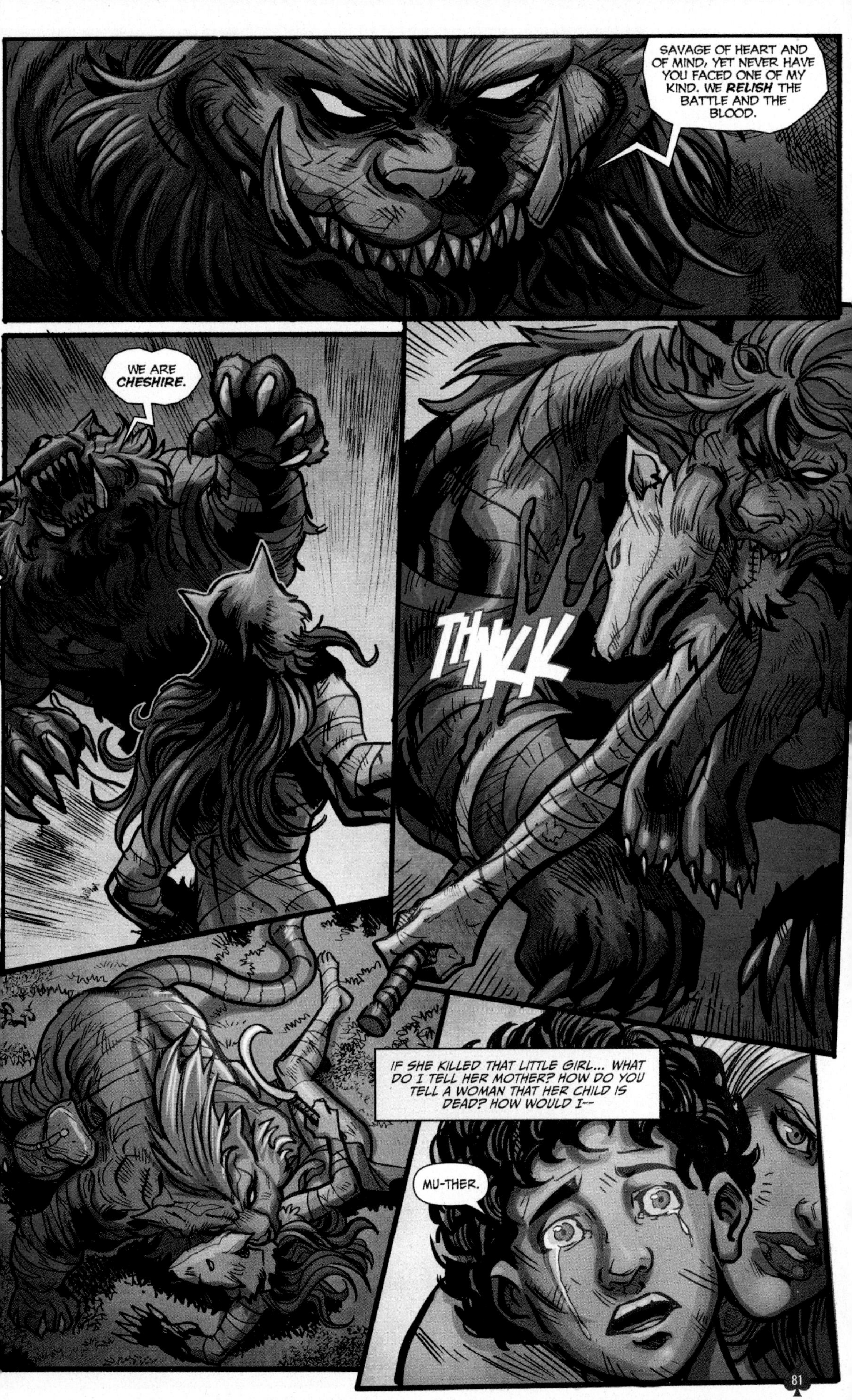
SAVAGE OF HEART AND OF MIND, YET NEVER HAVE YOU FACED ONE OF MY KIND. WE **RELISH** THE BATTLE AND THE BLOOD.
WE ARE **CHESHIRE.**
THNKK
IF SHE KILLED THAT LITTLE GIRL... WHAT DO I TELL HER MOTHER? HOW DO YOU TELL A WOMAN THAT HER CHILD IS DEAD? HOW WOULD I--
MU-THER.

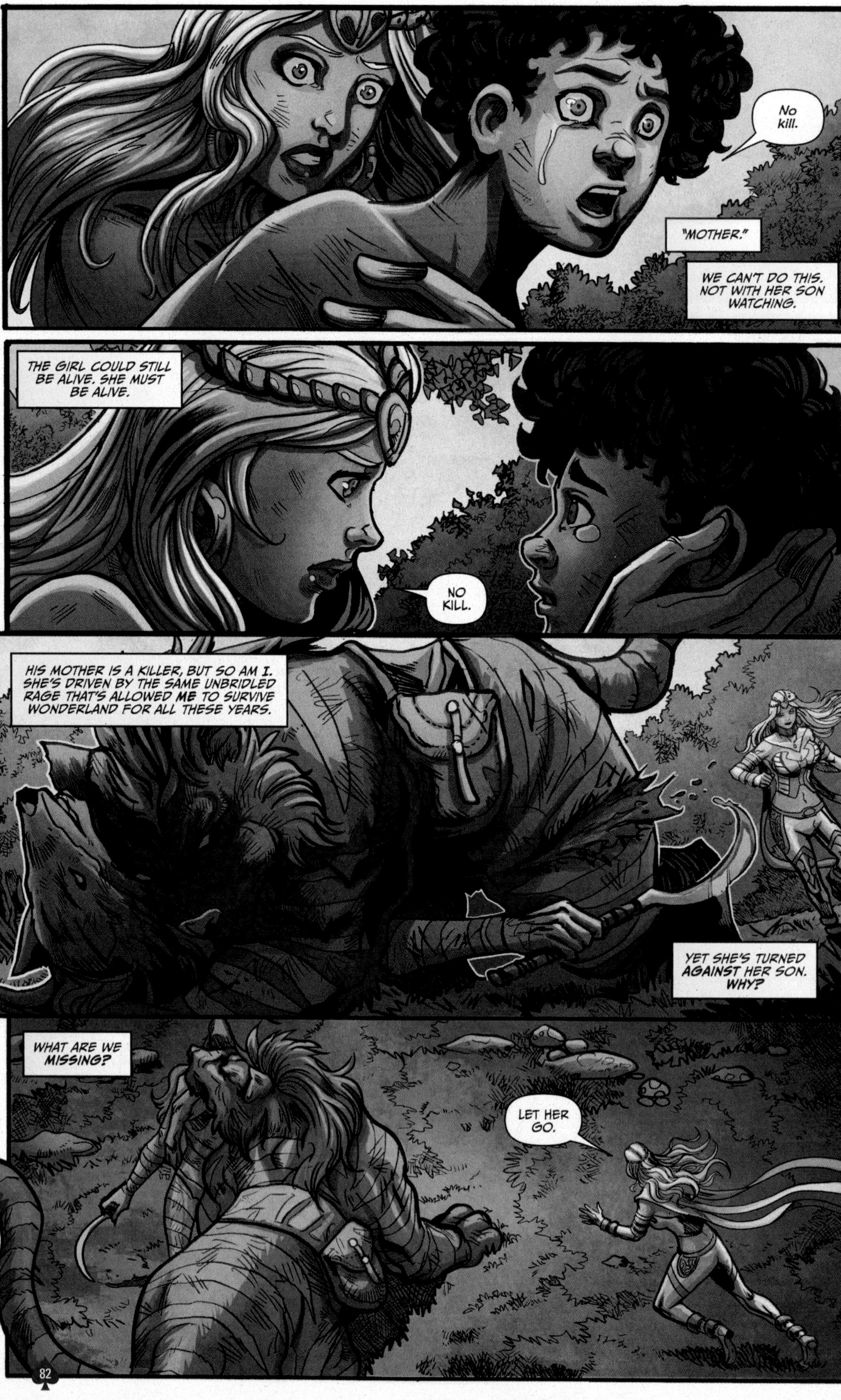
No kill.
"MOTHER."
WE CAN'T DO THIS. NOT WITH HER SON WATCHING.
THE GIRL COULD STILL BE ALIVE. SHE MUST BE ALIVE.
NO KILL.
HIS MOTHER IS A KILLER, BUT SO AM I. SHE'S DRIVEN BY THE SAME UNBRIDLED RAGE THAT'S ALLOWED ME TO SURVIVE WONDERLAND FOR ALL THESE YEARS.
YET SHE'S TURNED AGAINST HER SON. WHY?
WHAT ARE WE MISSING?
LET HER GO.

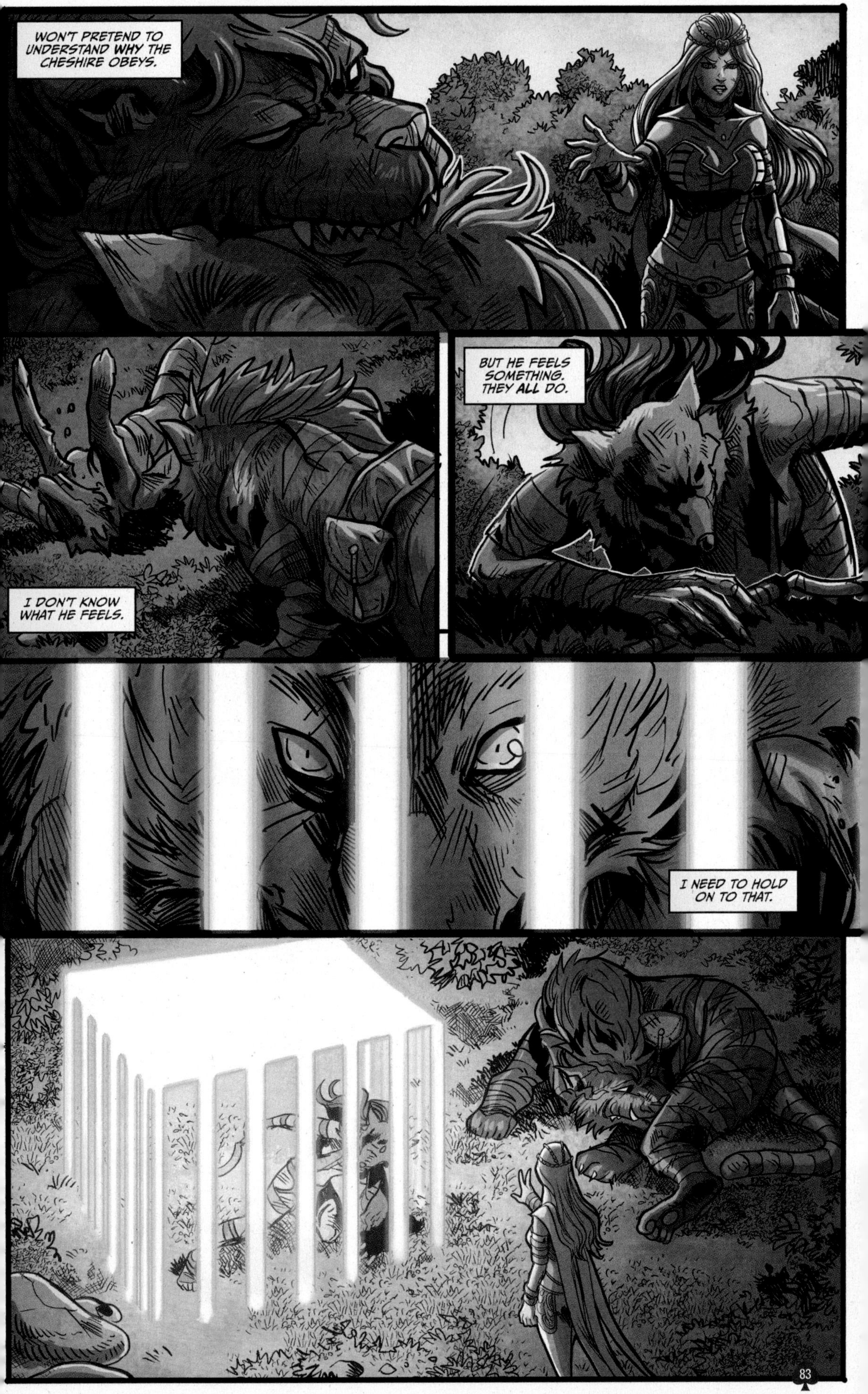
WON'T PRETEND TO UNDERSTAND WHY THE CHESHIRE OBEYS.
I DON'T KNOW WHAT HE FEELS.
BUT HE FEELS SOMETHING. THEY ALL DO.
I NEED TO HOLD ON TO THAT.

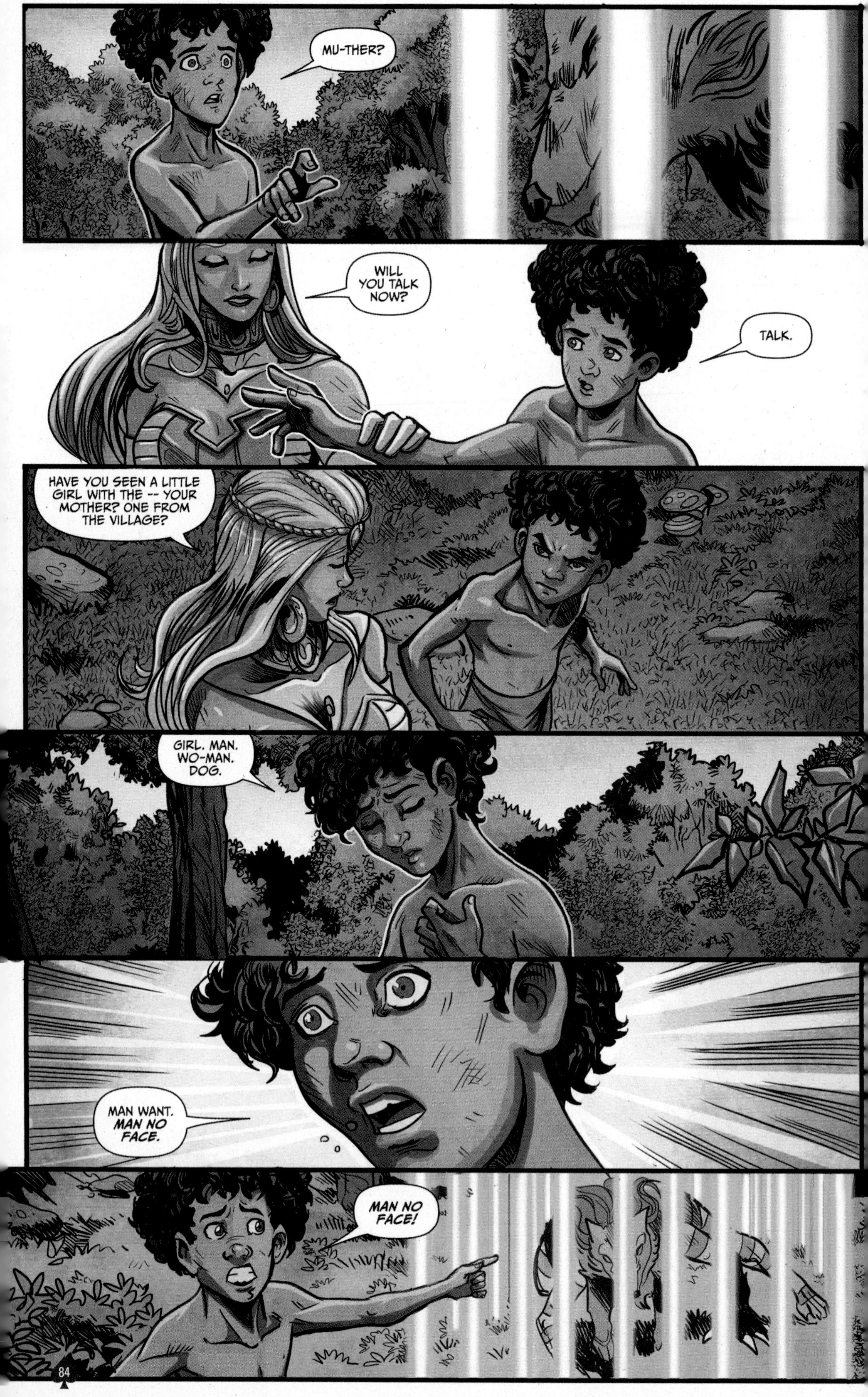
MU-THER?
WILL YOU TALK NOW?
TALK.
HAVE YOU SEEN A LITTLE GIRL WITH THE -- YOUR MOTHER? ONE FROM THE VILLAGE?
GIRL. MAN. WO-MAN. DOG.
MAN WANT. *MAN NO FACE.*
MAN NO FACE!

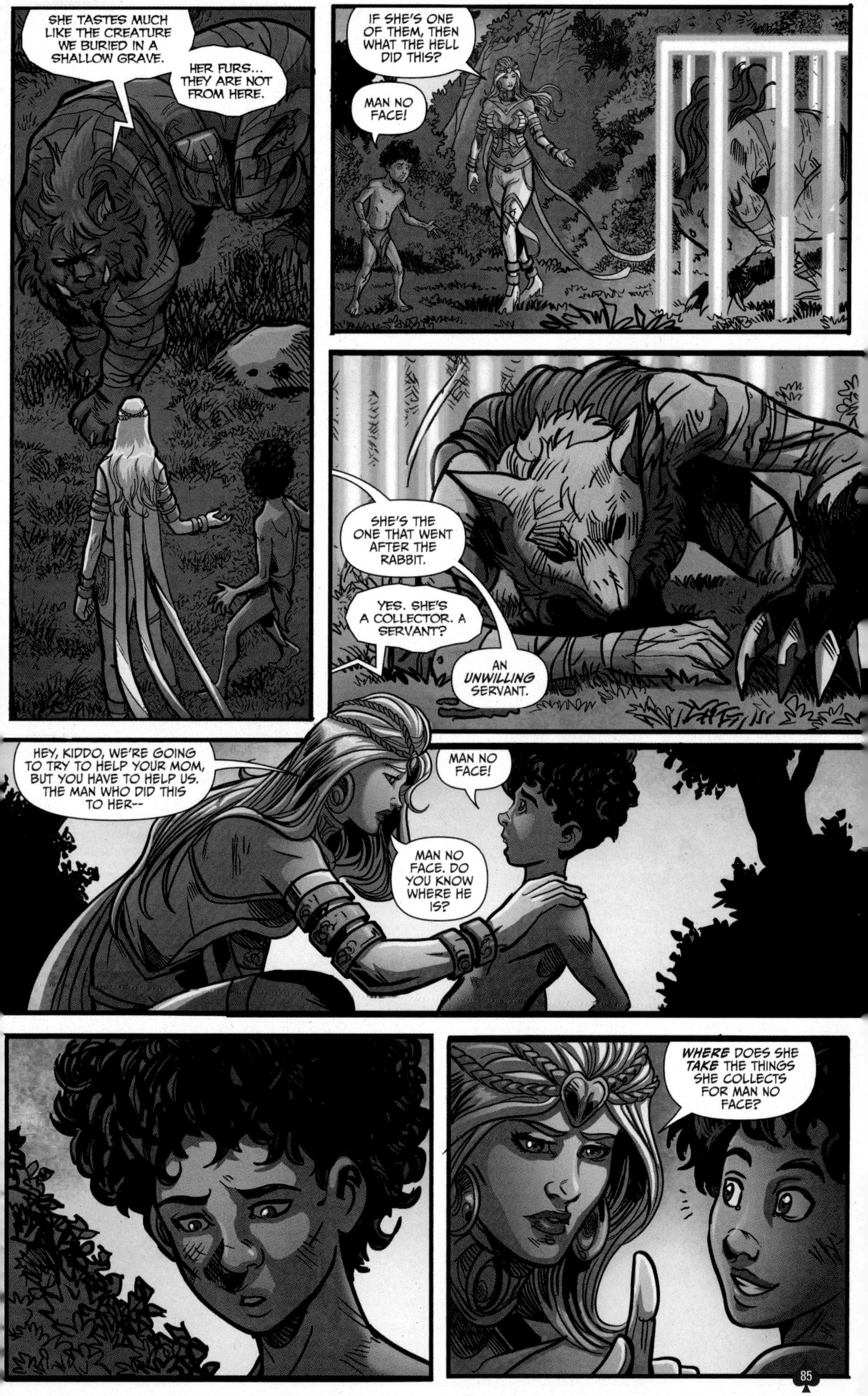
SHE TASTES MUCH LIKE THE CREATURE WE BURIED IN A SHALLOW GRAVE.
HER FURS... THEY ARE NOT FROM HERE.
IF SHE'S ONE OF THEM, THEN WHAT THE HELL DID THIS?
MAN NO FACE!
SHE'S THE ONE THAT WENT AFTER THE RABBIT.
YES. SHE'S A COLLECTOR. A SERVANT?
AN *UNWILLING* SERVANT.
HEY, KIDDO, WE'RE GOING TO TRY TO HELP YOUR MOM, BUT YOU HAVE TO HELP US. THE MAN WHO DID THIS TO HER--
MAN NO FACE!
MAN NO FACE. DO YOU KNOW WHERE HE IS?
WHERE DOES SHE *TAKE* THE THINGS SHE COLLECTS FOR MAN NO FACE?

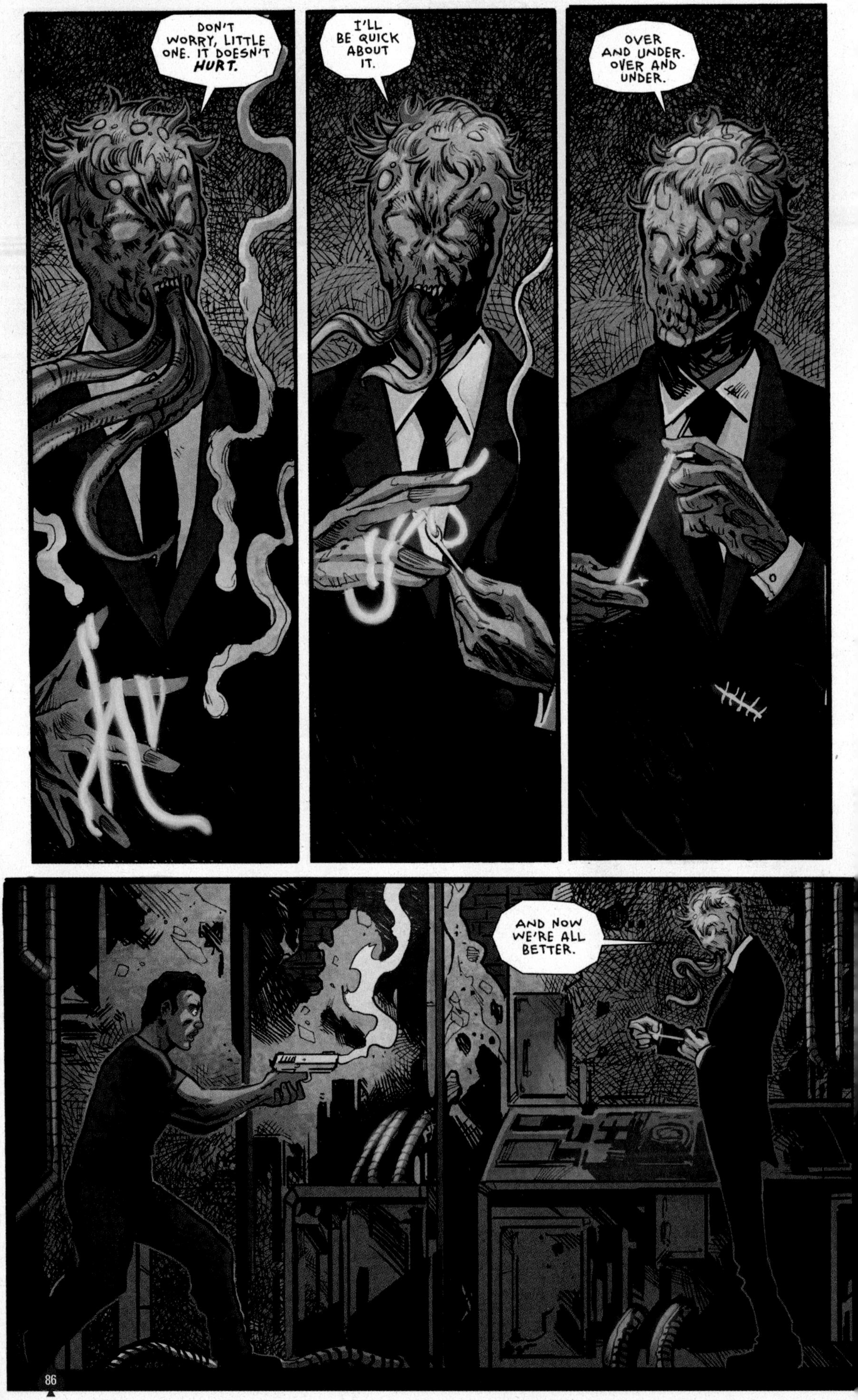

DON'T WORRY, LITTLE ONE. IT DOESN'T HURT.
I'LL BE QUICK ABOUT IT.
OVER AND UNDER. OVER AND UNDER.
AND NOW WE'RE ALL BETTER.

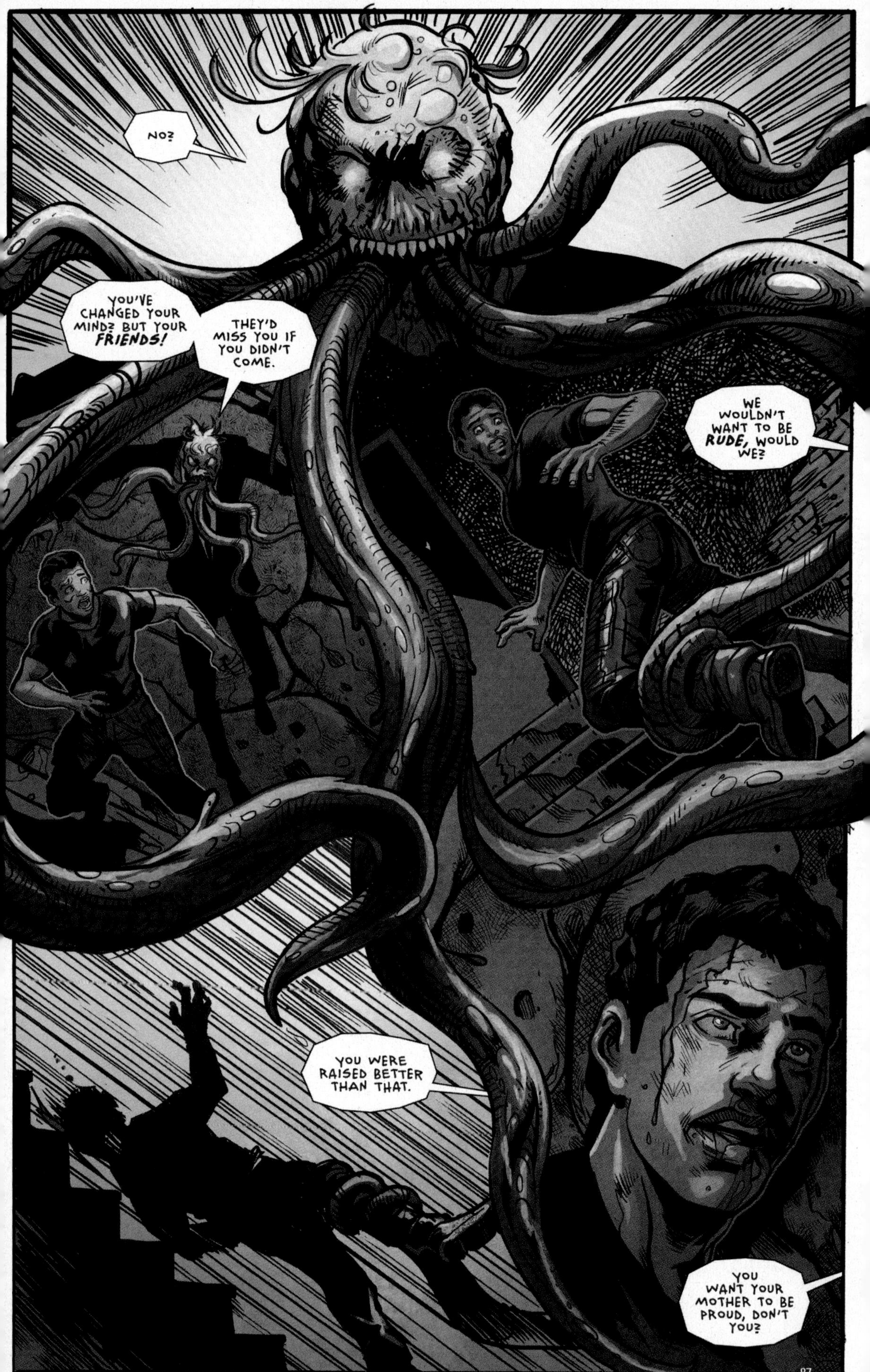
NO?
YOU'VE CHANGED YOUR MIND? BUT YOUR FRIENDS!
THEY'D MISS YOU IF YOU DIDN'T COME.
WE WOULDN'T WANT TO BE RUDE, WOULD WE?
YOU WERE RAISED BETTER THAN THAT.
YOU WANT YOUR MOTHER TO BE PROUD, DON'T YOU?

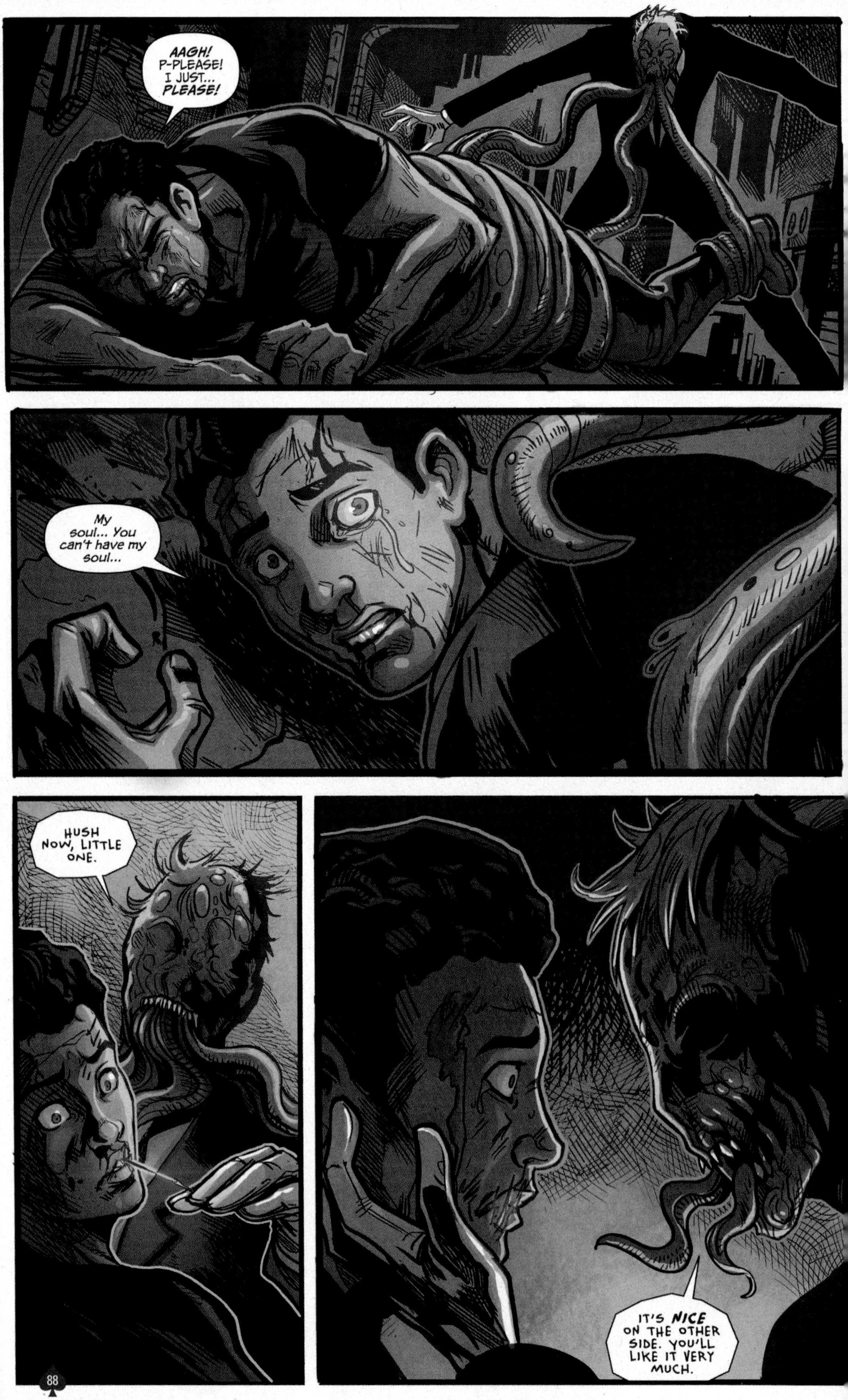
AAGH! P-PLEASE! I JUST... PLEASE!
My soul... You can't have my soul...
HUSH NOW, LITTLE ONE.
IT'S NICE ON THE OTHER SIDE. YOU'LL LIKE IT VERY MUCH.

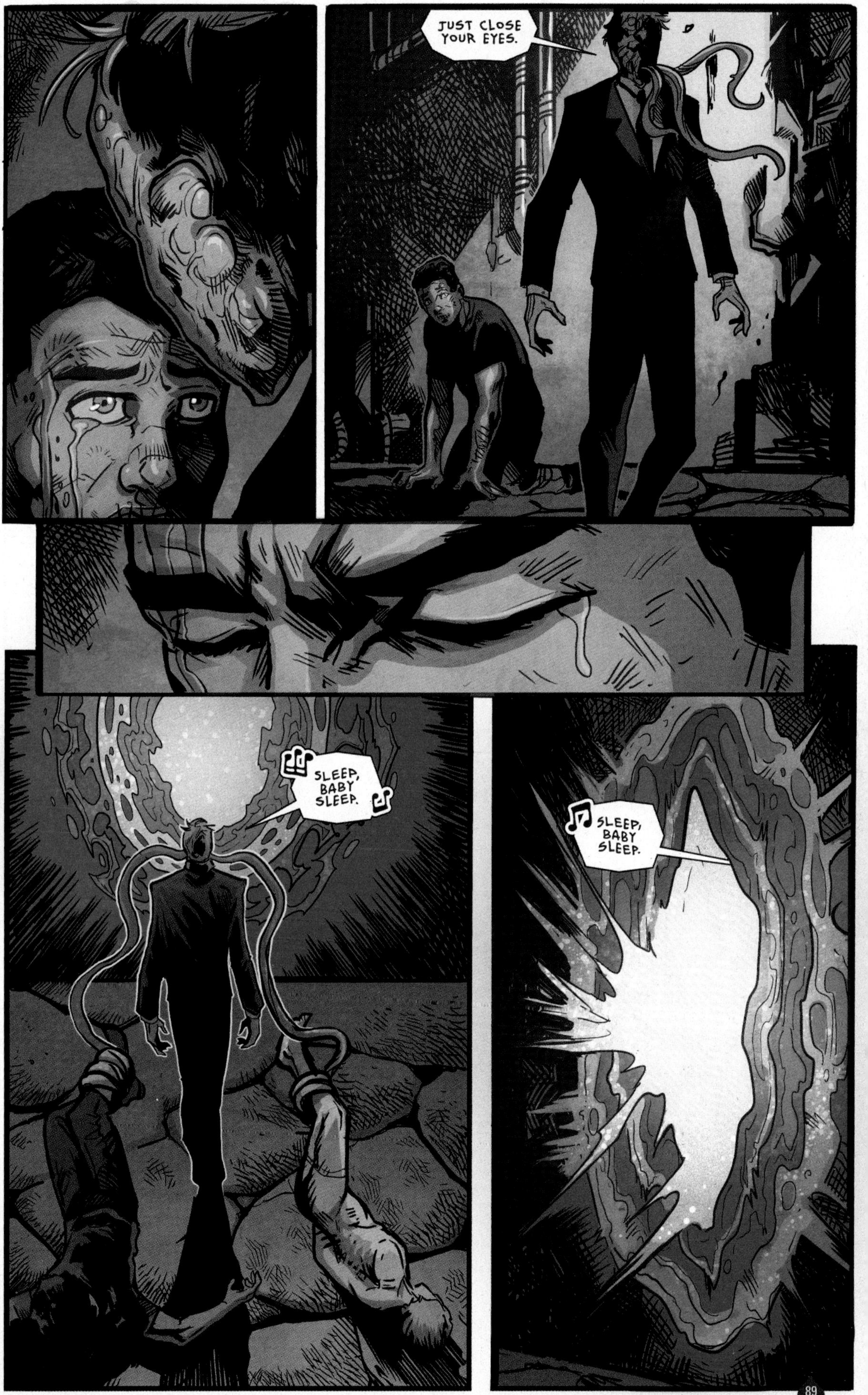
JUST CLOSE YOUR EYES.
SLEEP, BABY SLEEP.
SLEEP, BABY SLEEP.

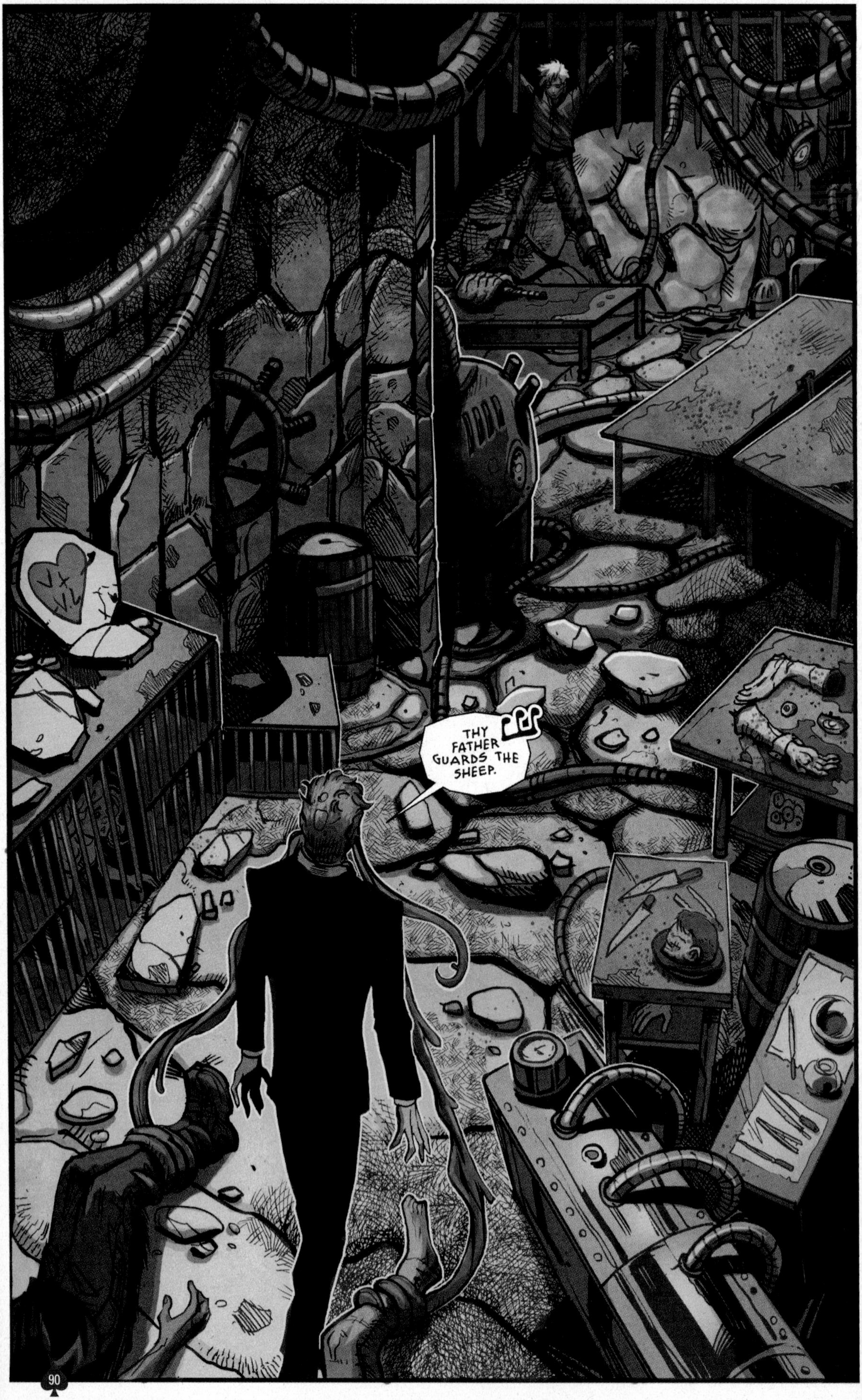
THY FATHER GUARDS THE SHEEP.

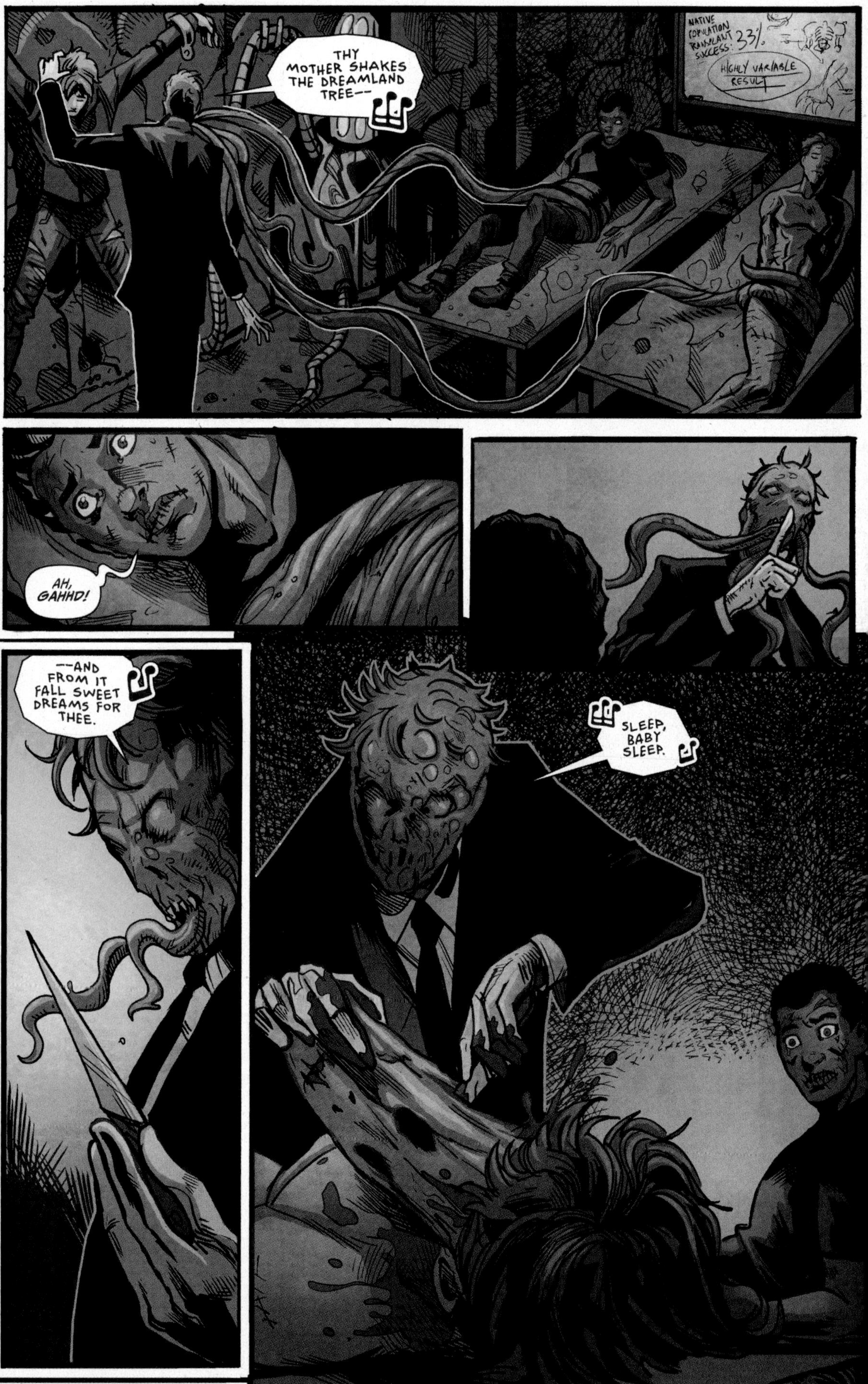
NATIVE POPULATION TRANSPLANT SUCCESS: 33%
HIGHLY VARIABLE RESULT
THY MOTHER SHAKES THE DREAMLAND TREE--
AH, GAHHD!
--AND FROM IT FALL SWEET DREAMS FOR THEE.
SLEEP, BABY SLEEP.

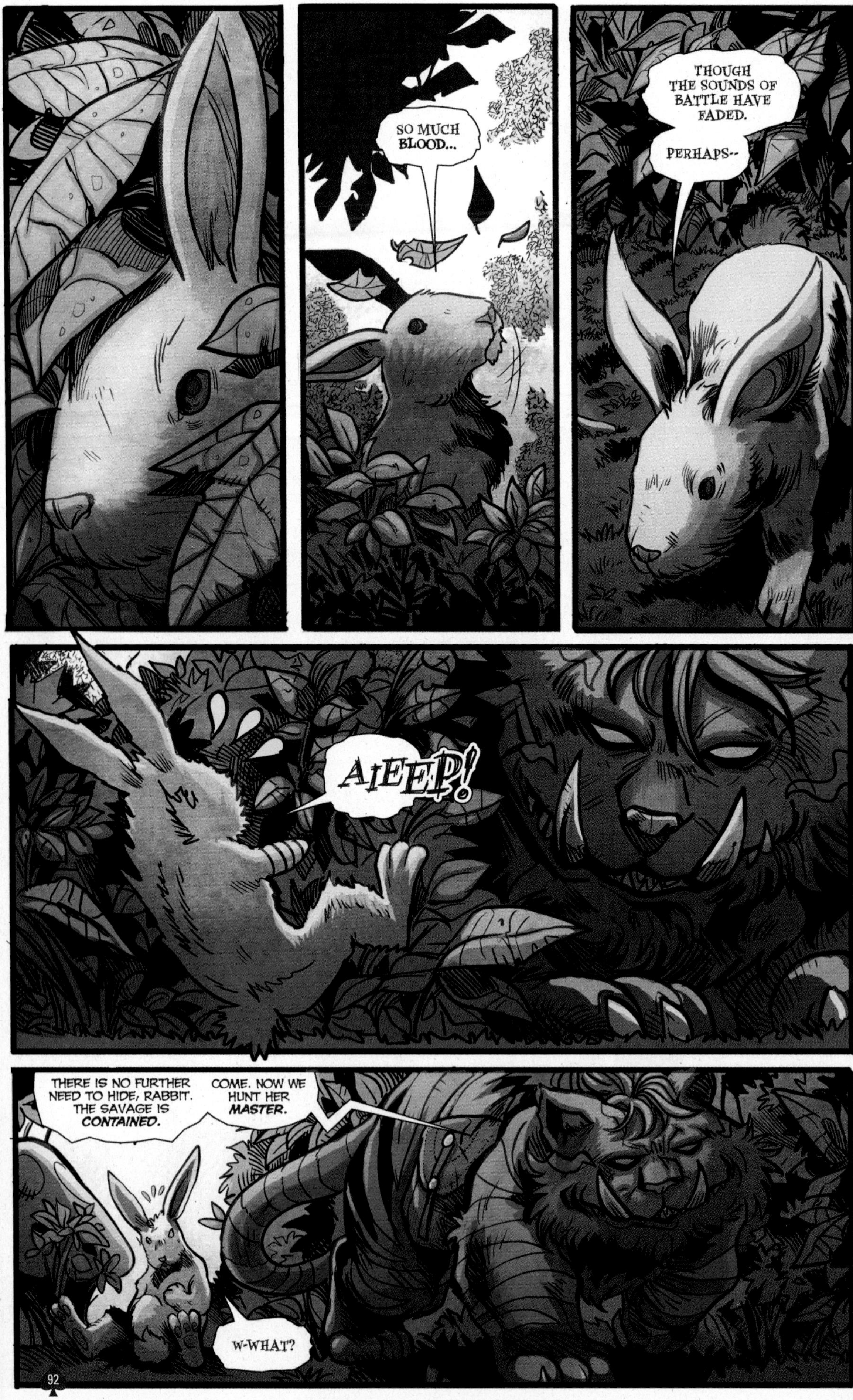
SO MUCH BLOOD...
THOUGH THE SOUNDS OF BATTLE HAVE FADED.
PERHAPS--
AIEEP!
THERE IS NO FURTHER NEED TO HIDE, RABBIT. THE SAVAGE IS CONTAINED.
COME. NOW WE HUNT HER MASTER.
W-WHAT?

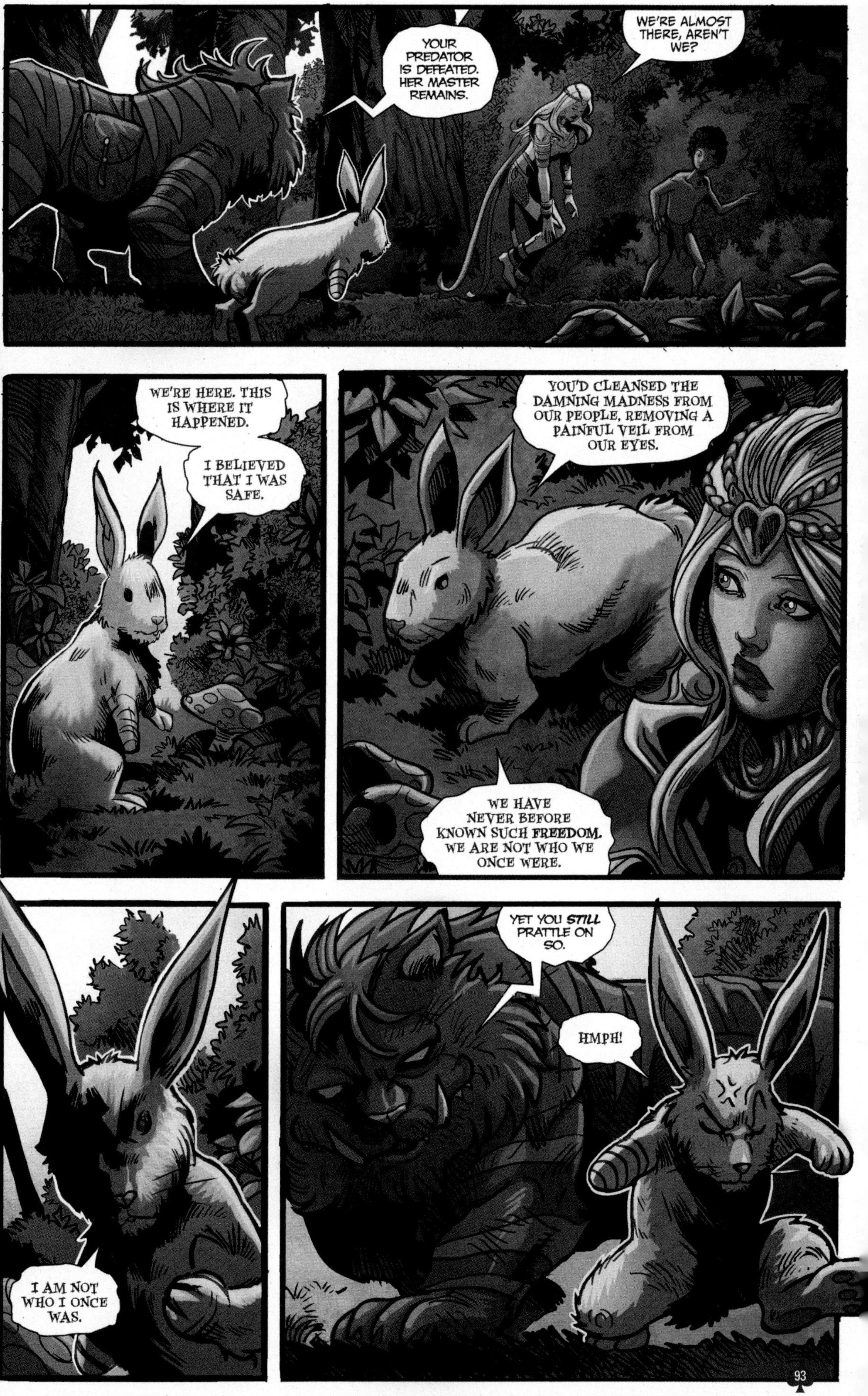
YOUR PREDATOR IS DEFEATED. HER MASTER REMAINS.
WE'RE ALMOST THERE, AREN'T WE?
WE'RE HERE. THIS IS WHERE IT HAPPENED.
I BELIEVED THAT I WAS SAFE.
YOU'D CLEANSED THE DAMNING MADNESS FROM OUR PEOPLE, REMOVING A PAINFUL VEIL FROM OUR EYES.
WE HAVE NEVER BEFORE KNOWN SUCH FREEDOM. WE ARE NOT WHO WE ONCE WERE.
I AM NOT WHO I ONCE WAS.
YET YOU STILL PRATTLE ON SO.
HMPH!

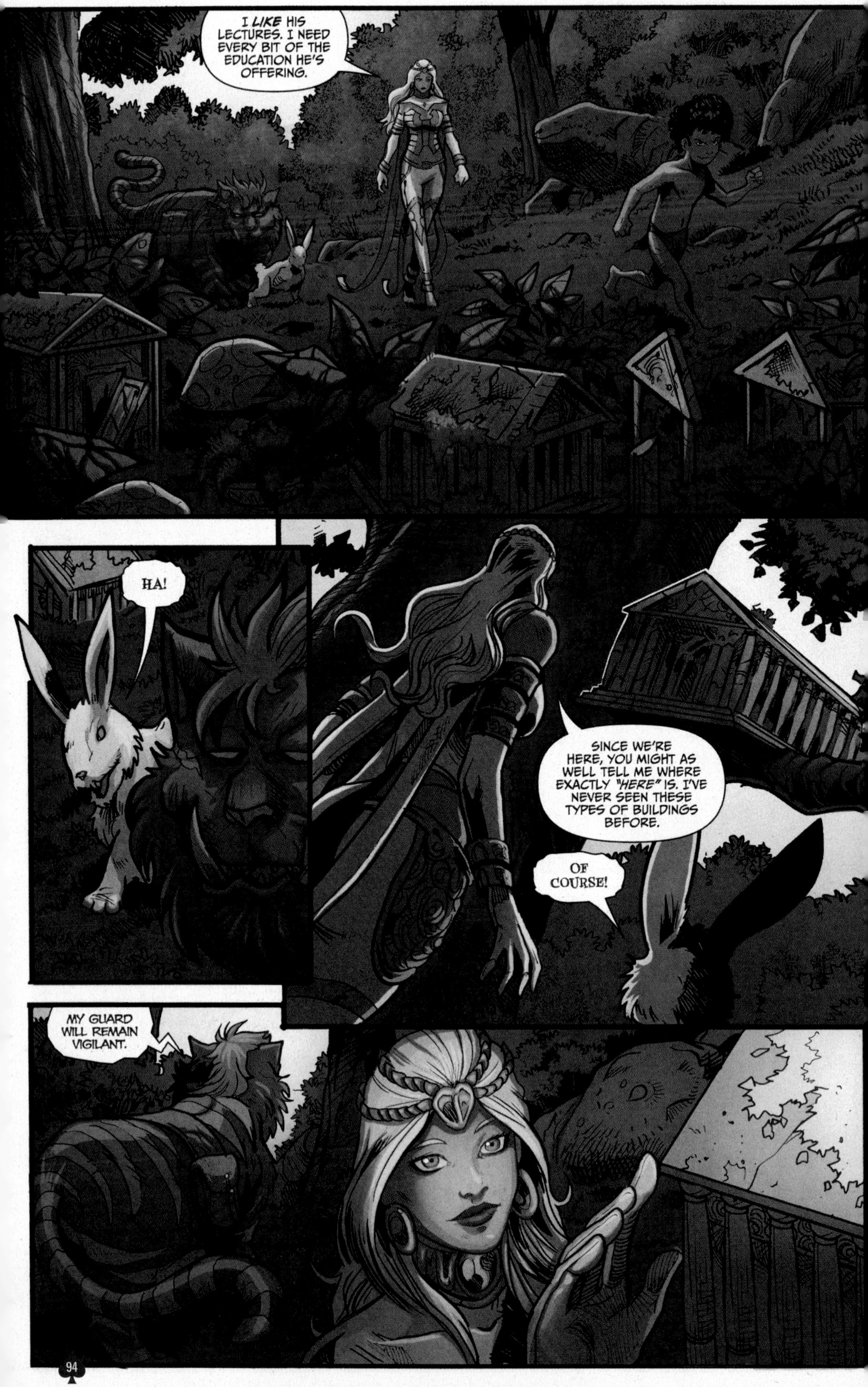
I LIKE HIS LECTURES. I NEED EVERY BIT OF THE EDUCATION HE'S OFFERING.
HA!
SINCE WE'RE HERE, YOU MIGHT AS WELL TELL ME WHERE EXACTLY "HERE" IS. I'VE NEVER SEEN THESE TYPES OF BUILDINGS BEFORE.
OF COURSE!
MY GUARD WILL REMAIN VIGILANT.

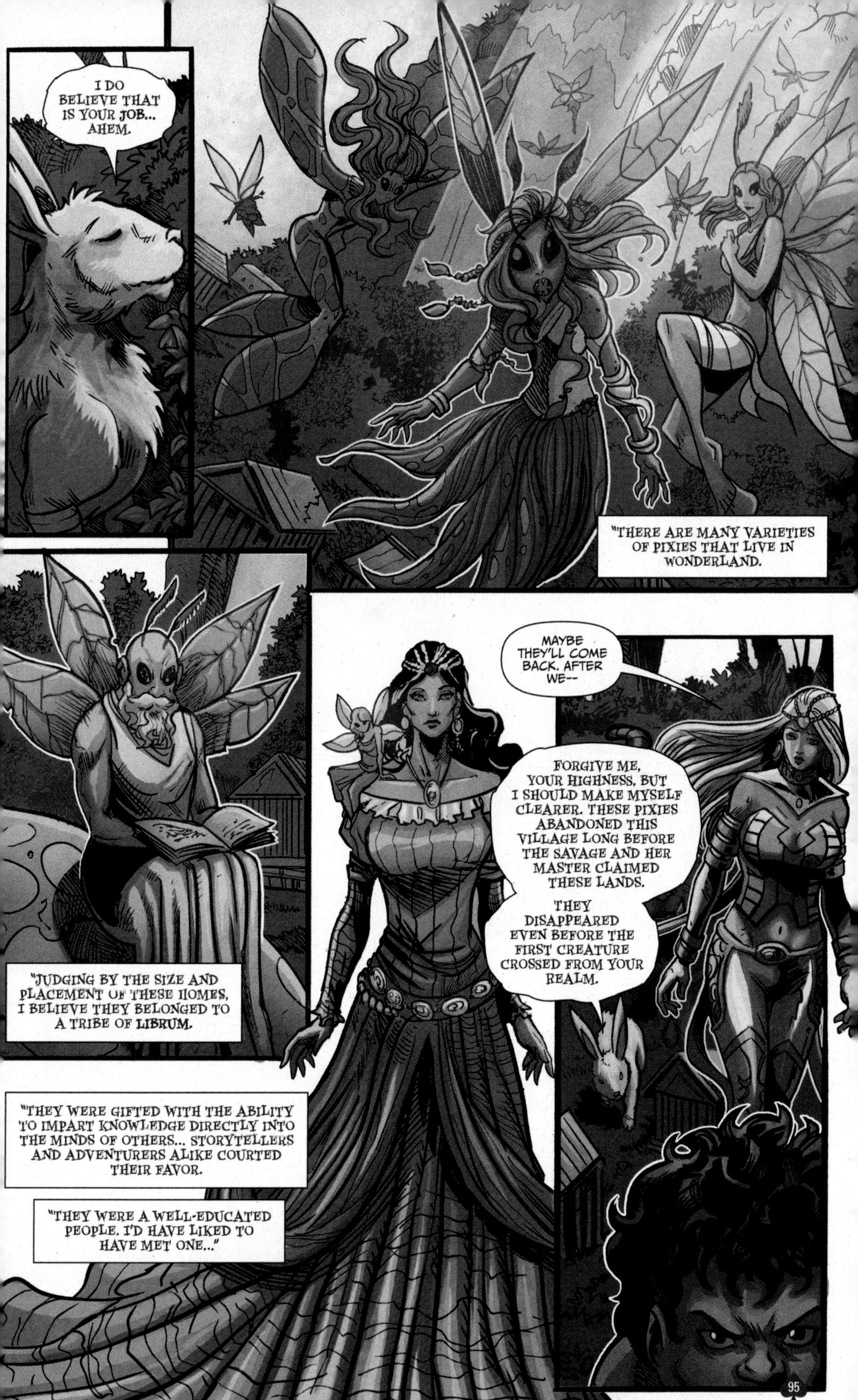

I DO BELIEVE THAT IS YOUR JOB... AHEM.
"THERE ARE MANY VARIETIES OF PIXIES THAT LIVE IN WONDERLAND.
"JUDGING BY THE SIZE AND PLACEMENT OF THESE HOMES, I BELIEVE THEY BELONGED TO A TRIBE OF LIBRUM.
MAYBE THEY'LL COME BACK. AFTER WE--
FORGIVE ME, YOUR HIGHNESS, BUT I SHOULD MAKE MYSELF CLEARER. THESE PIXIES ABANDONED THIS VILLAGE LONG BEFORE THE SAVAGE AND HER MASTER CLAIMED THESE LANDS.
THEY DISAPPEARED EVEN BEFORE THE FIRST CREATURE CROSSED FROM YOUR REALM.
"THEY WERE GIFTED WITH THE ABILITY TO IMPART KNOWLEDGE DIRECTLY INTO THE MINDS OF OTHERS... STORYTELLERS AND ADVENTURERS ALIKE COURTED THEIR FAVOR.
"THEY WERE A WELL-EDUCATED PEOPLE. I'D HAVE LIKED TO HAVE MET ONE..."

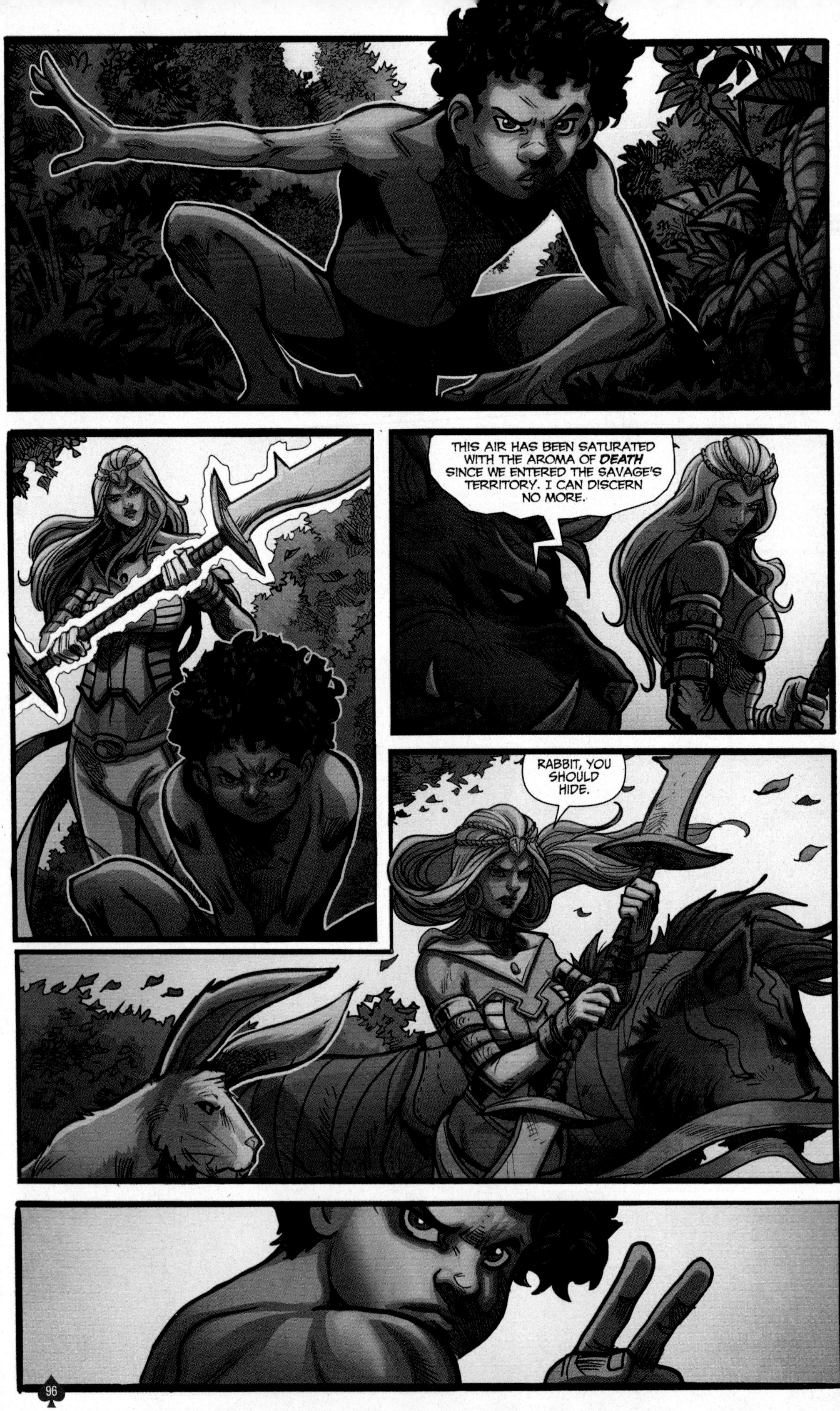
THIS AIR HAS BEEN SATURATED WITH THE AROMA OF DEATH SINCE WE ENTERED THE SAVAGE'S TERRITORY. I CAN DISCERN NO MORE.
RABBIT, YOU SHOULD HIDE.

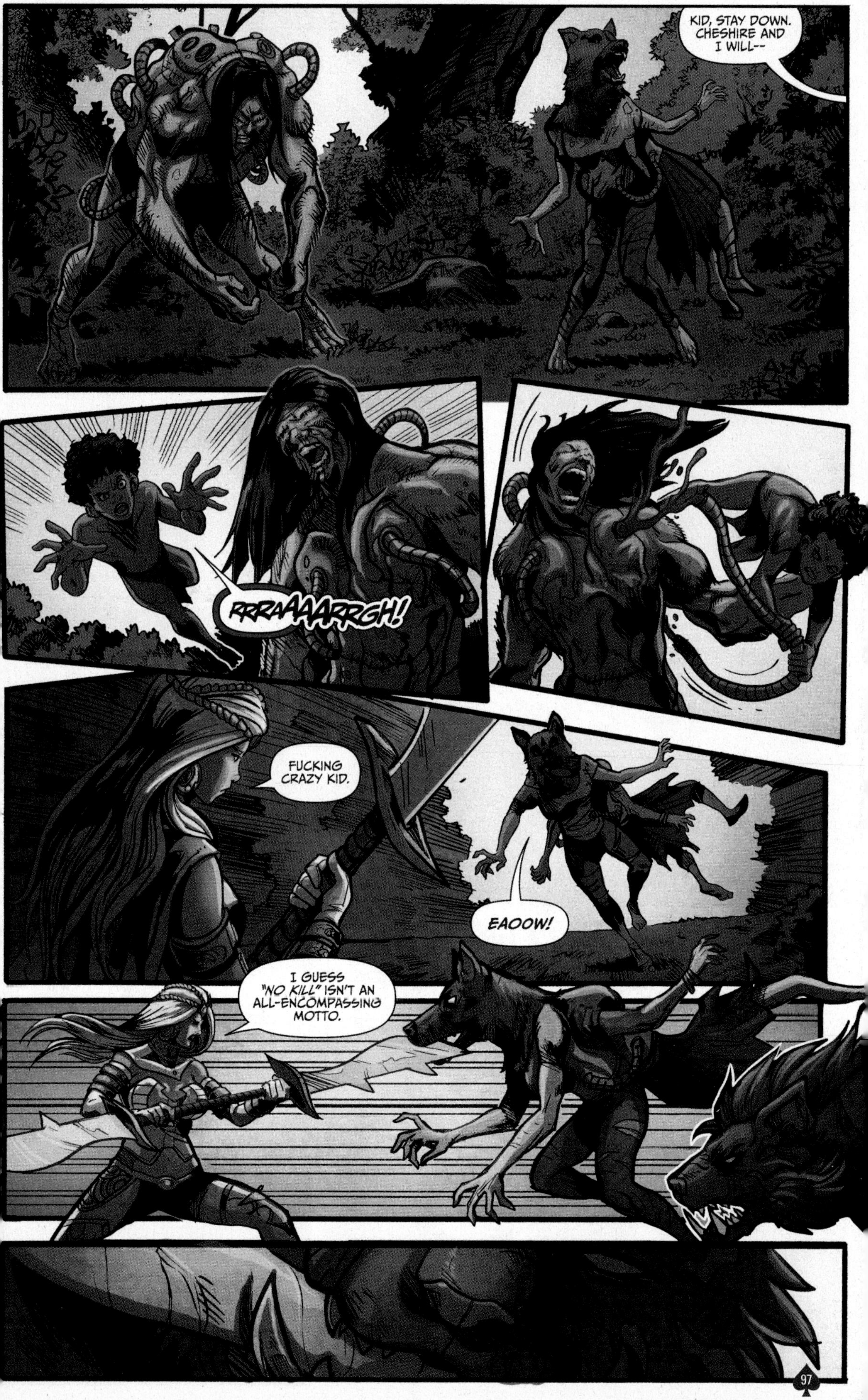
KID, STAY DOWN. CHESHIRE AND I WILL--
RRRAAAAARRGH!
FUCKING CRAZY KID.
EAOOW!
I GUESS "NO KILL" ISN'T AN ALL-ENCOMPASSING MOTTO.

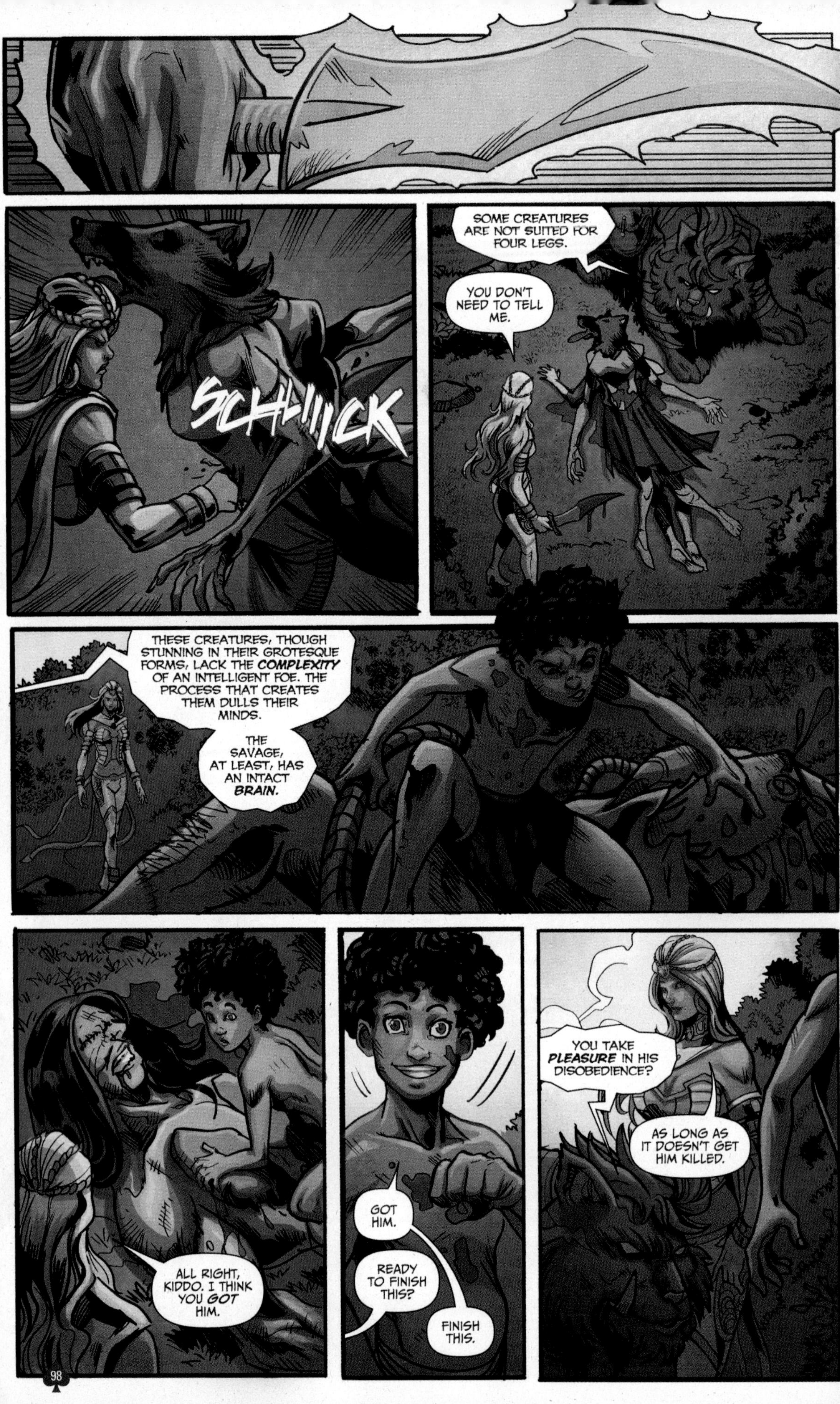

SCHLIIICK
SOME CREATURES ARE NOT SUITED FOR FOUR LEGS.
YOU DON'T NEED TO TELL ME.
THESE CREATURES, THOUGH STUNNING IN THEIR GROTESQUE FORMS, LACK THE *COMPLEXITY* OF AN INTELLIGENT FOE. THE PROCESS THAT CREATES THEM DULLS THEIR MINDS.
THE SAVAGE, AT LEAST, HAS AN INTACT *BRAIN.*
ALL RIGHT, KIDDO. I THINK YOU *GOT* HIM.
GOT HIM.
READY TO FINISH THIS?
FINISH THIS.
YOU TAKE *PLEASURE* IN HIS DISOBEDIENCE?
AS LONG AS IT DOESN'T GET HIM KILLED.

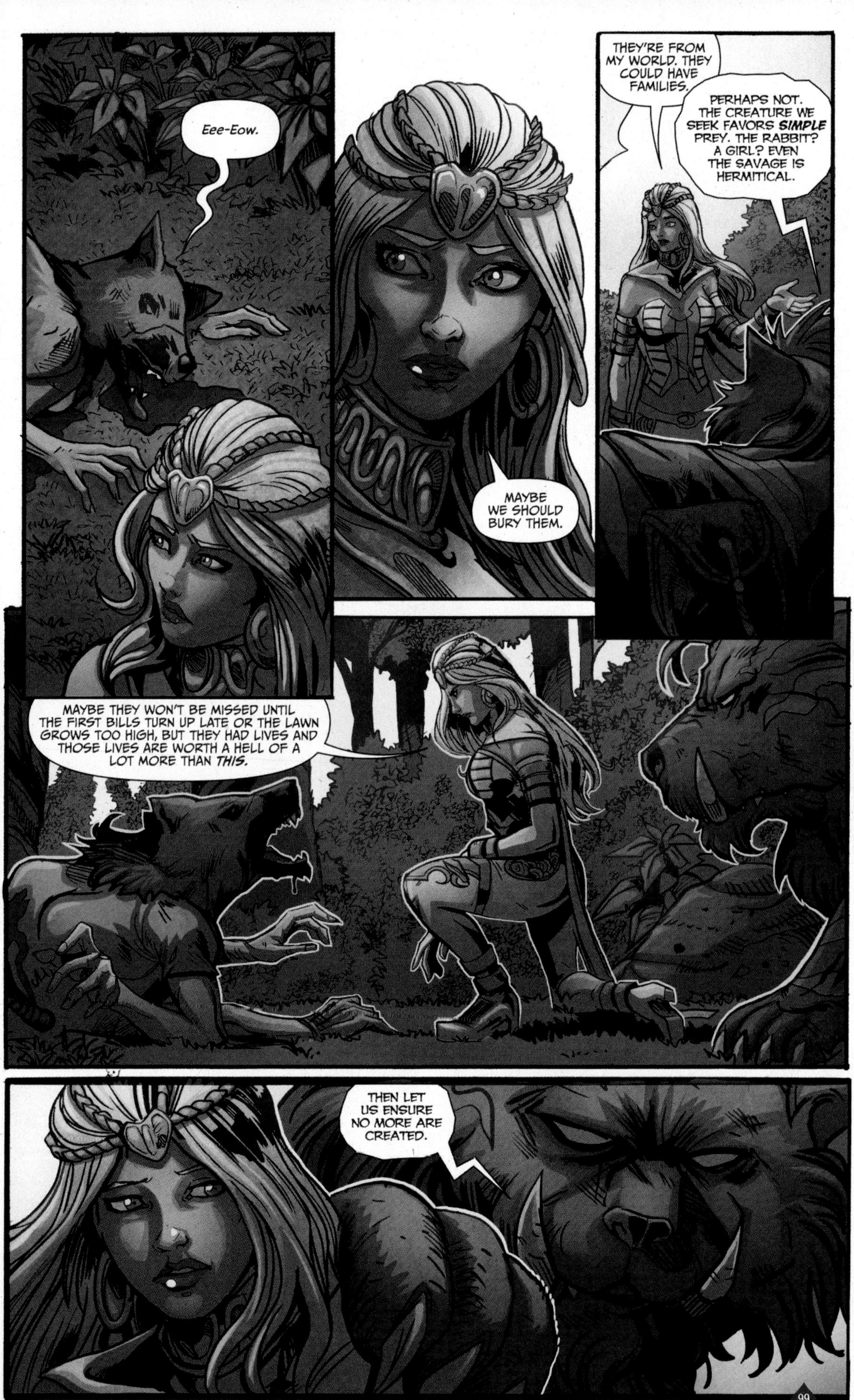

Eee-Eow.
MAYBE WE SHOULD BURY THEM.
THEY'RE FROM MY WORLD. THEY COULD HAVE FAMILIES.
PERHAPS NOT. THE CREATURE WE SEEK FAVORS SIMPLE PREY. THE RABBIT? A GIRL? EVEN THE SAVAGE IS HERMITICAL.
MAYBE THEY WON'T BE MISSED UNTIL THE FIRST BILLS TURN UP LATE OR THE LAWN GROWS TOO HIGH, BUT THEY HAD LIVES AND THOSE LIVES ARE WORTH A HELL OF A LOT MORE THAN THIS.
THEN LET US ENSURE NO MORE ARE CREATED.

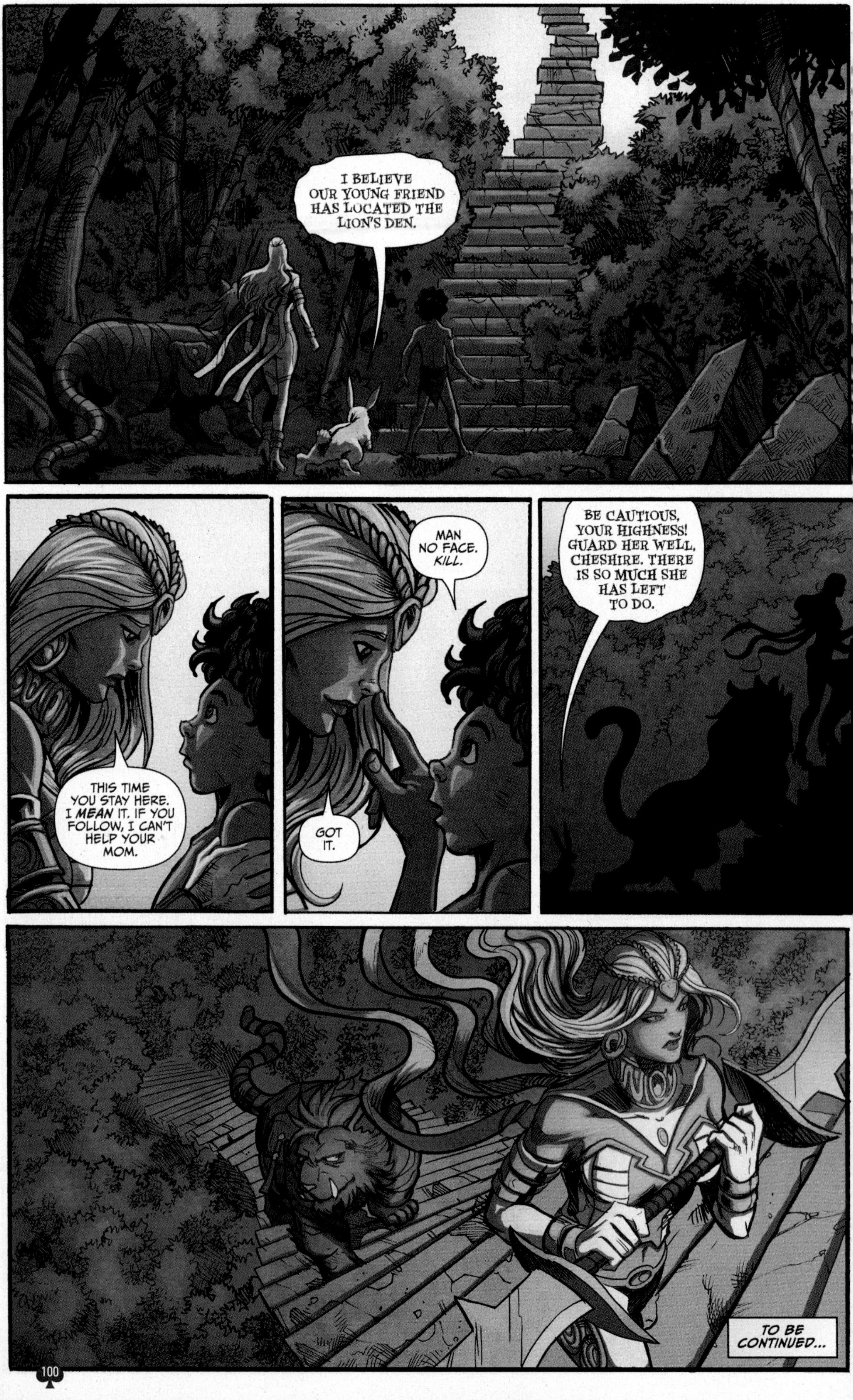

I BELIEVE OUR YOUNG FRIEND HAS LOCATED THE LION'S DEN.
THIS TIME YOU STAY HERE. I *MEAN* IT. IF YOU FOLLOW, I CAN'T HELP YOUR MOM.
MAN NO FACE. *KILL.*
GOT IT.
BE CAUTIOUS, YOUR HIGHNESS! GUARD HER WELL, CHESHIRE. THERE IS SO MUCH SHE HAS LEFT TO DO.
TO BE CONTINUED...

END CHAPTER

RENAISSANCE

PART FIVE

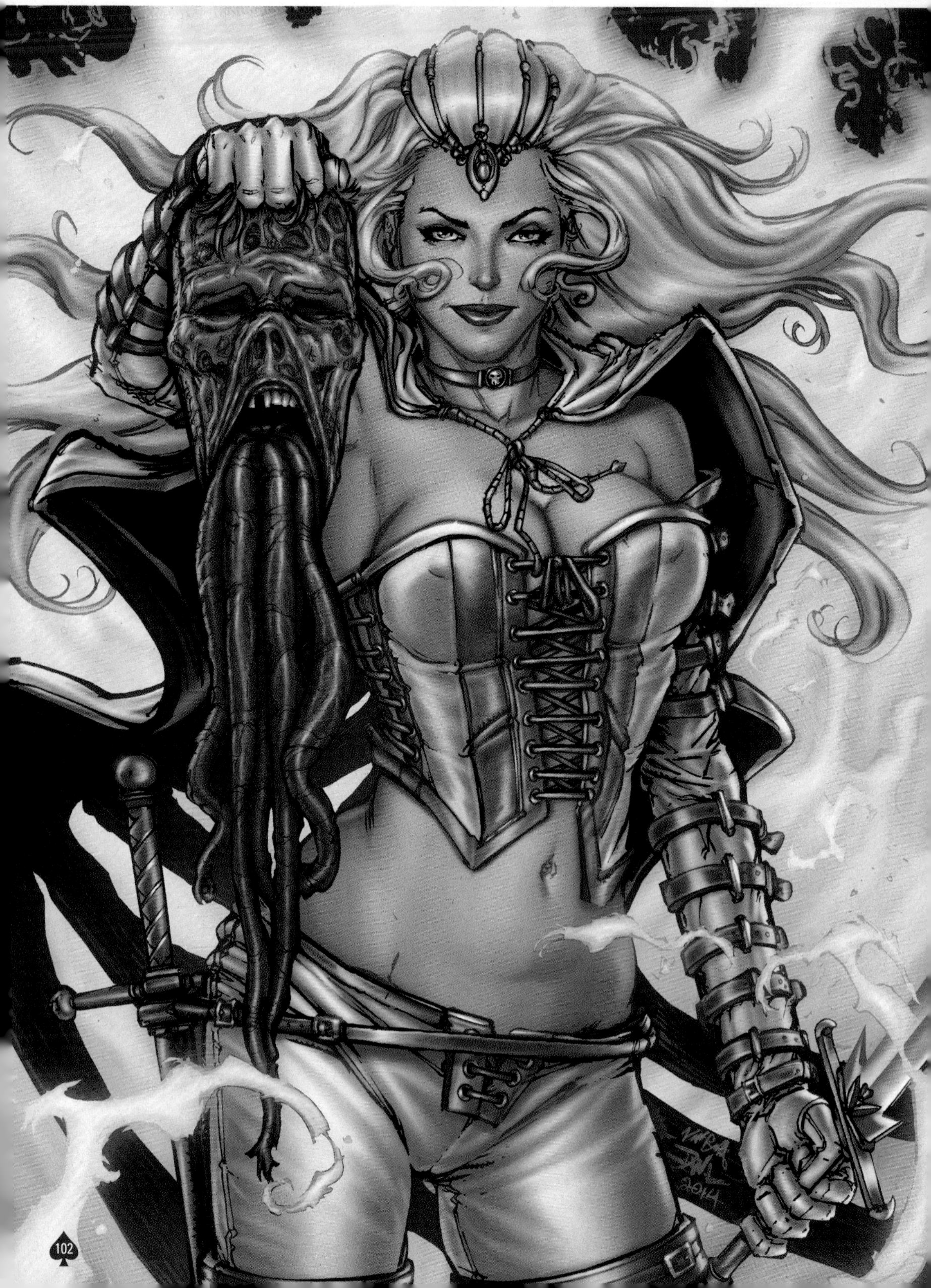

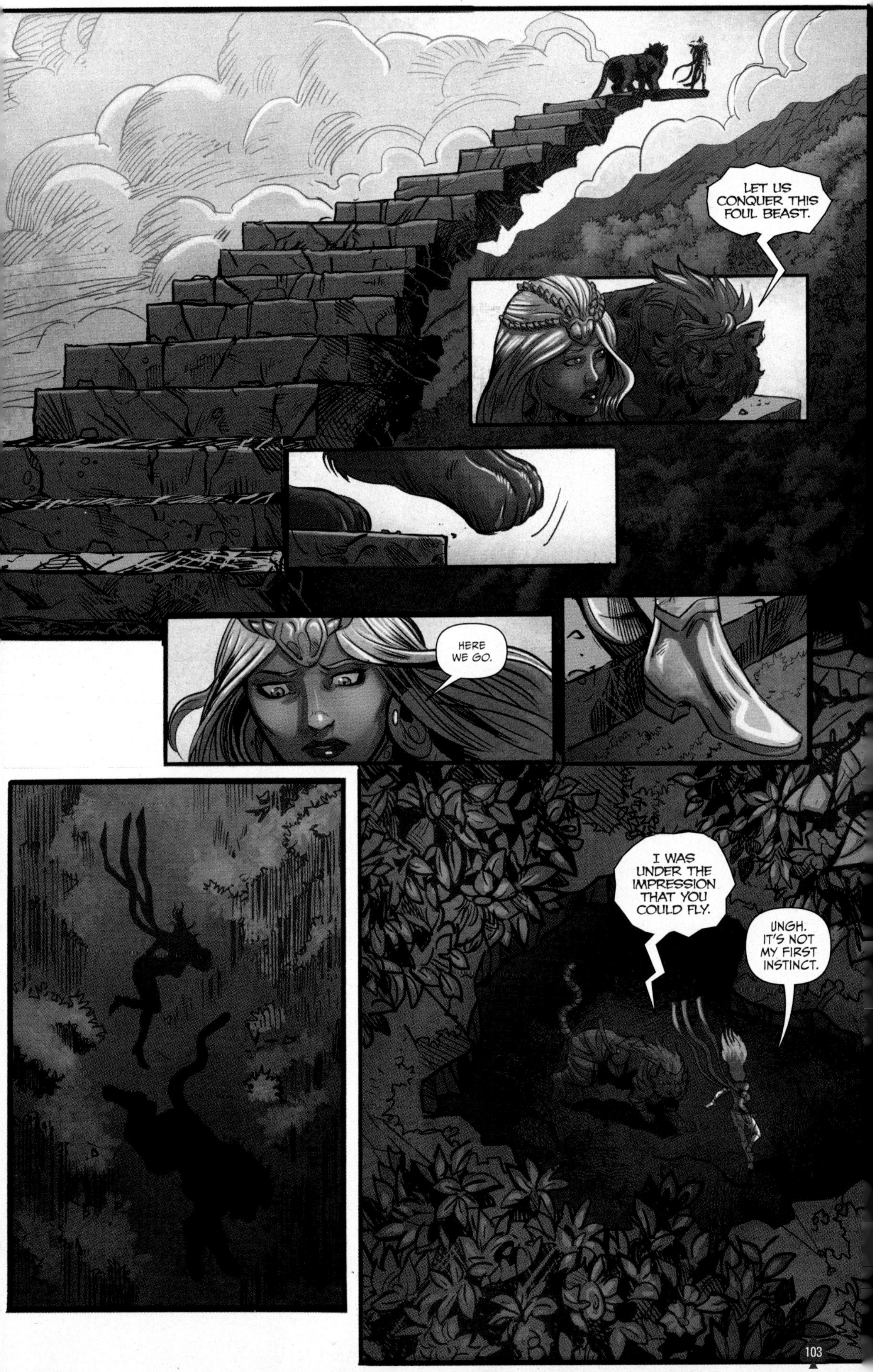
LET US CONQUER THIS FOUL BEAST.
HERE WE GO.
I WAS UNDER THE IMPRESSION THAT YOU COULD FLY.
UNGH. IT'S NOT MY FIRST INSTINCT.

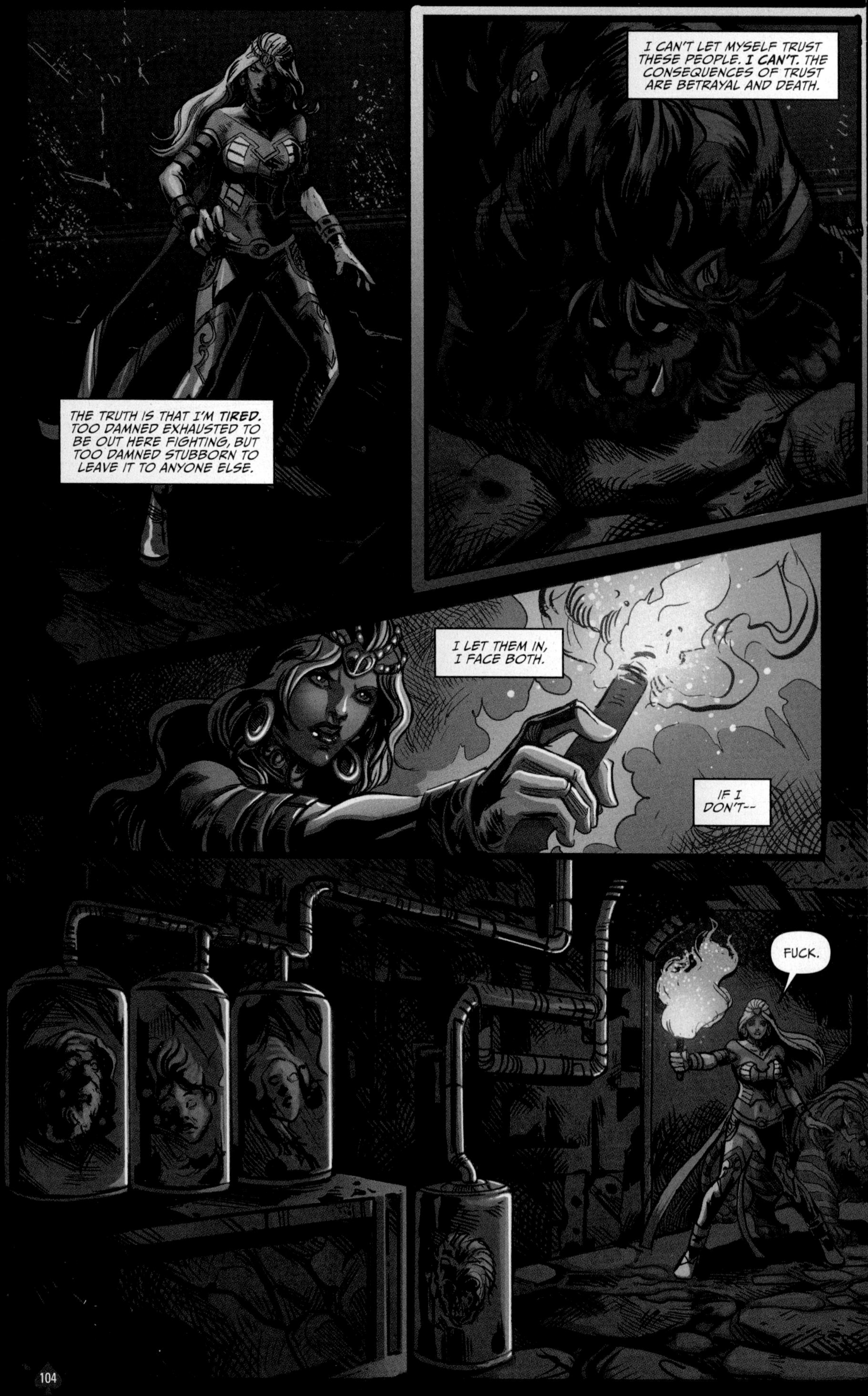
THE TRUTH IS THAT I'M **TIRED.** TOO DAMNED EXHAUSTED TO BE OUT HERE FIGHTING, BUT TOO DAMNED STUBBORN TO LEAVE IT TO ANYONE ELSE.
I CAN'T LET MYSELF TRUST THESE PEOPLE. **I CAN'T.** THE CONSEQUENCES OF TRUST ARE BETRAYAL AND DEATH.
I LET THEM IN, I FACE BOTH.
IF I DON'T--
FUCK.

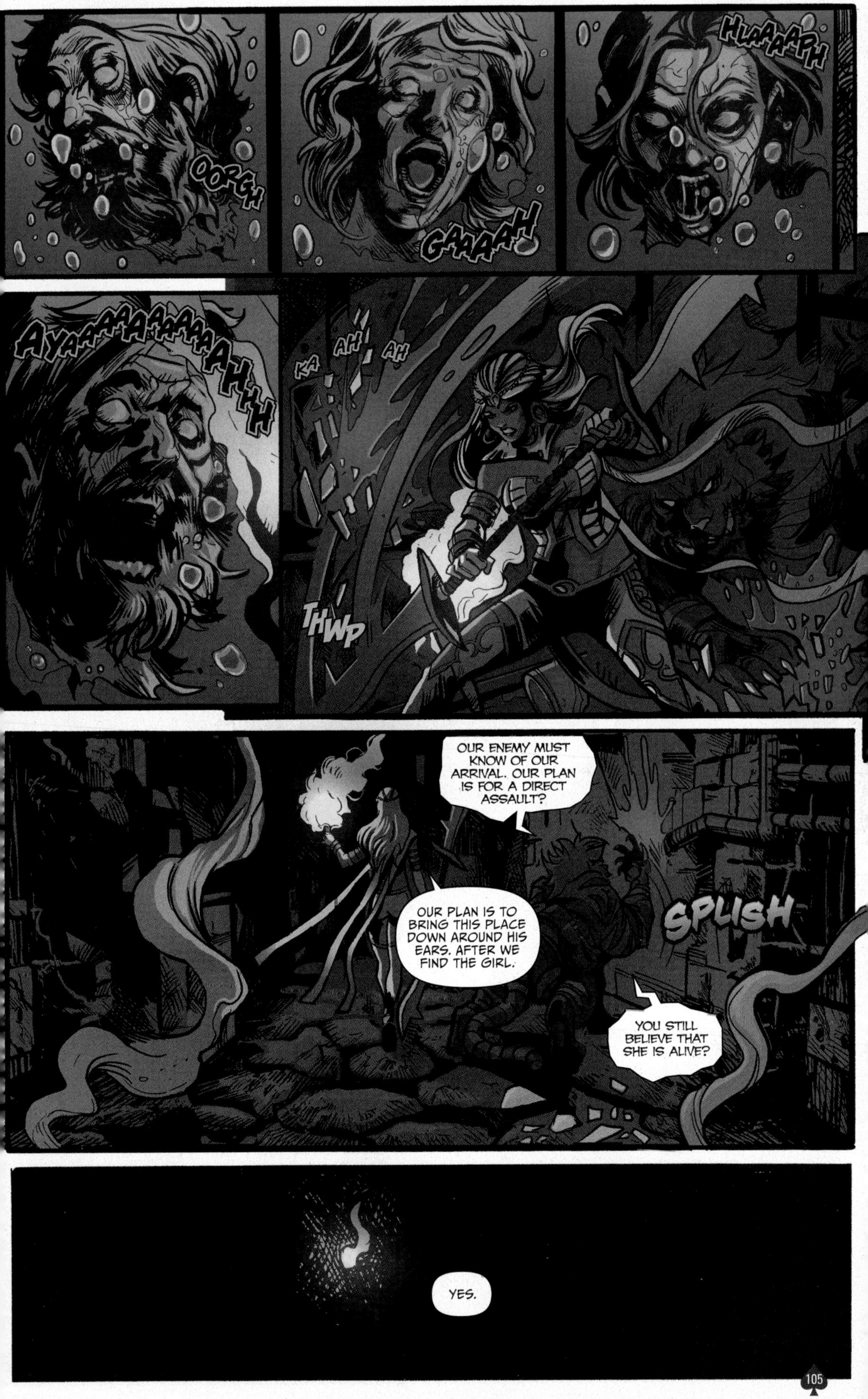
OORGH
GAAAAAH
HLAAAAPH
AYAAAAAAAAAAAAAHHH
KA AH AH
THWP
OUR ENEMY MUST KNOW OF OUR ARRIVAL. OUR PLAN IS FOR A DIRECT ASSAULT?
OUR PLAN IS TO BRING THIS PLACE DOWN AROUND HIS EARS. AFTER WE FIND THE GIRL.
SPLISH
YOU STILL BELIEVE THAT SHE IS ALIVE?
YES.

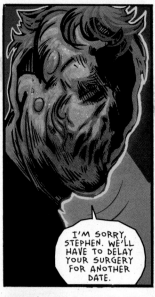

I'M SORRY, STEPHEN. WE'LL HAVE TO DELAY YOUR SURGERY FOR ANOTHER DATE.

HAVE NO WORRIES, MY SON.

I'VE PERFECTED THE PROCESS.

AFTER YOUR NEW LUNGS ARE IN PLACE, I'LL TAKE YOU OUT INTO THE YARD. I THINK YOU'LL ENJOY OUR NEW HOME.

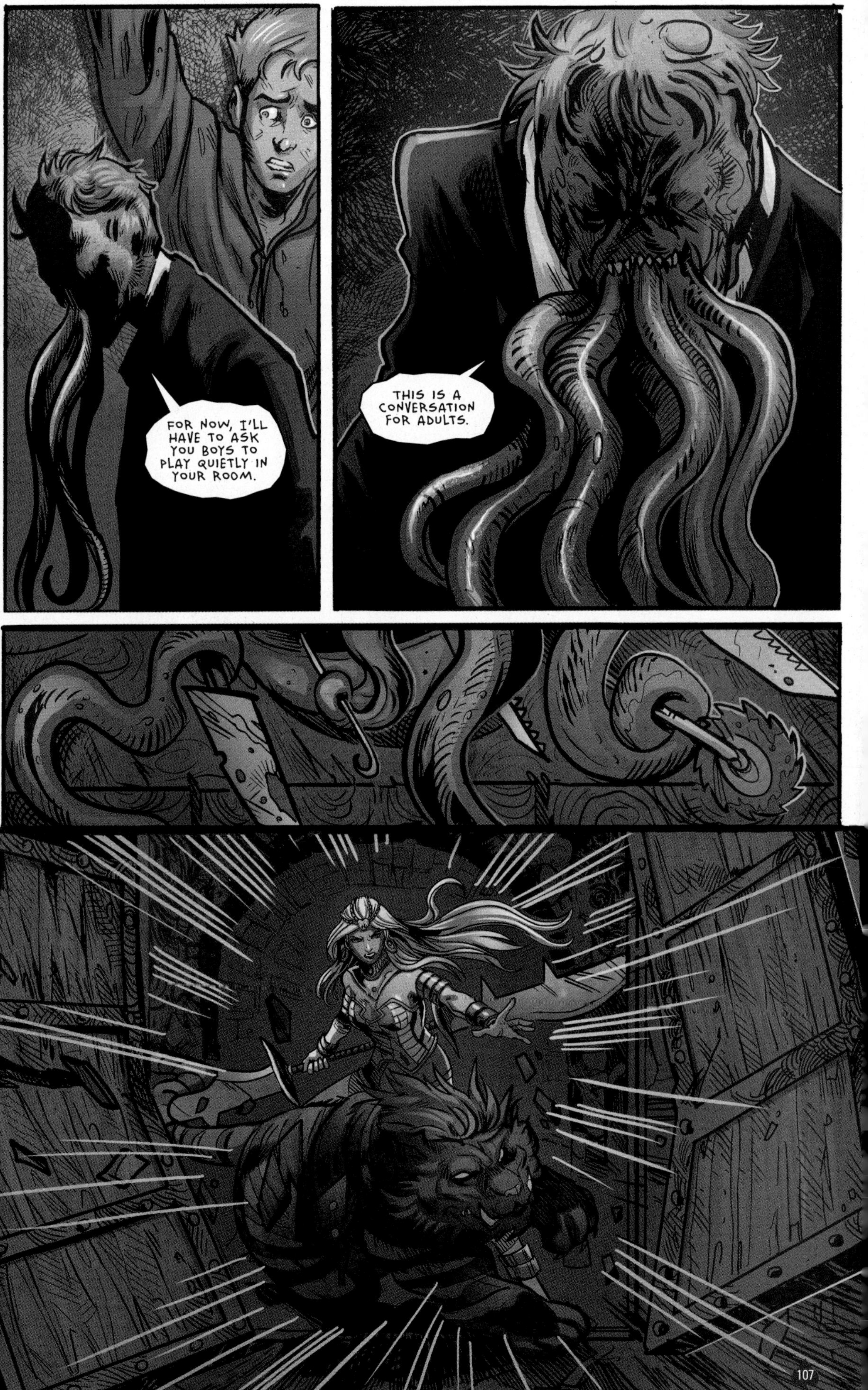
FOR NOW, I'LL HAVE TO ASK YOU BOYS TO PLAY QUIETLY IN YOUR ROOM.
THIS IS A CONVERSATION FOR ADULTS.

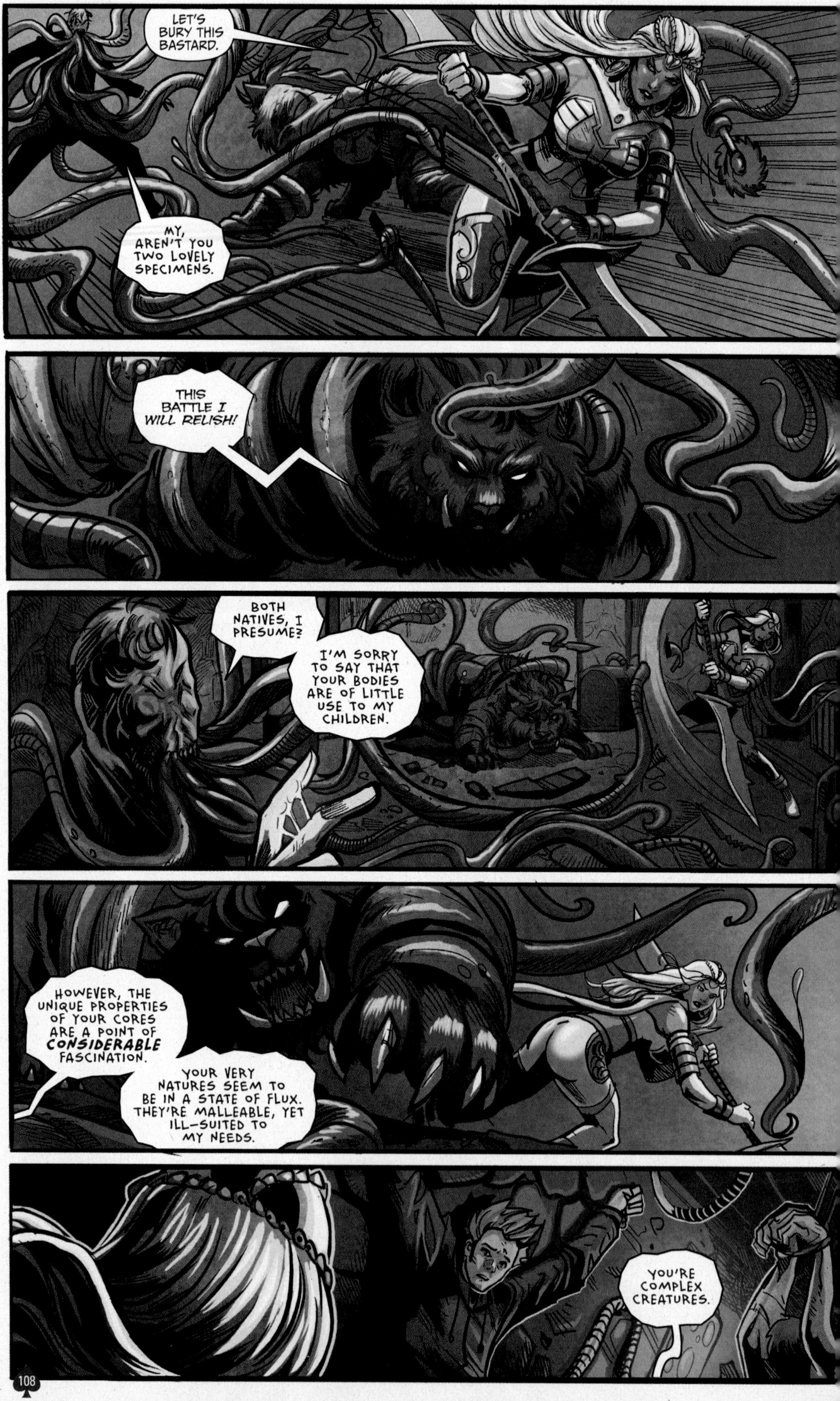
LET'S BURY THIS BASTARD.
MY, AREN'T YOU TWO LOVELY SPECIMENS.
THIS BATTLE I WILL RELISH!
BOTH NATIVES, I PRESUME?
I'M SORRY TO SAY THAT YOUR BODIES ARE OF LITTLE USE TO MY CHILDREN.
HOWEVER, THE UNIQUE PROPERTIES OF YOUR CORES ARE A POINT OF CONSIDERABLE FASCINATION.
YOUR VERY NATURES SEEM TO BE IN A STATE OF FLUX. THEY'RE MALLEABLE, YET ILL-SUITED TO MY NEEDS.
YOU'RE COMPLEX CREATURES.

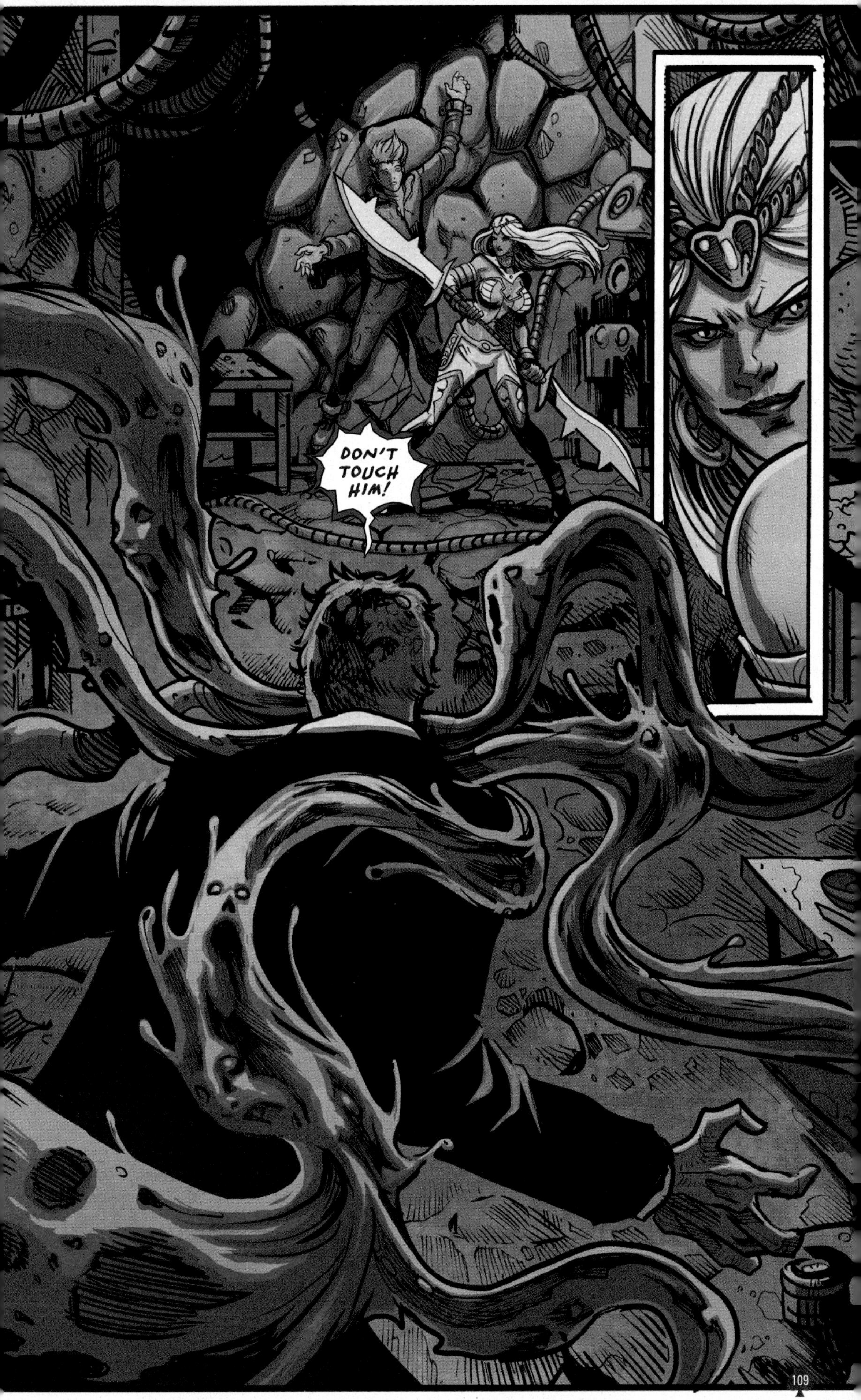
DON'T TOUCH HIM!

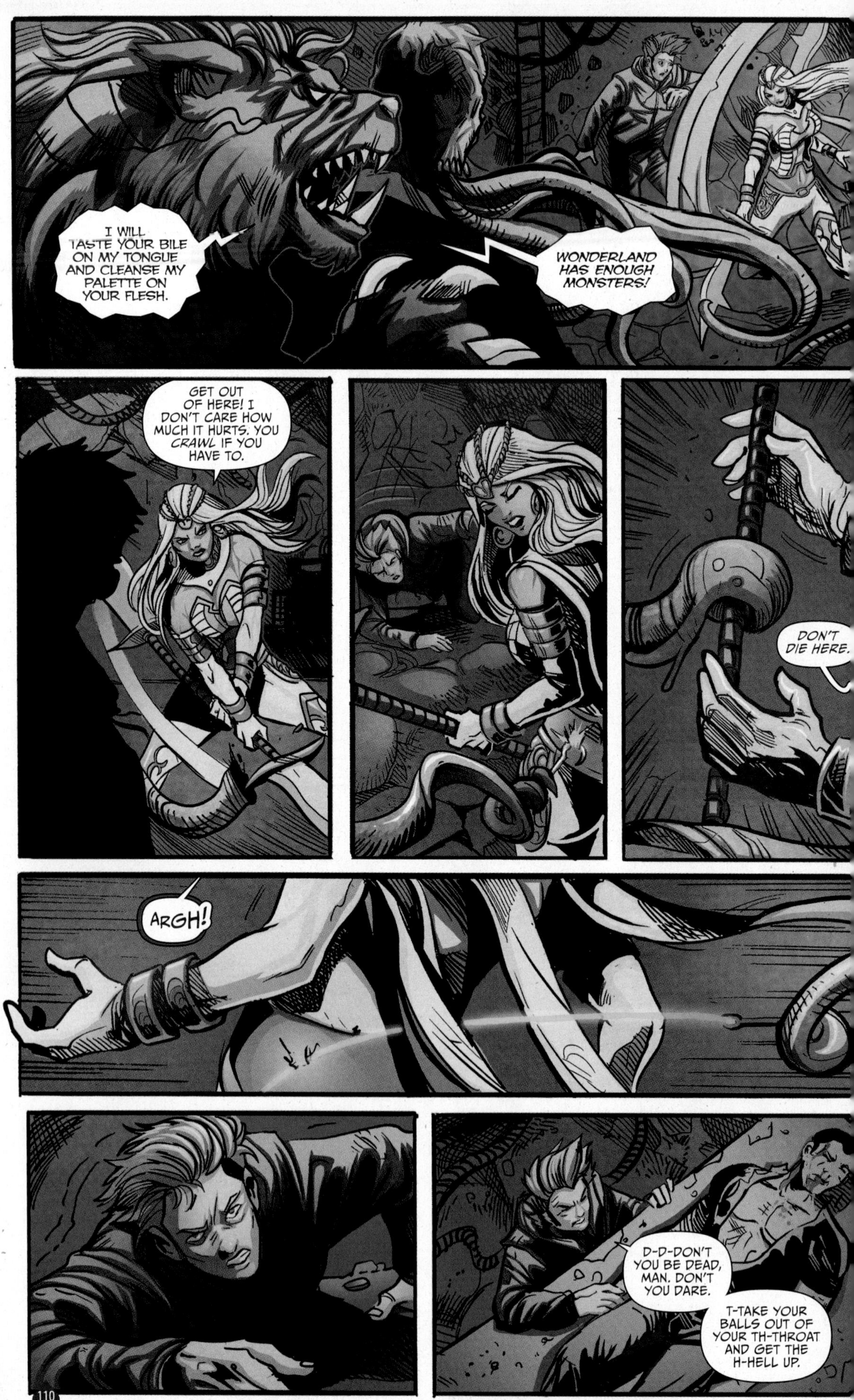

I WILL TASTE YOUR BILE ON MY TONGUE AND CLEANSE MY PALETTE ON YOUR FLESH.
WONDERLAND HAS ENOUGH MONSTERS!
GET OUT OF HERE! I DON'T CARE HOW MUCH IT HURTS. YOU CRAWL IF YOU HAVE TO.
DON'T DIE HERE.
ARGH!
D-D-DON'T YOU BE DEAD, MAN. DON'T YOU DARE.
T-TAKE YOUR BALLS OUT OF YOUR TH-THROAT AND GET THE H-HELL UP.

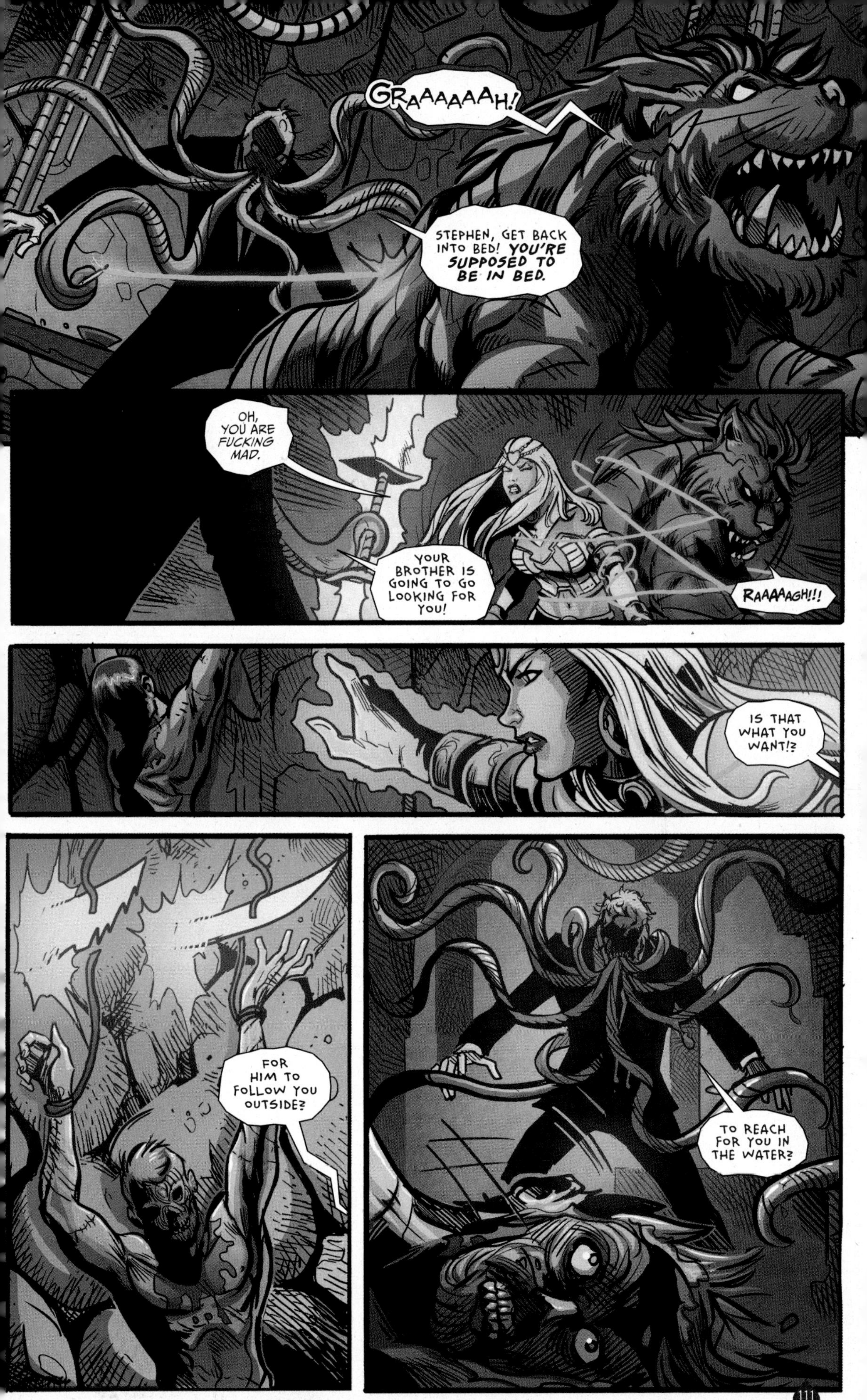
GRAAAAAAH!
STEPHEN, GET BACK INTO BED! YOU'RE SUPPOSED TO BE IN BED.
OH, YOU ARE FUCKING MAD.
YOUR BROTHER IS GOING TO GO LOOKING FOR YOU!
RAAAAAGH!!!
IS THAT WHAT YOU WANT!?
FOR HIM TO FOLLOW YOU OUTSIDE?
TO REACH FOR YOU IN THE WATER?

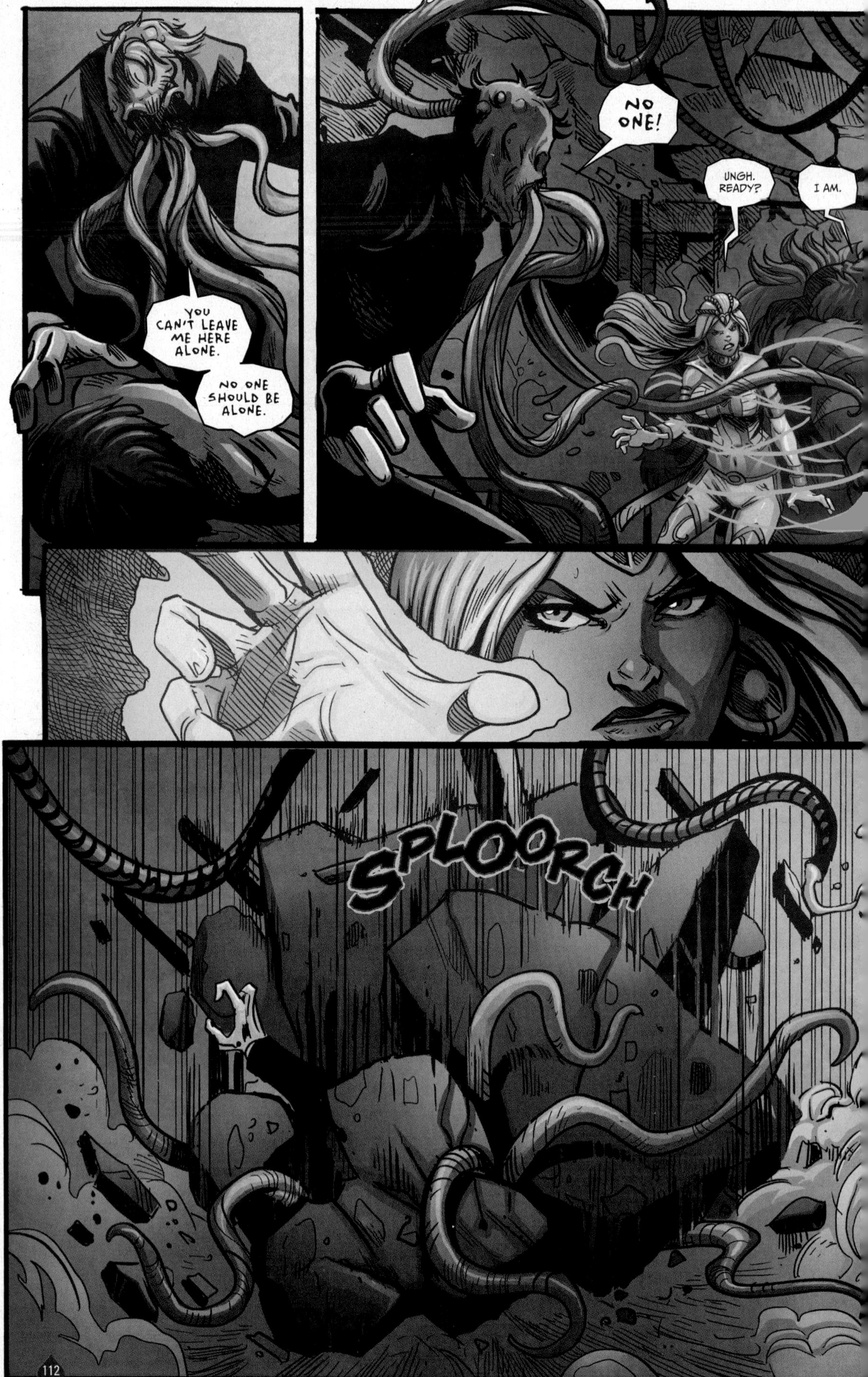

YOU CAN'T LEAVE ME HERE ALONE.
NO ONE SHOULD BE ALONE.
NO ONE!
UNGH. READY?
I AM.
SPLOORCH

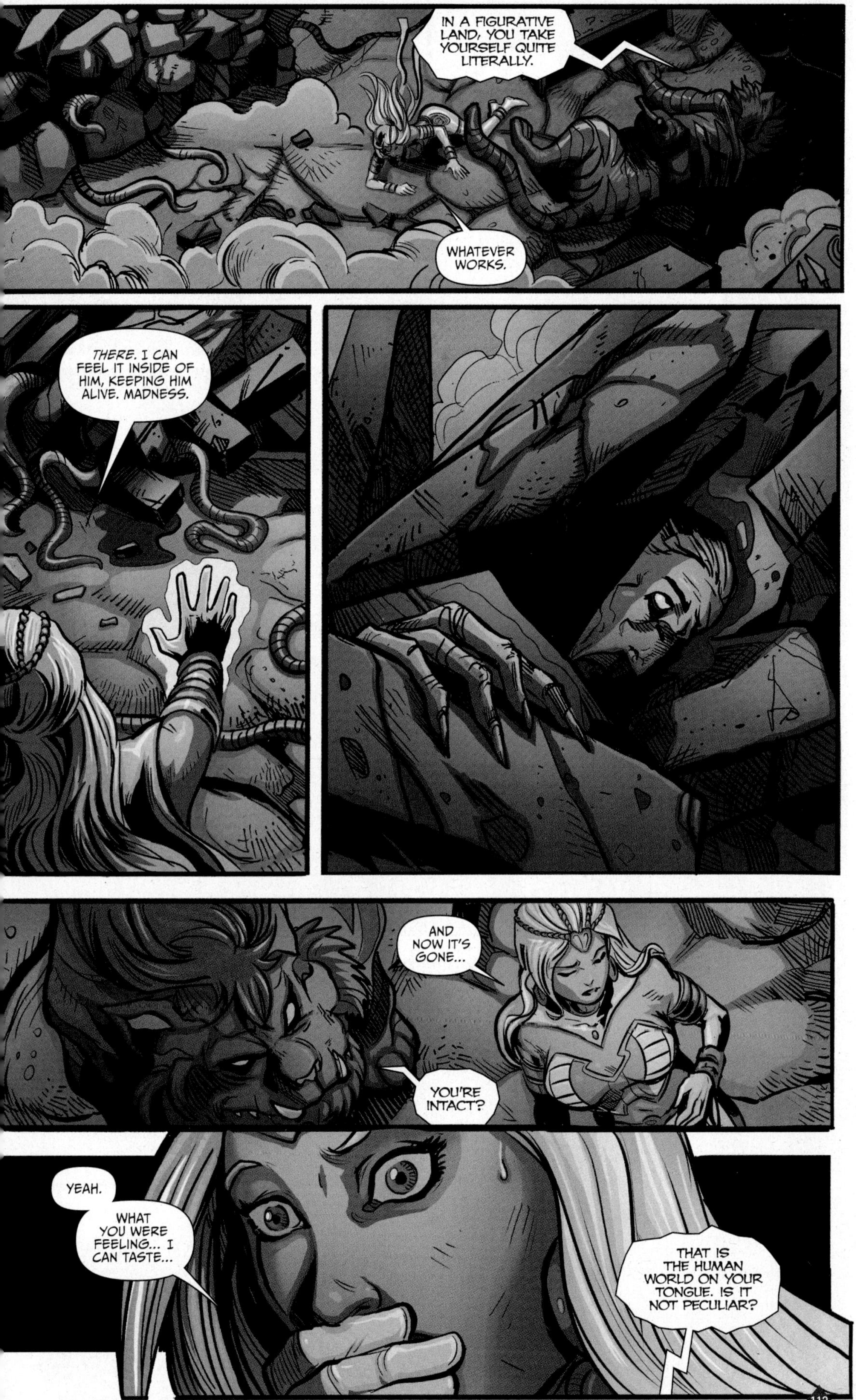
IN A FIGURATIVE LAND, YOU TAKE YOURSELF QUITE LITERALLY.
WHATEVER WORKS.
THERE. I CAN FEEL IT INSIDE OF HIM, KEEPING HIM ALIVE. MADNESS.
AND NOW IT'S GONE...
YOU'RE INTACT?
YEAH.
WHAT YOU WERE FEELING... I CAN TASTE...
THAT IS THE HUMAN WORLD ON YOUR TONGUE. IS IT NOT PECULIAR?

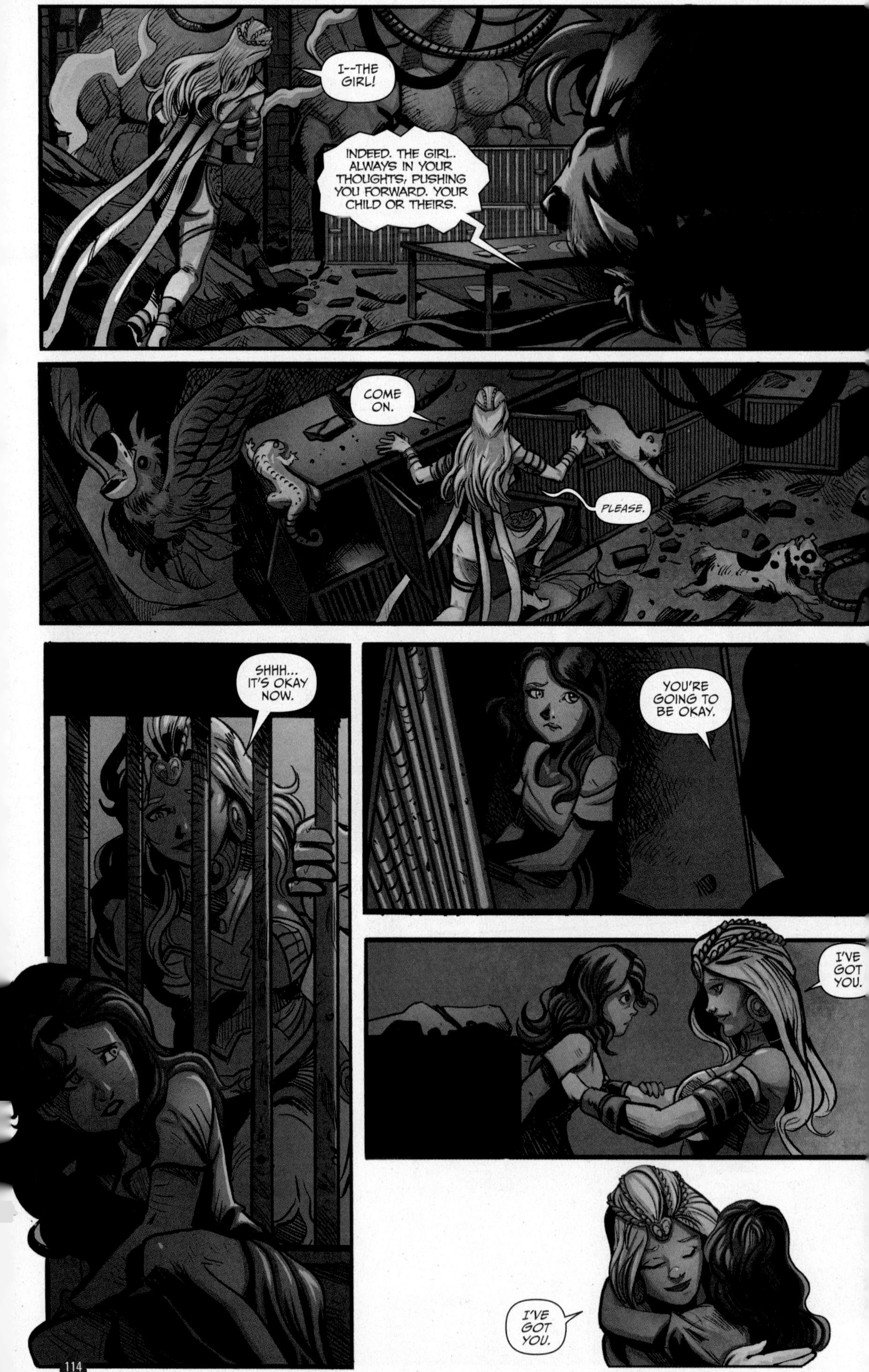
I--THE GIRL!
INDEED. THE GIRL. ALWAYS IN YOUR THOUGHTS, PUSHING YOU FORWARD. YOUR CHILD OR THEIRS.
COME ON.
PLEASE.
SHHH... IT'S OKAY NOW.
YOU'RE GOING TO BE OKAY.
I'VE GOT YOU.
I'VE GOT YOU.

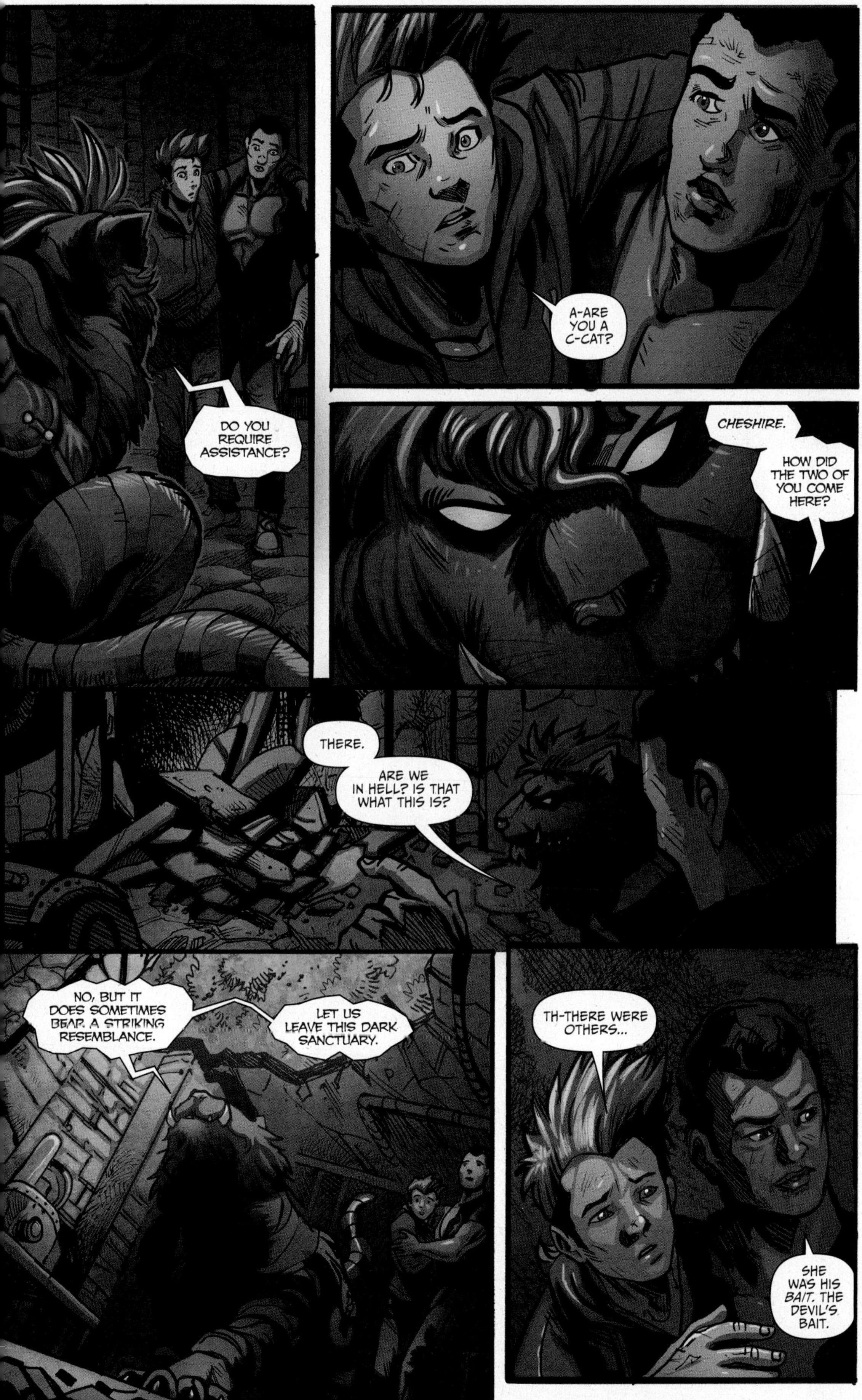
DO YOU REQUIRE ASSISTANCE?
A-ARE YOU A C-CAT?
CHESHIRE.
HOW DID THE TWO OF YOU COME HERE?
THERE.
ARE WE IN HELL? IS THAT WHAT THIS IS?
NO, BUT IT DOES SOMETIMES BEAR A STRIKING RESEMBLANCE.
LET US LEAVE THIS DARK SANCTUARY.
TH-THERE WERE OTHERS...
SHE WAS HIS *BAIT*. THE DEVIL'S BAIT.

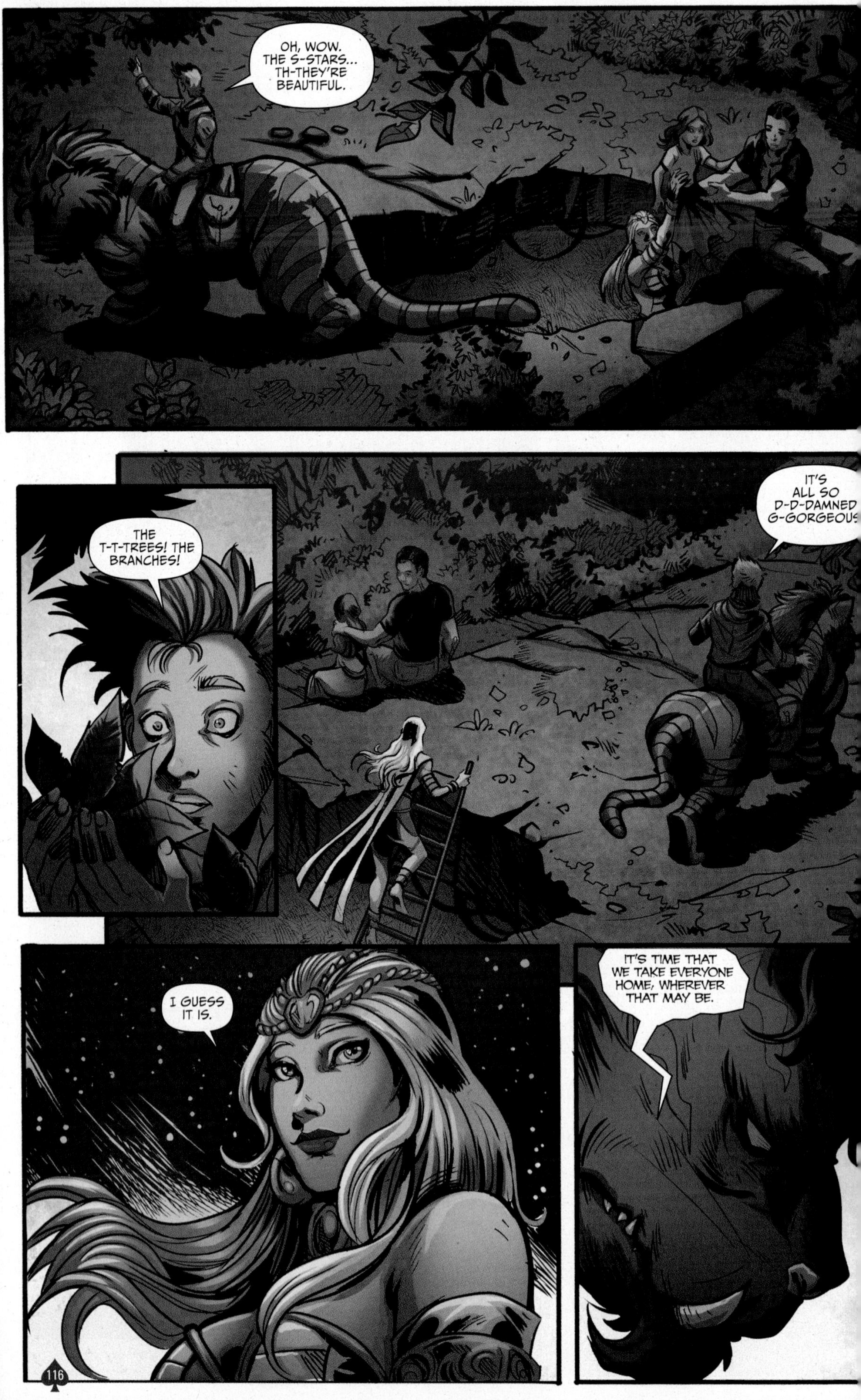
OH, WOW. THE S-STARS... TH-THEY'RE BEAUTIFUL.
THE T-T-TREES! THE BRANCHES!
IT'S ALL SO D-D-DAMNED G-GORGEOUS
I GUESS IT IS.
IT'S TIME THAT WE TAKE EVERYONE HOME, WHEREVER THAT MAY BE.

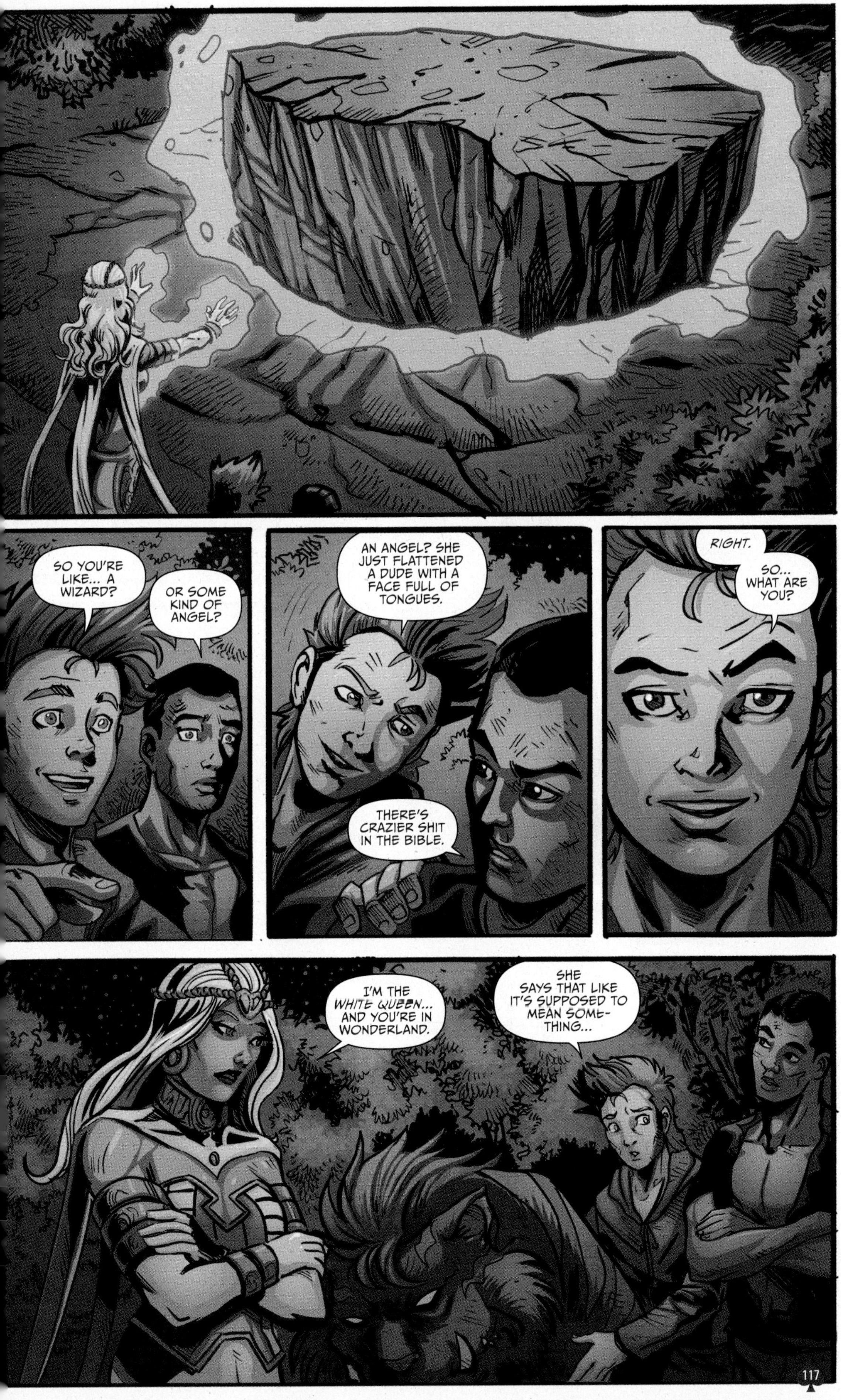
SO YOU'RE LIKE... A WIZARD?
OR SOME KIND OF ANGEL?
AN ANGEL? SHE JUST FLATTENED A DUDE WITH A FACE FULL OF TONGUES.
THERE'S CRAZIER SHIT IN THE BIBLE.
RIGHT.
SO... WHAT ARE YOU?
I'M THE *WHITE QUEEN*... AND YOU'RE IN WONDERLAND.
SHE SAYS THAT LIKE IT'S SUPPOSED TO MEAN SOME-THING...

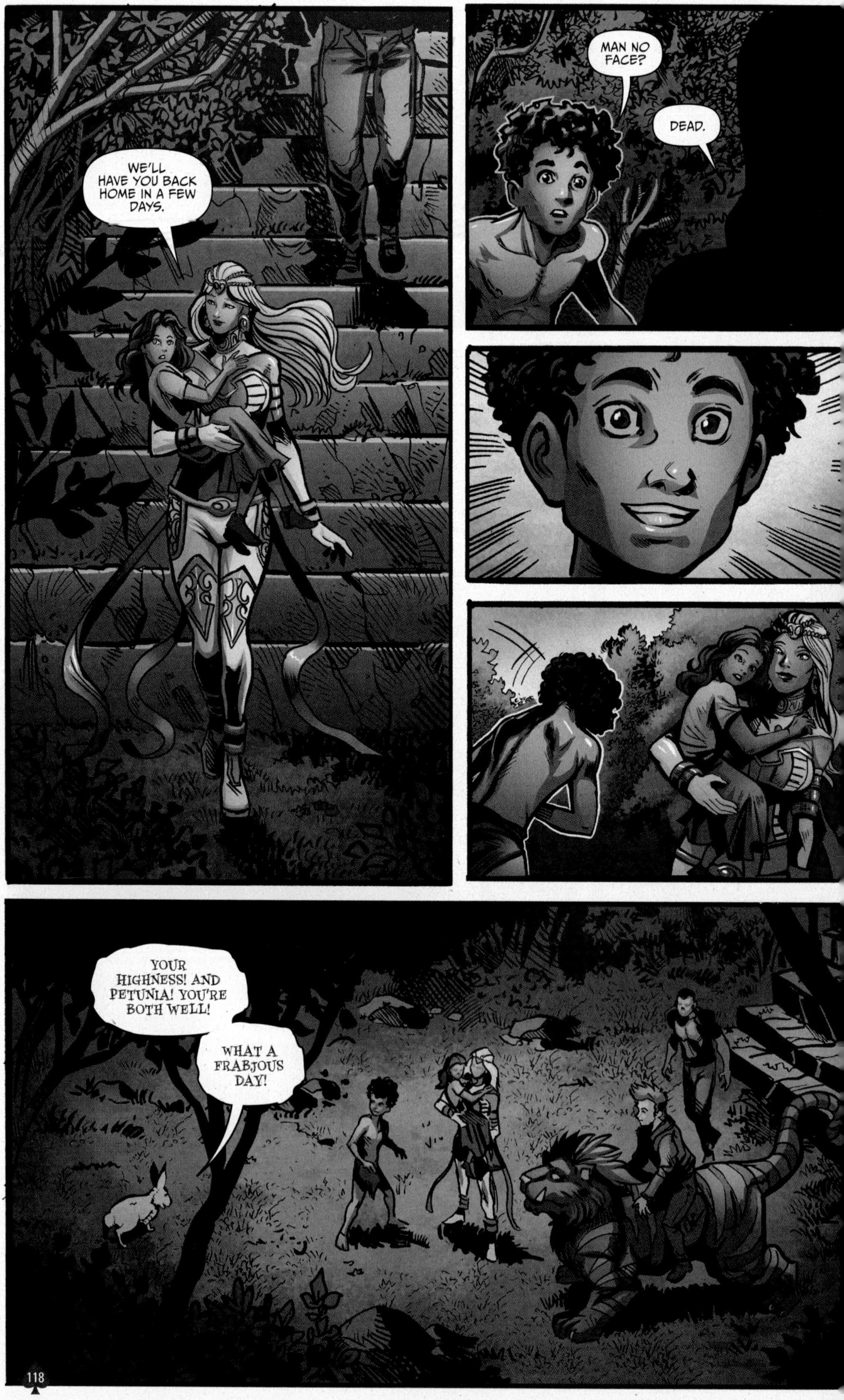
WE'LL HAVE YOU BACK HOME IN A FEW DAYS.
MAN NO FACE?
DEAD.
YOUR HIGHNESS! AND PETUNIA! YOU'RE BOTH WELL!
WHAT A FRABJOUS DAY!

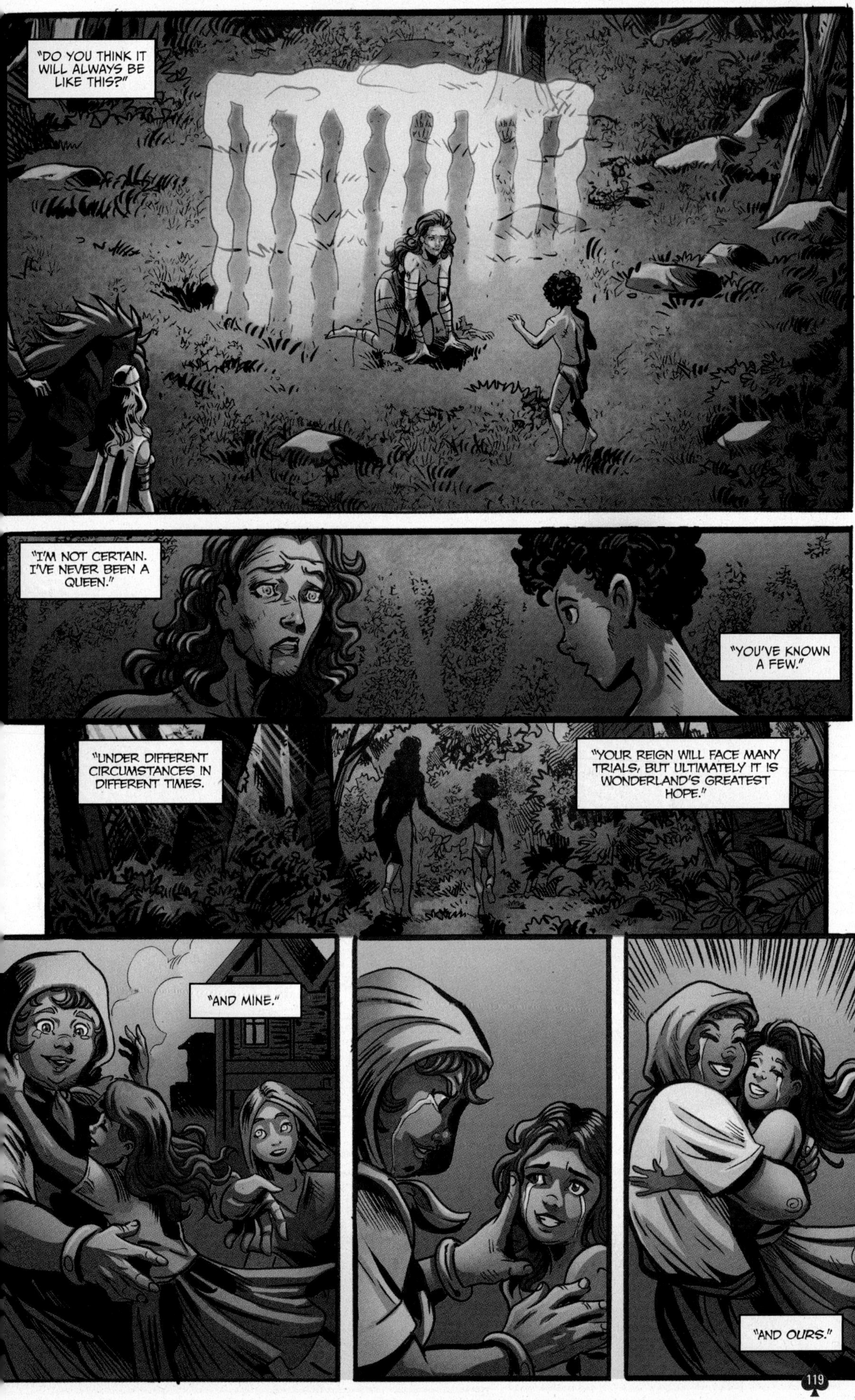
"DO YOU THINK IT WILL ALWAYS BE LIKE THIS?"
"I'M NOT CERTAIN. I'VE NEVER BEEN A QUEEN."
"YOU'VE KNOWN A FEW."
"UNDER DIFFERENT CIRCUMSTANCES IN DIFFERENT TIMES.
"YOUR REIGN WILL FACE MANY TRIALS, BUT ULTIMATELY IT IS WONDERLAND'S GREATEST HOPE."
"AND MINE."
"AND OURS."

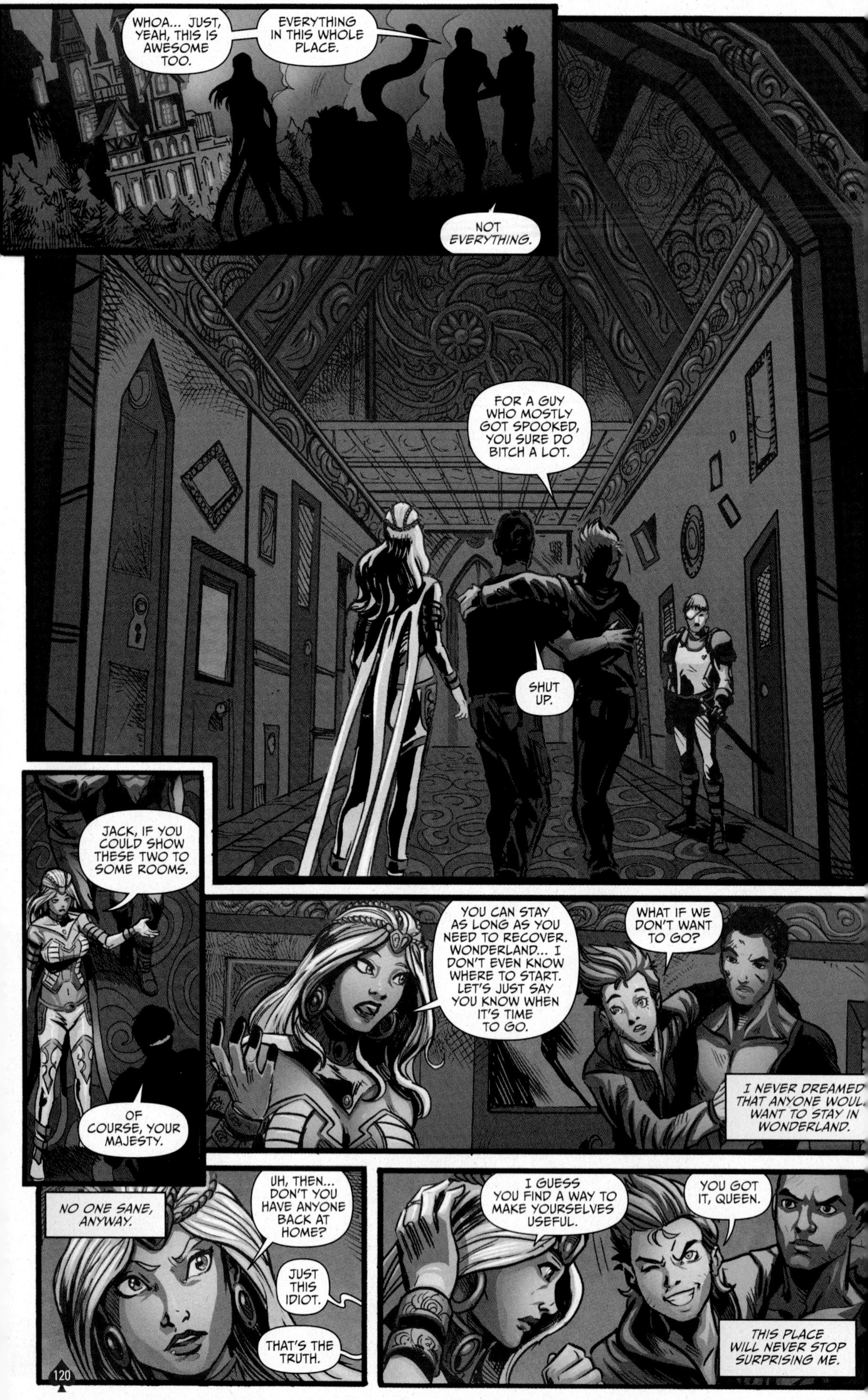
WHOA... JUST, YEAH, THIS IS AWESOME TOO.
EVERYTHING IN THIS WHOLE PLACE.
NOT EVERYTHING.
FOR A GUY WHO MOSTLY GOT SPOOKED, YOU SURE DO BITCH A LOT.
SHUT UP.
JACK, IF YOU COULD SHOW THESE TWO TO SOME ROOMS.
OF COURSE, YOUR MAJESTY.
YOU CAN STAY AS LONG AS YOU NEED TO RECOVER. WONDERLAND... I DON'T EVEN KNOW WHERE TO START. LET'S JUST SAY YOU KNOW WHEN IT'S TIME TO GO.
WHAT IF WE DON'T WANT TO GO?
I NEVER DREAMED THAT ANYONE WOUL WANT TO STAY IN WONDERLAND.
NO ONE SANE, ANYWAY.
UH, THEN... DON'T YOU HAVE ANYONE BACK AT HOME?
JUST THIS IDIOT.
THAT'S THE TRUTH.
I GUESS YOU FIND A WAY TO MAKE YOURSELVES USEFUL.
YOU GOT IT, QUEEN.
THIS PLACE WILL NEVER STOP SURPRISING ME.

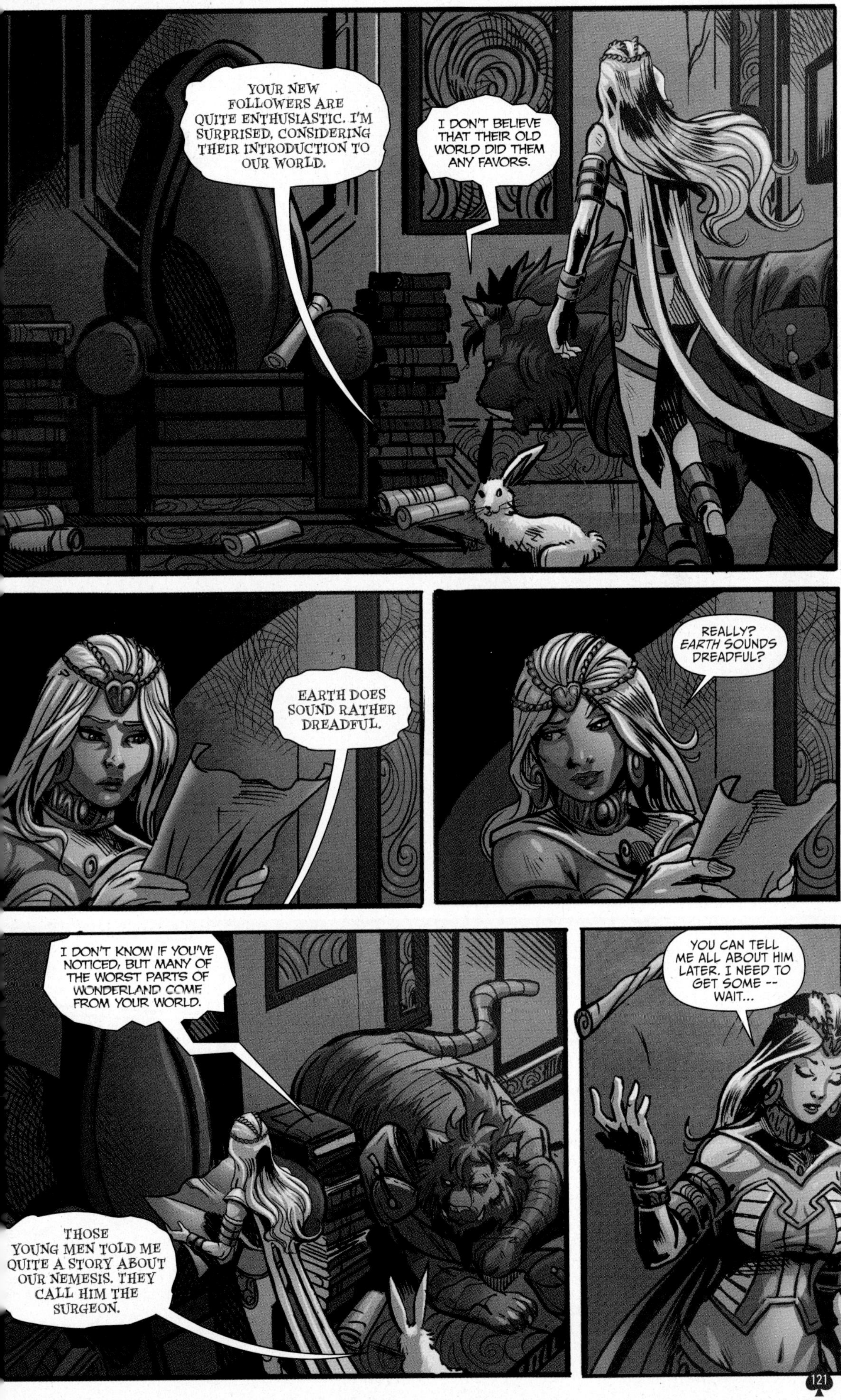
YOUR NEW FOLLOWERS ARE QUITE ENTHUSIASTIC. I'M SURPRISED, CONSIDERING THEIR INTRODUCTION TO OUR WORLD.
I DON'T BELIEVE THAT THEIR OLD WORLD DID THEM ANY FAVORS.
EARTH DOES SOUND RATHER DREADFUL.
REALLY? EARTH SOUNDS DREADFUL?
I DON'T KNOW IF YOU'VE NOTICED, BUT MANY OF THE WORST PARTS OF WONDERLAND COME FROM YOUR WORLD.
THOSE YOUNG MEN TOLD ME QUITE A STORY ABOUT OUR NEMESIS. THEY CALL HIM THE SURGEON.
YOU CAN TELL ME ALL ABOUT HIM LATER. I NEED TO GET SOME -- WAIT...

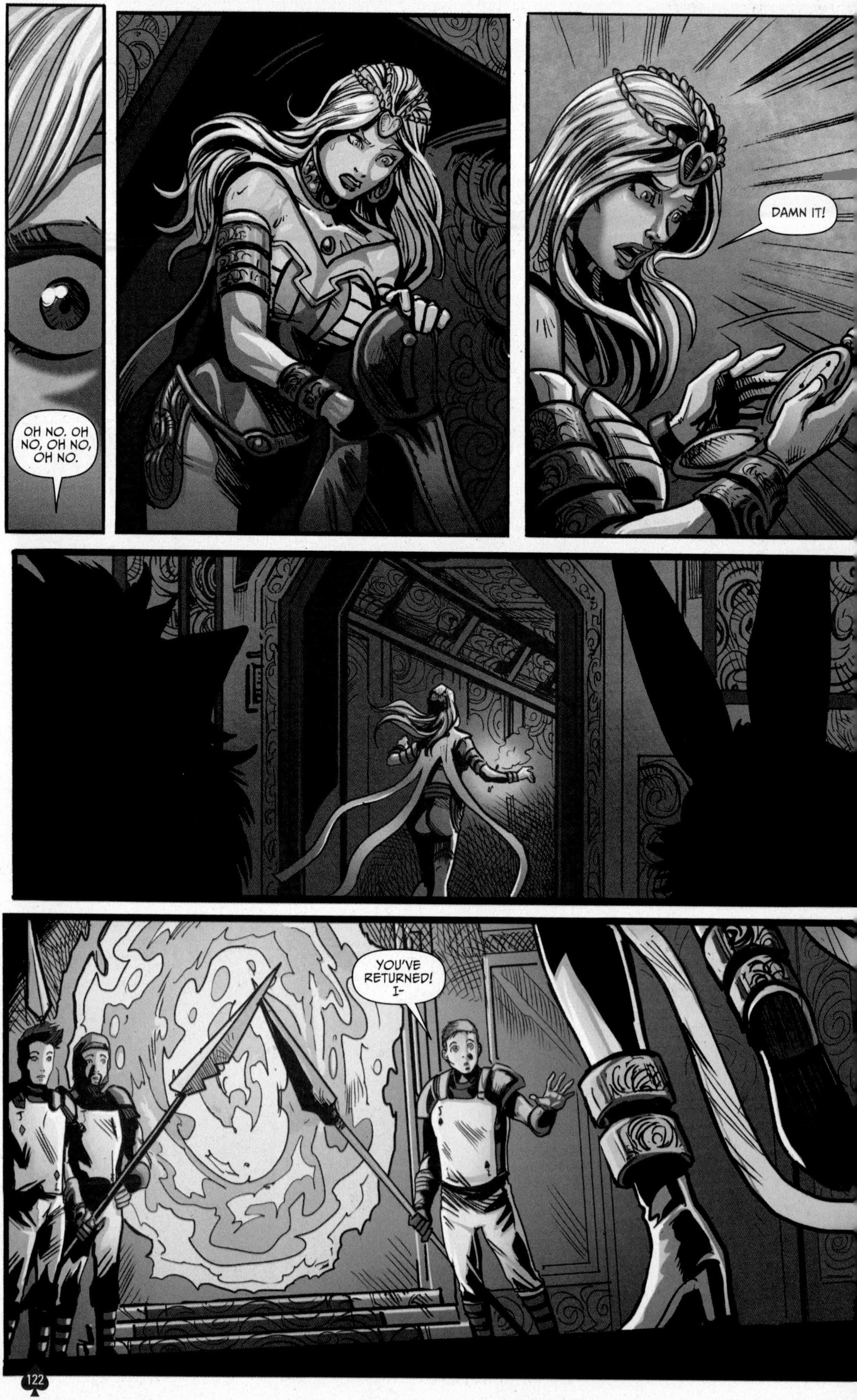
OH NO. OH NO, OH NO, OH NO.
DAMN IT!
YOU'VE RETURNED! I-

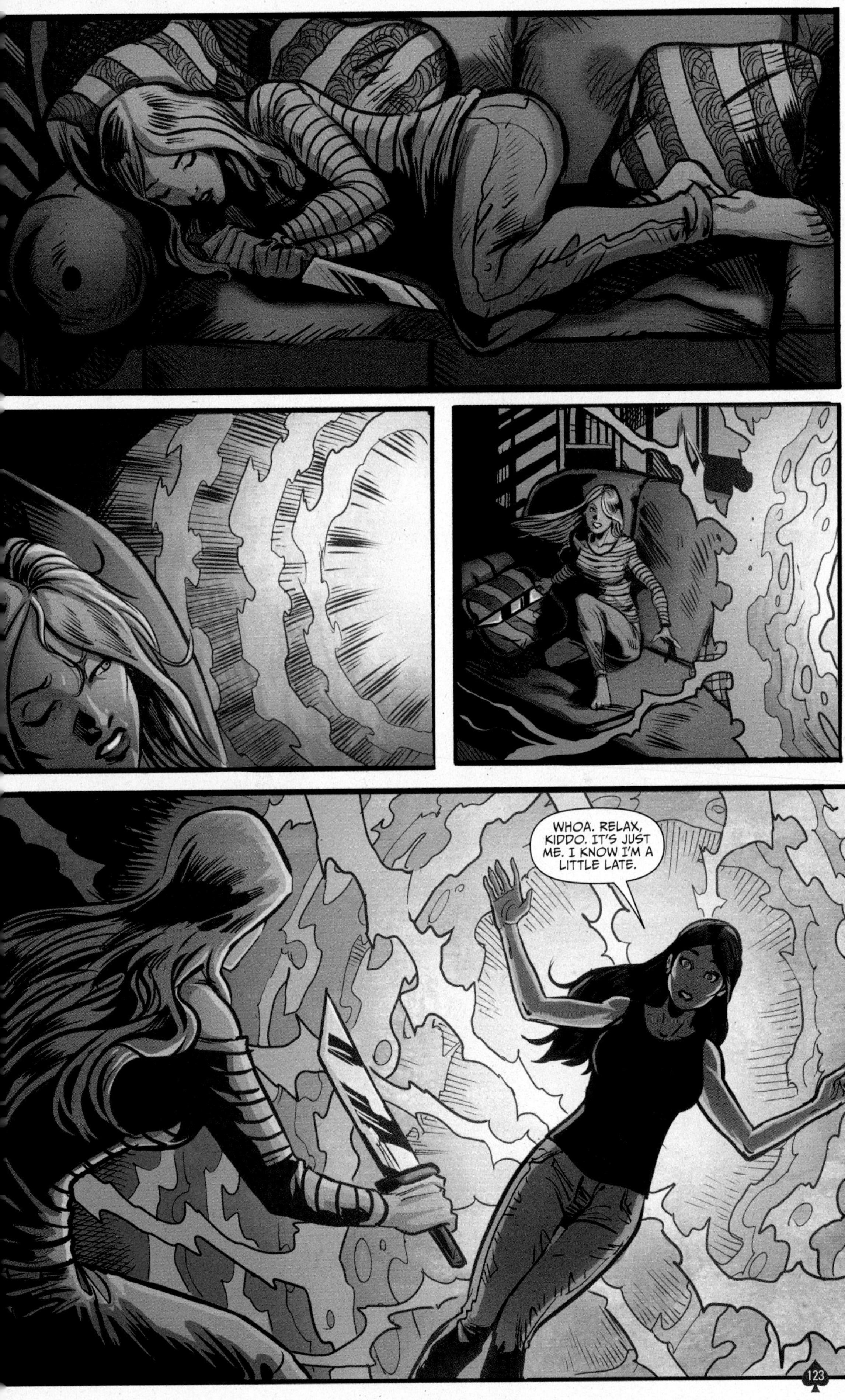
WHOA. RELAX, KIDDO. IT'S JUST ME. I KNOW I'M A LITTLE LATE.

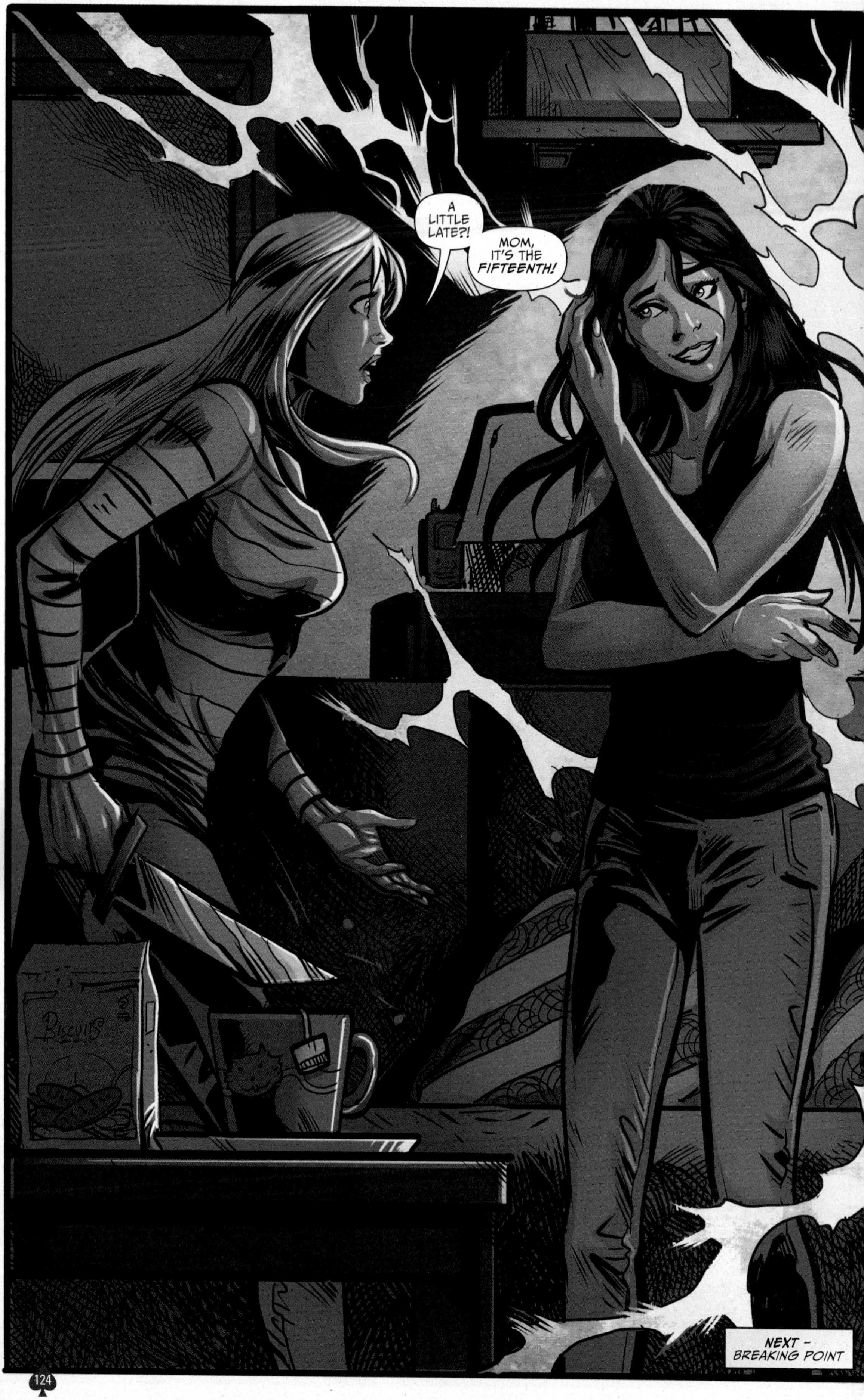
A LITTLE LATE?!
MOM, IT'S THE FIFTEENTH!
Biscuits
NEXT – BREAKING POINT

END CHAPTER

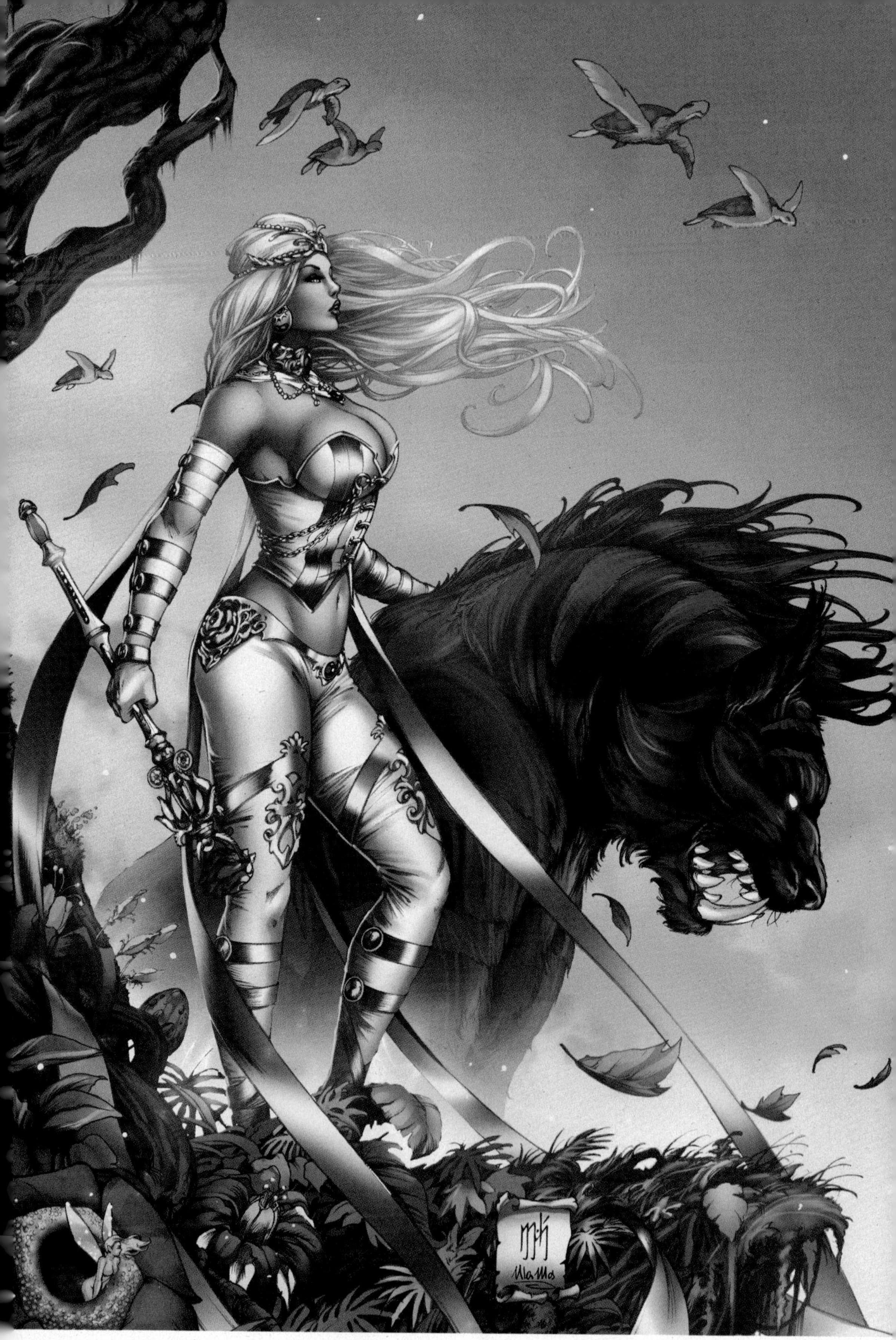

WONDERLAND 26 • COVER A
ARTWORK BY MIKE KROME • COLORS BY ULA MOS

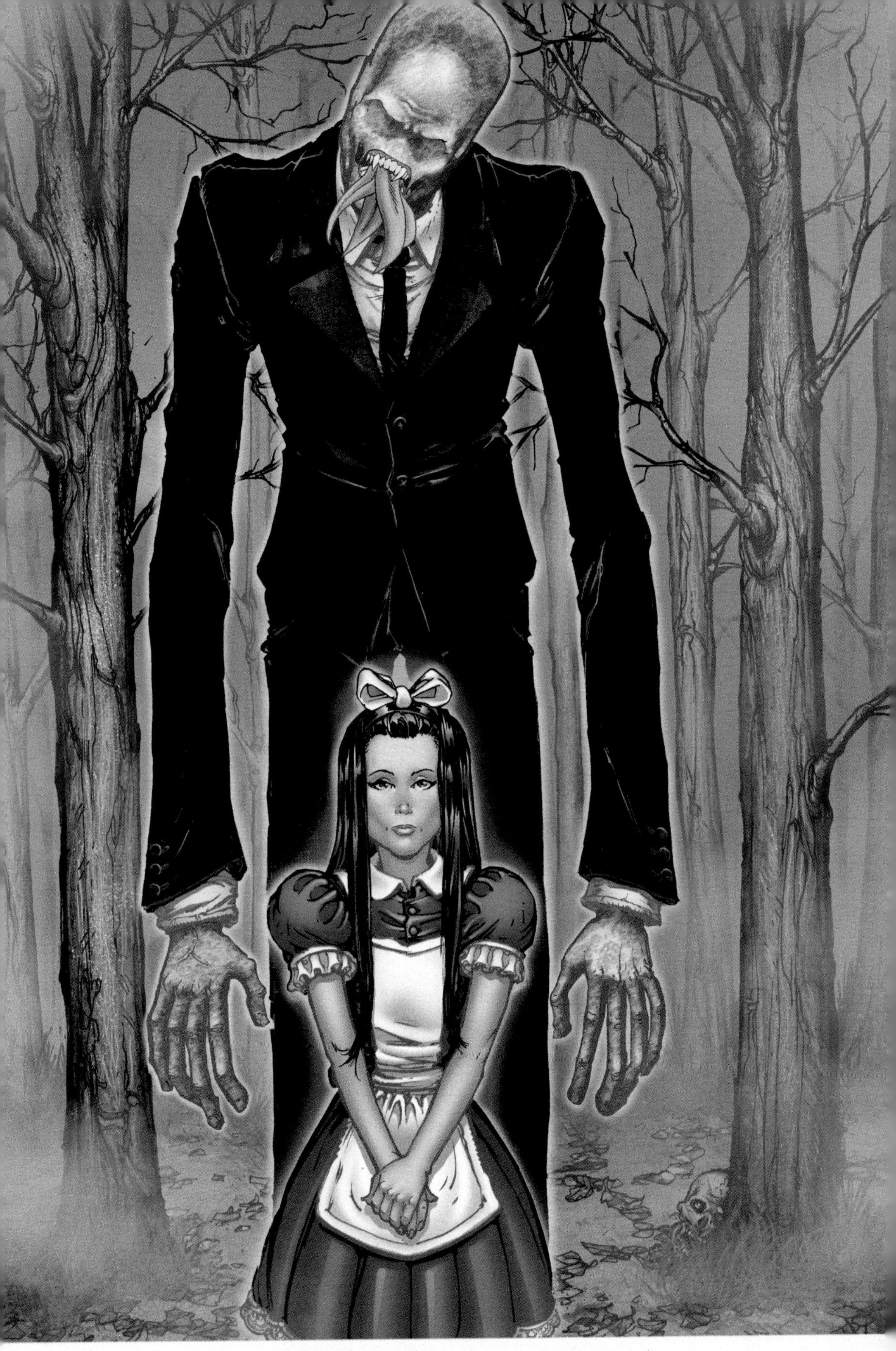

WONDERLAND 26 • COVER B
ARTWORK BY DANIEL LEISTER • COLORS BY WES HARTMAN

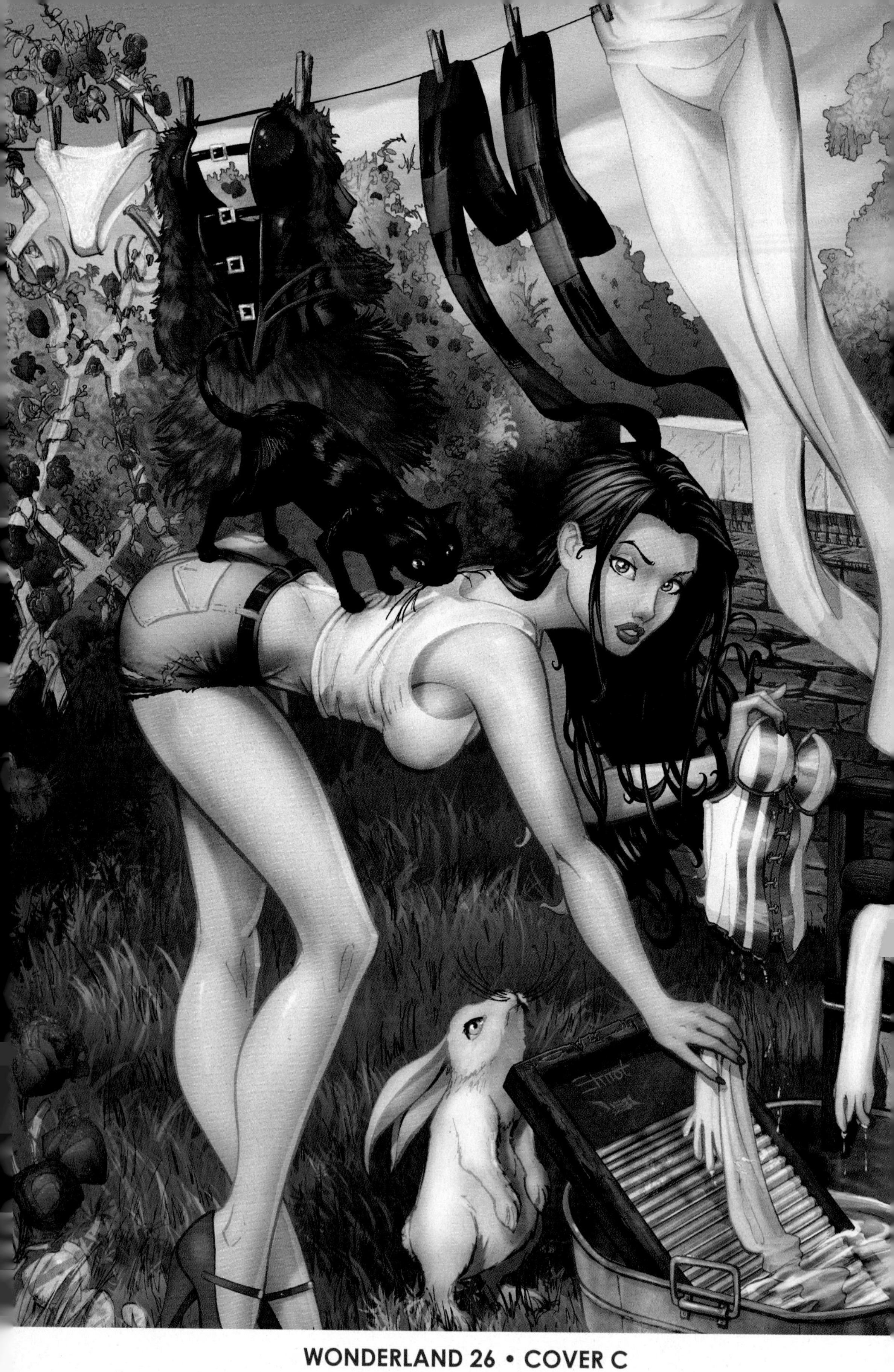

WONDERLAND 26 • COVER C

ARTWORK BY CHRIS EHNOT • COLORS BY DAVID DELANTY

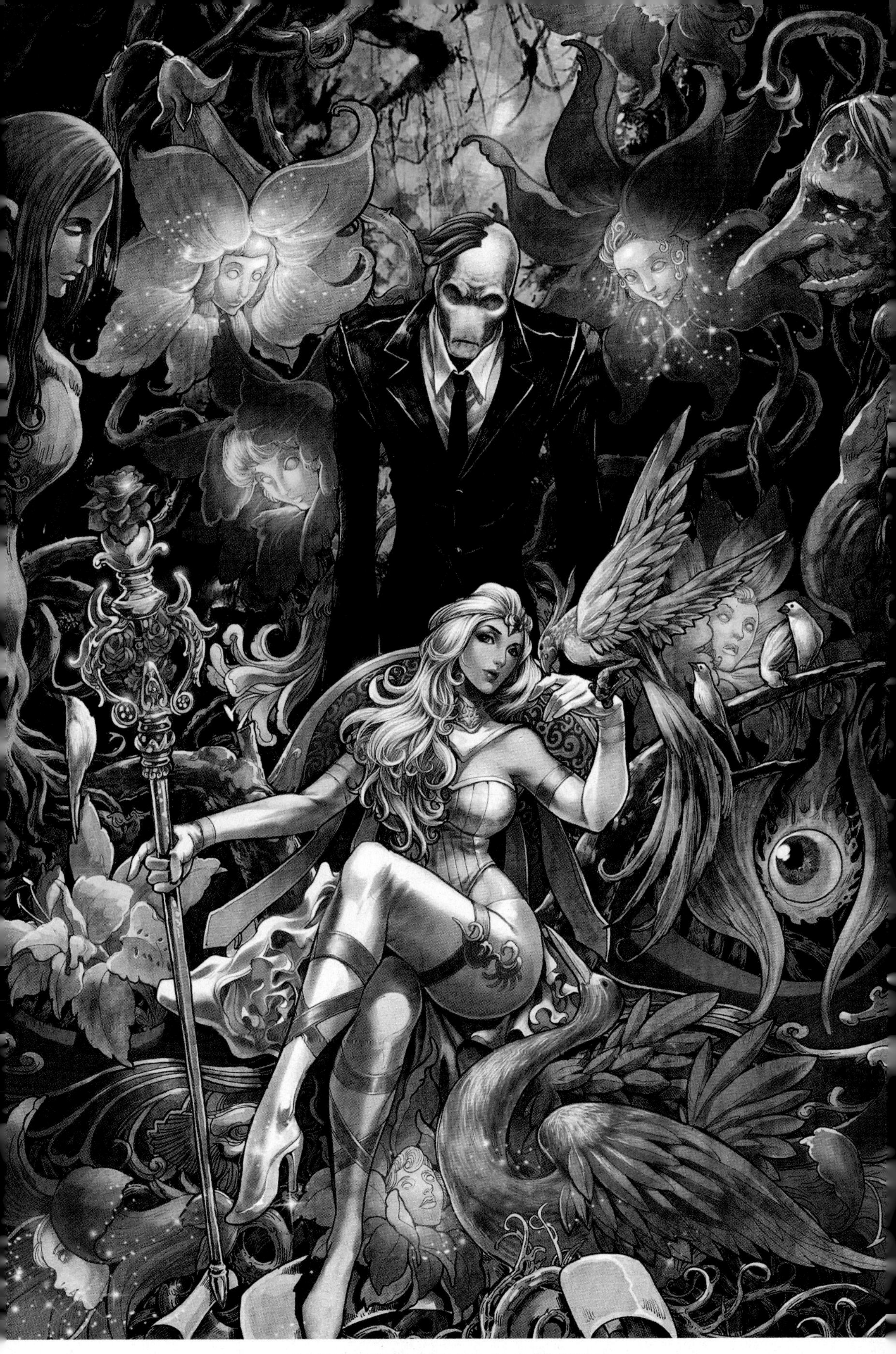

WONDERLAND 27 • COVER A
ARTWORK BY DAXIONG

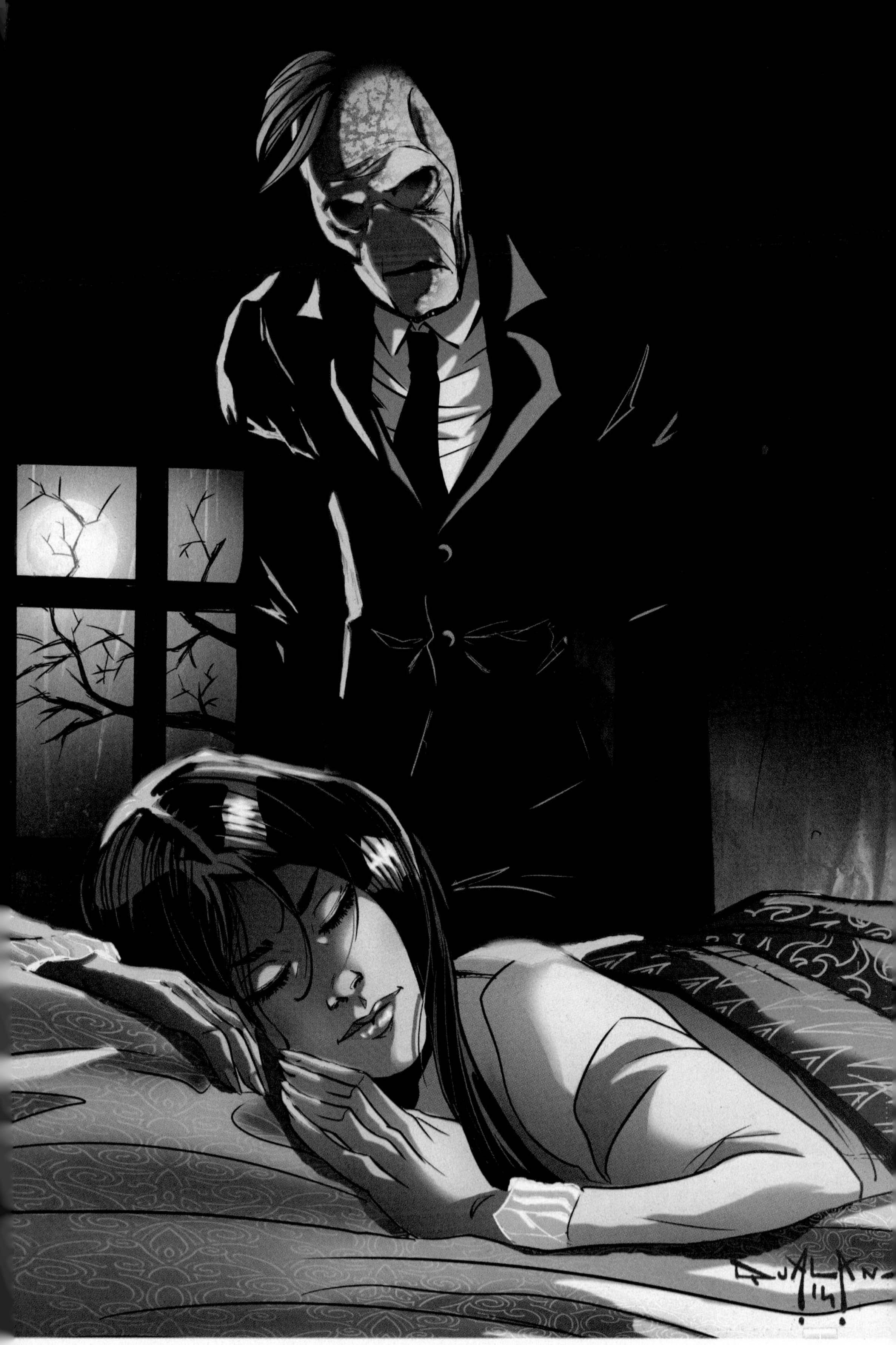
QUALANO '14

WONDERLAND 27 • COVER B

ARTWORK BY PASQUALE QUALANO • COLORS BY ALESSIA NOCERA

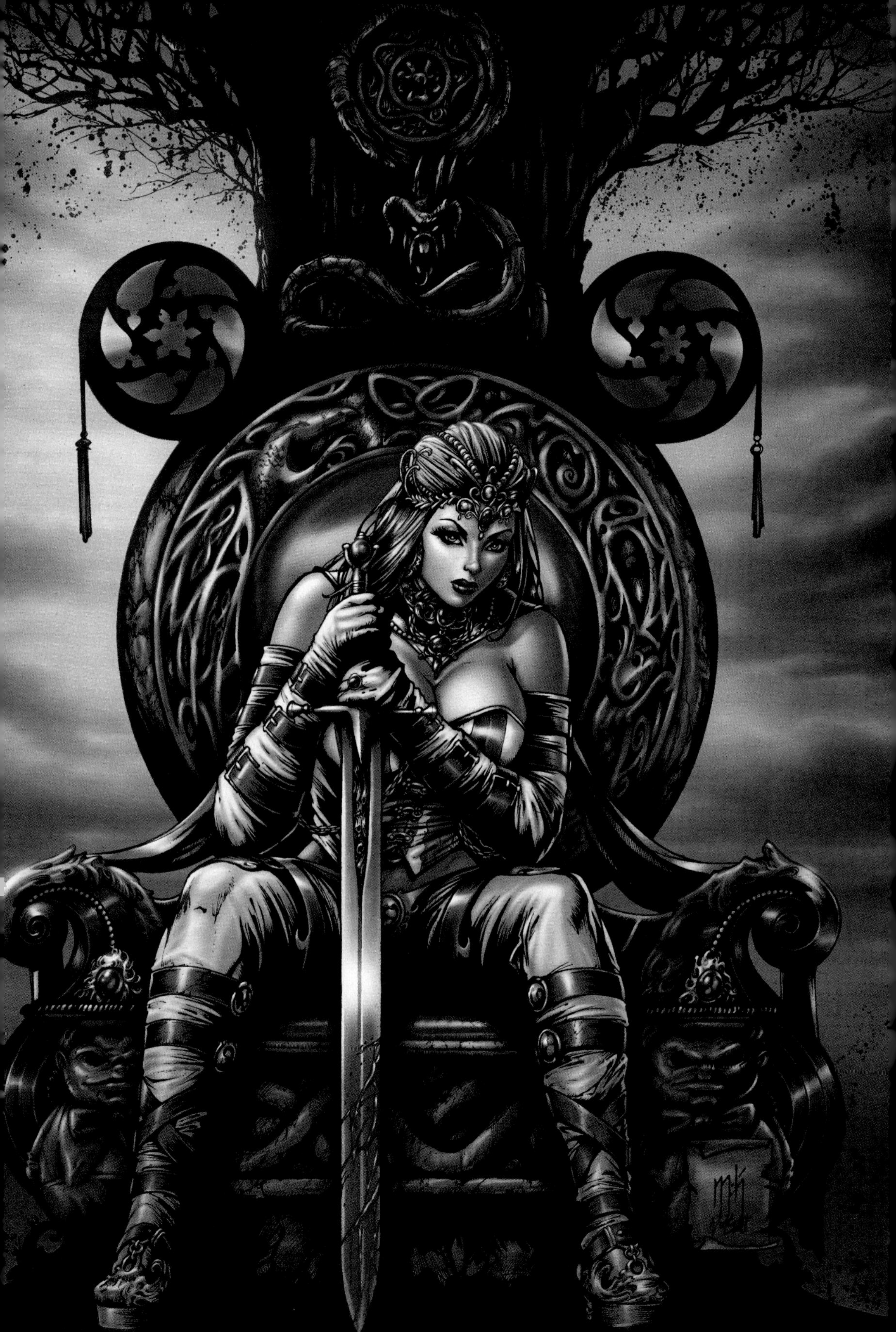

WONDERLAND 27 • COVER C

ARTWORK BY MIKE KROME • COLORS BY VICTOR BARTLETT

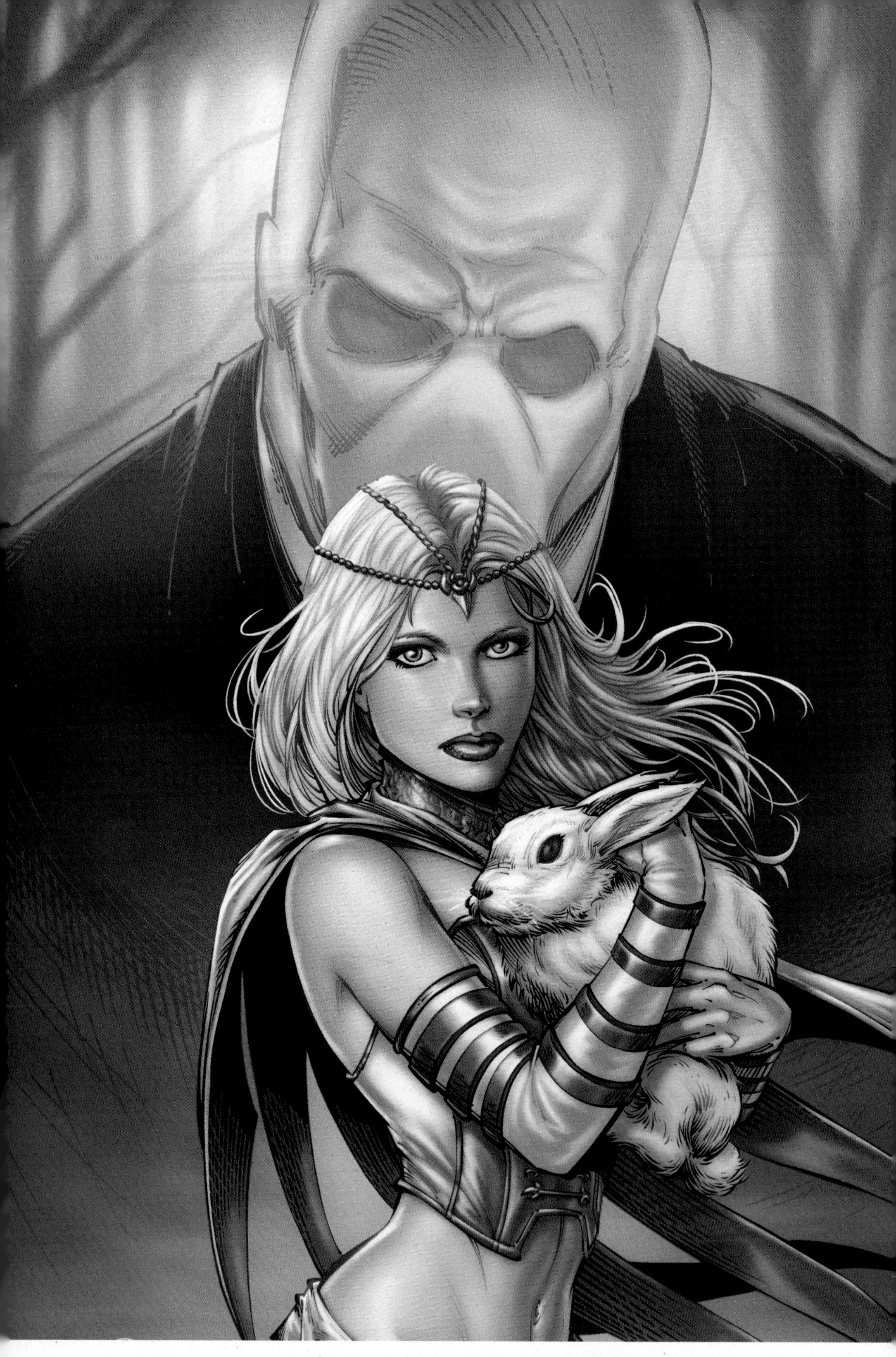

WONDERLAND 28 • COVER A
ARTWORK BY MARAT MYCHAELS • COLORS BY VICTOR BARTLETT

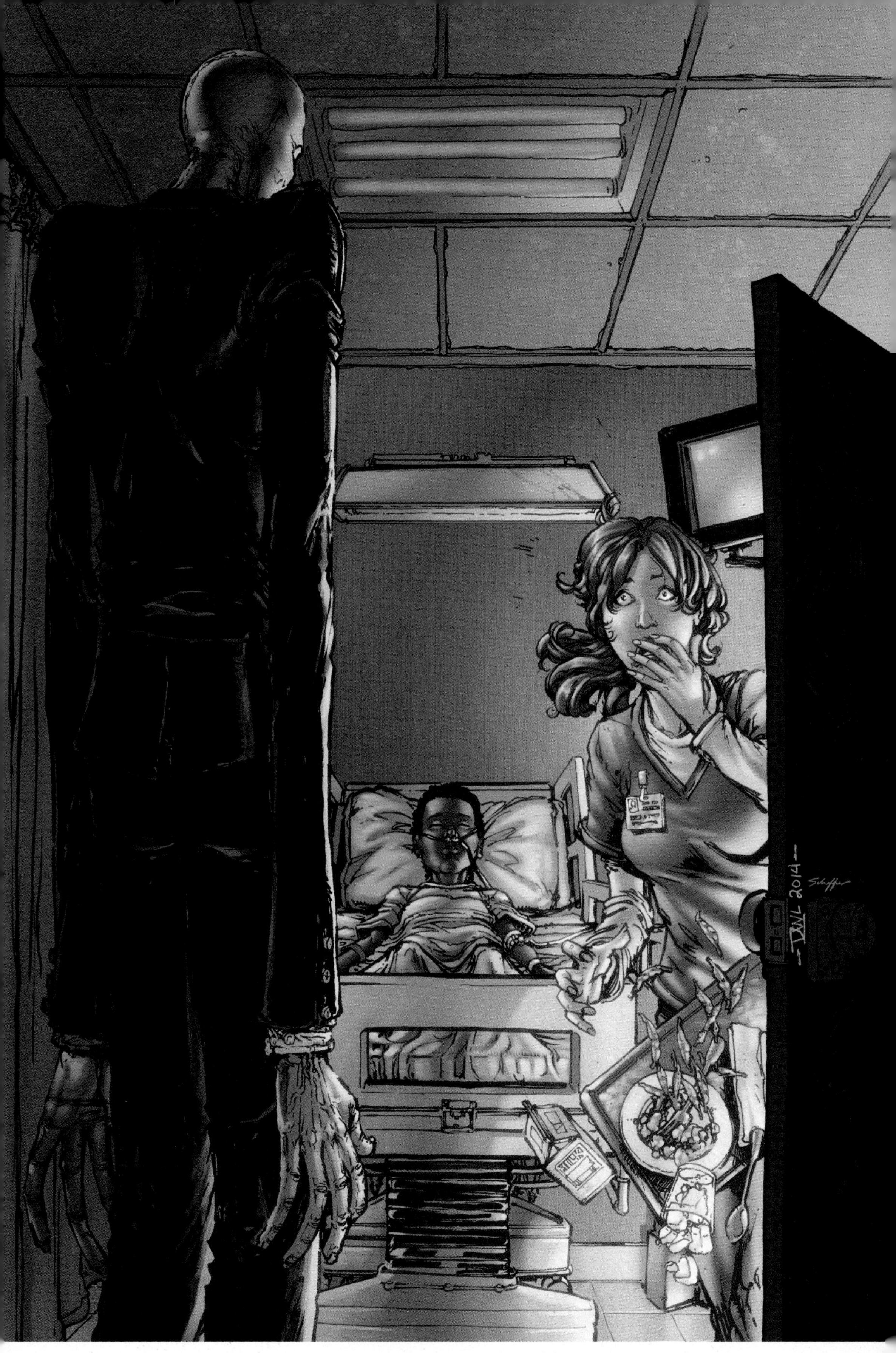

WONDERLAND 28 • COVER B

ARTWORK BY DANIEL LEISTER • COLORS BY STEPHEN SCHAFFER

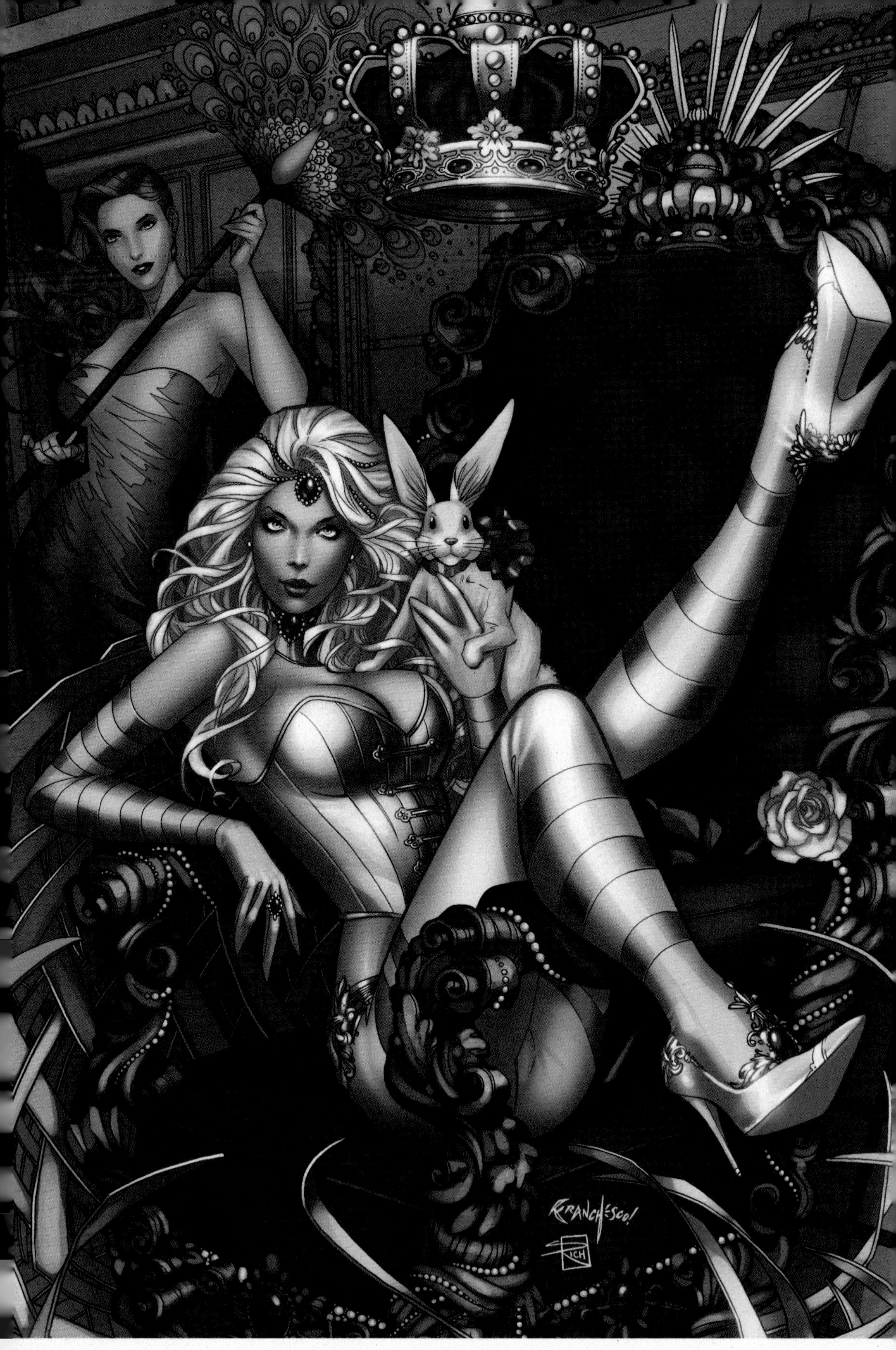
FRANCHESCO!
RICH

WONDERLAND 28 • COVER C

ARTWORK BY FRANCHESCO! • COLORS BY SABINE RICH

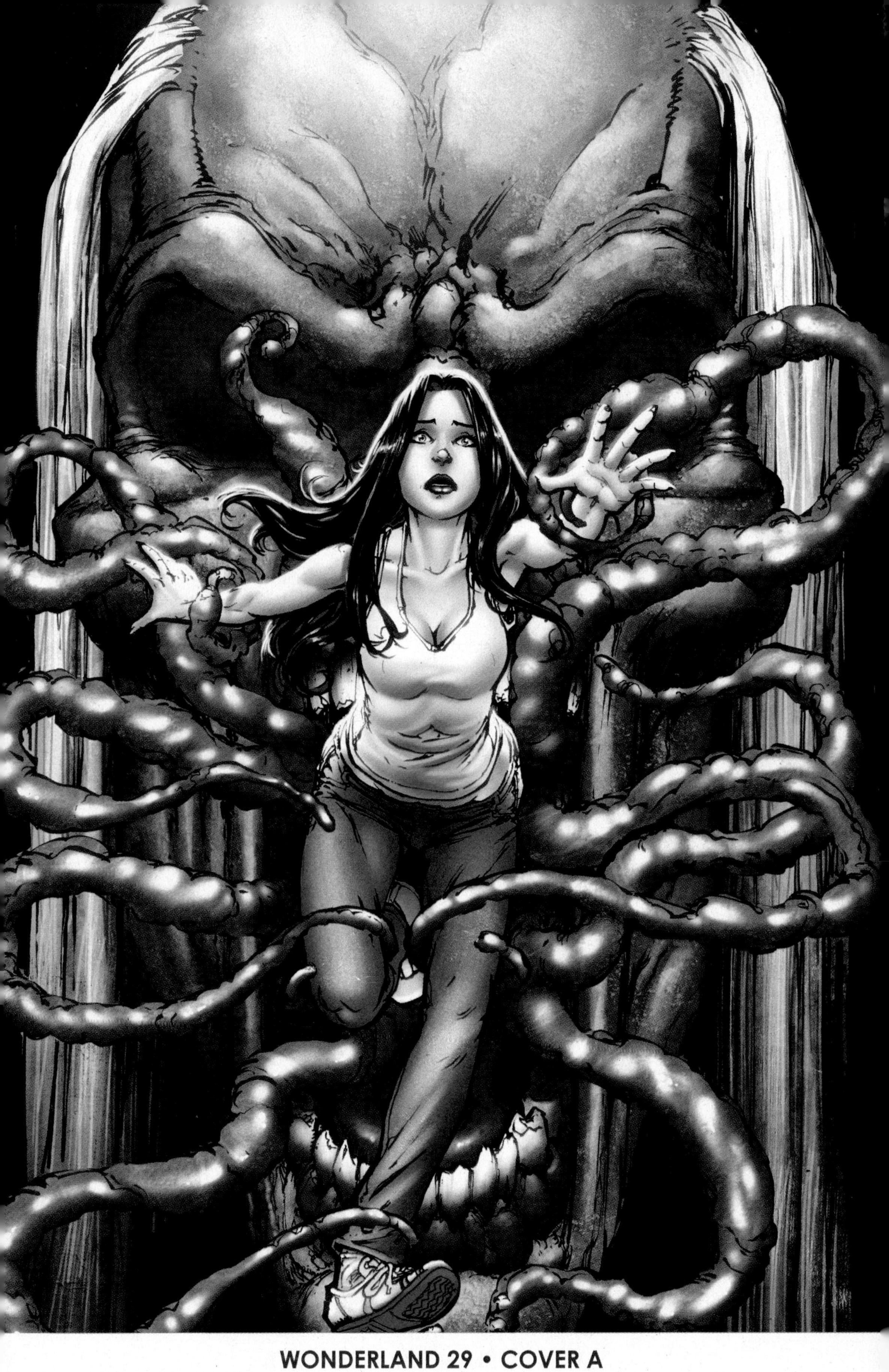

WONDERLAND 29 • COVER A

ARTWORK BY DANIEL LEISTER • COLORS BY STEPHEN SCHAFFER

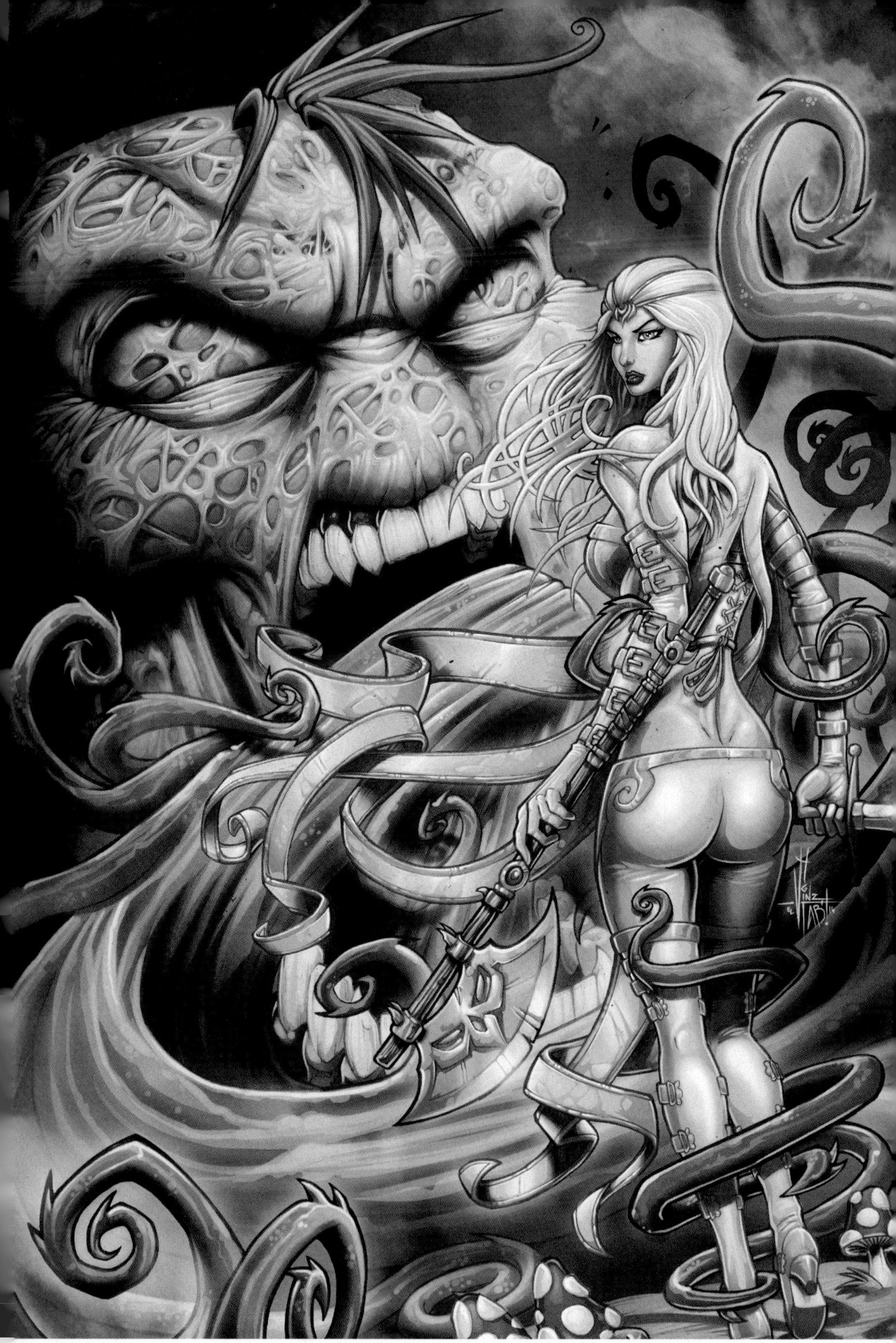

WONDERLAND 29 • COVER B
ARTWORK BY VINZ EL TABANAS

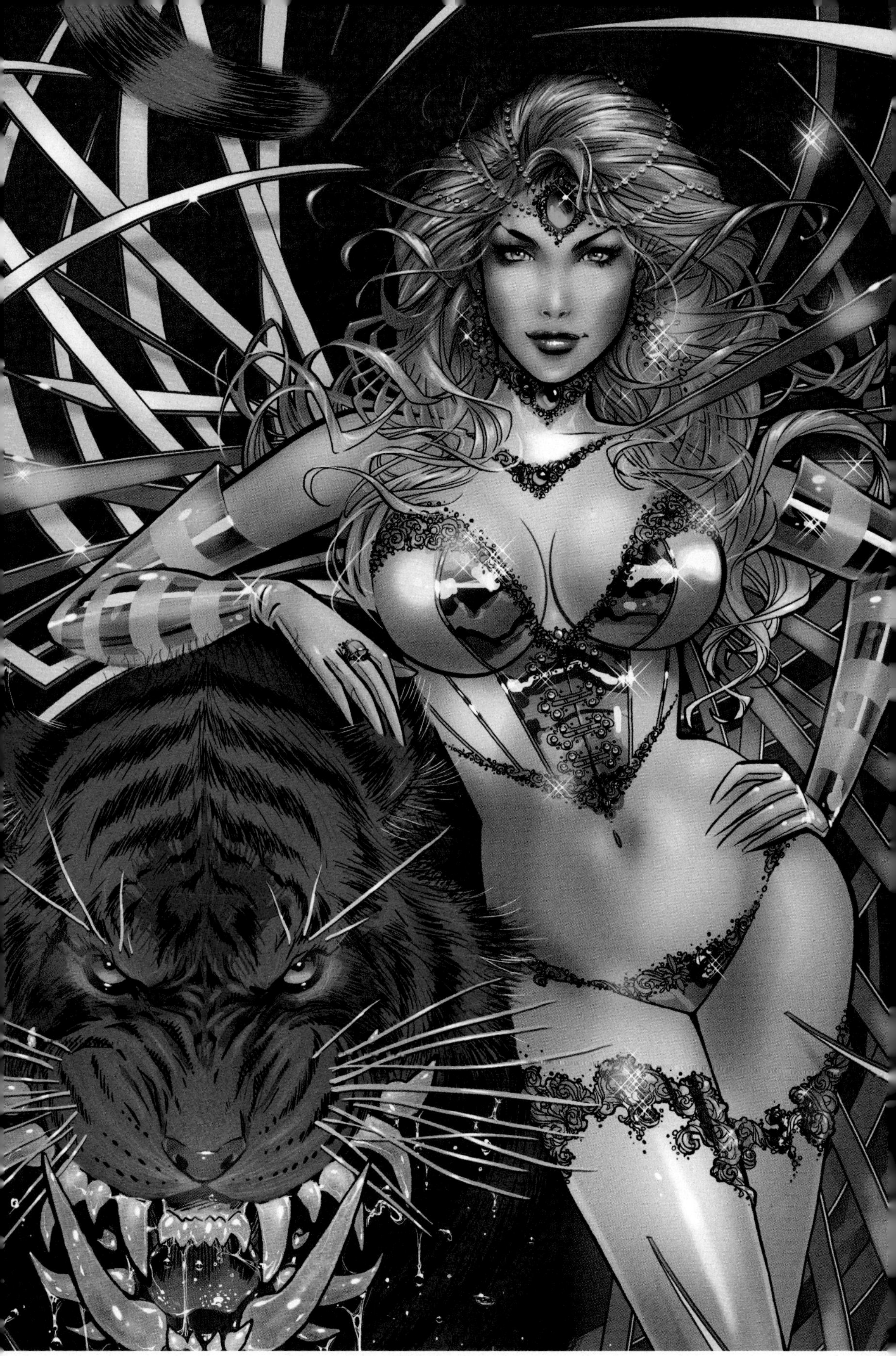

WONDERLAND 29 • COVER C
ARTWORK BY FRANCHESCO!

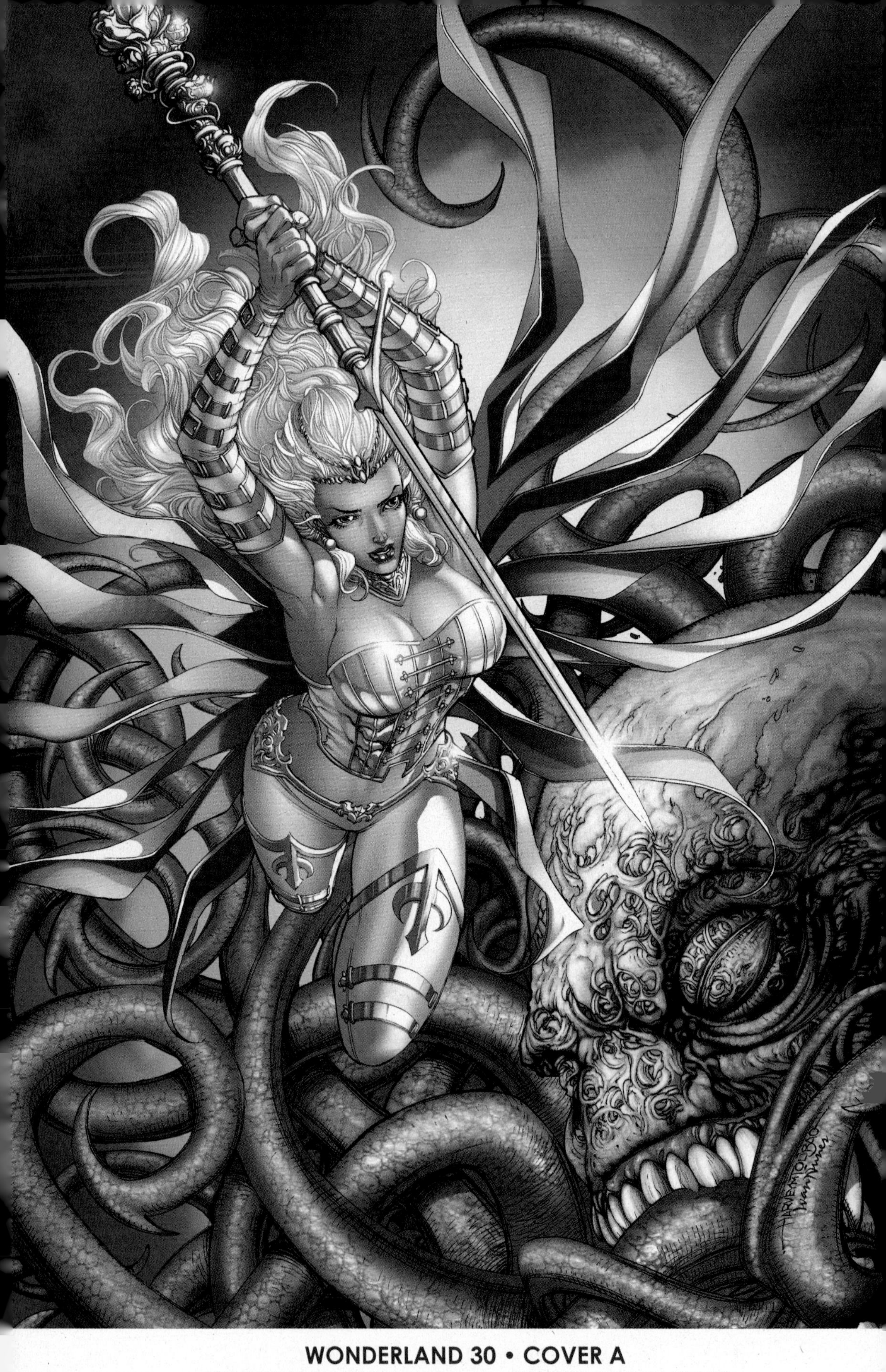

WONDERLAND 30 • COVER A

ARTWORK BY HARVEY TOLIBAO • COLORS BY IVAN NUNES

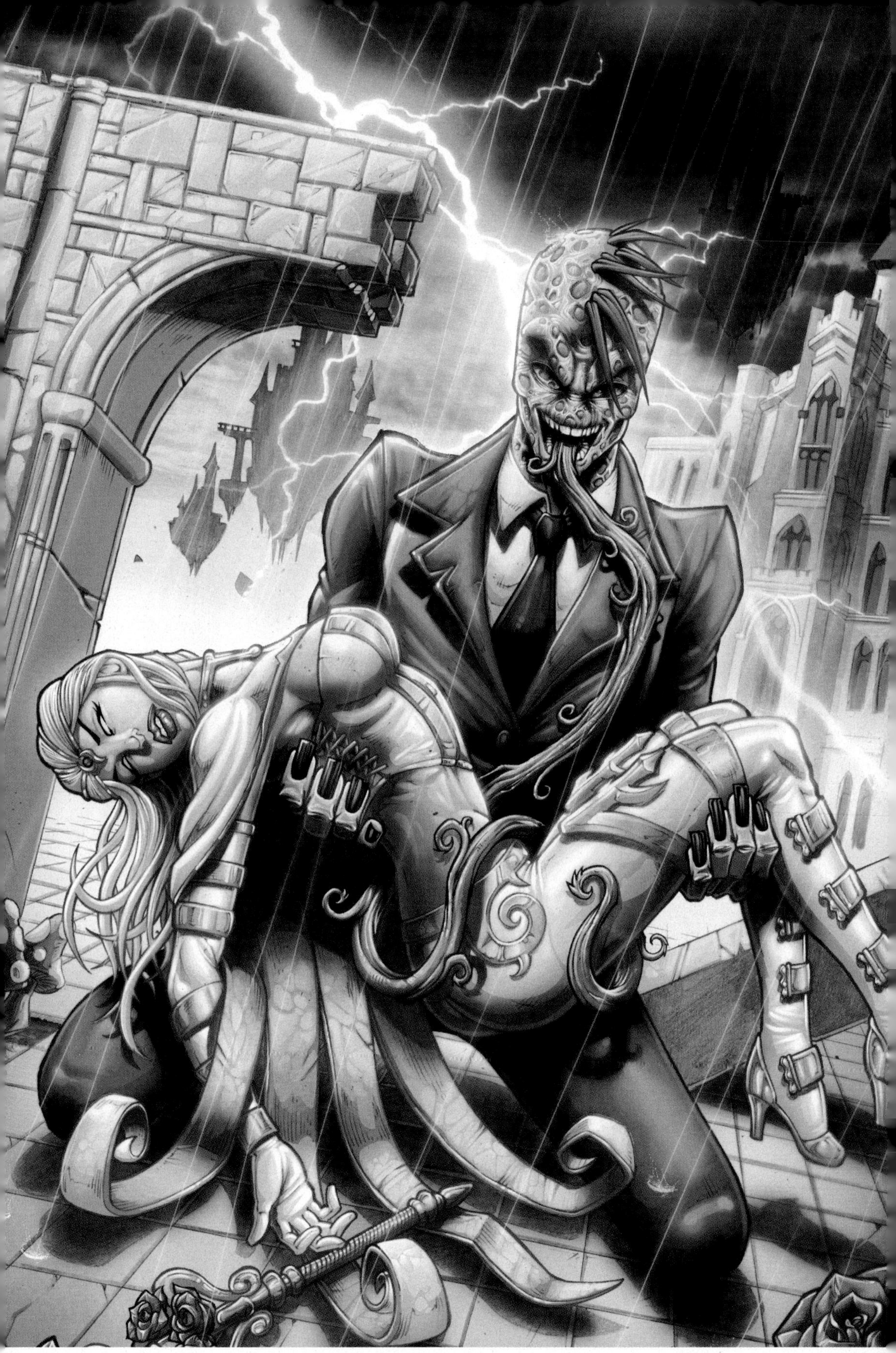

WONDERLAND 30 • COVER B
ARTWORK BY VINZ EL TABANAS

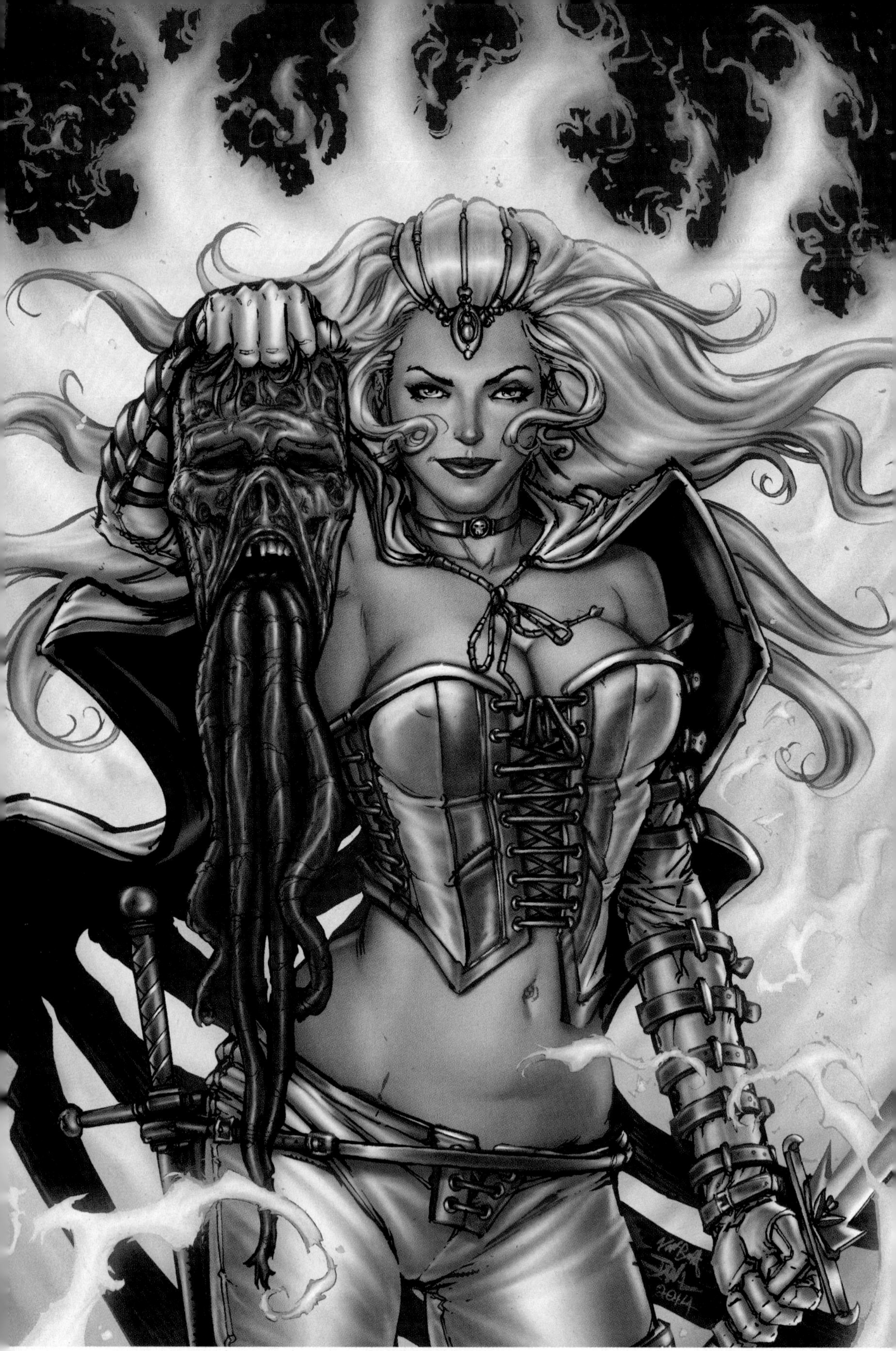

WONDERLAND 30 • COVER C

ARTWORK BY DANIEL LEISTER • COLORS BY VICTOR BARTLETT

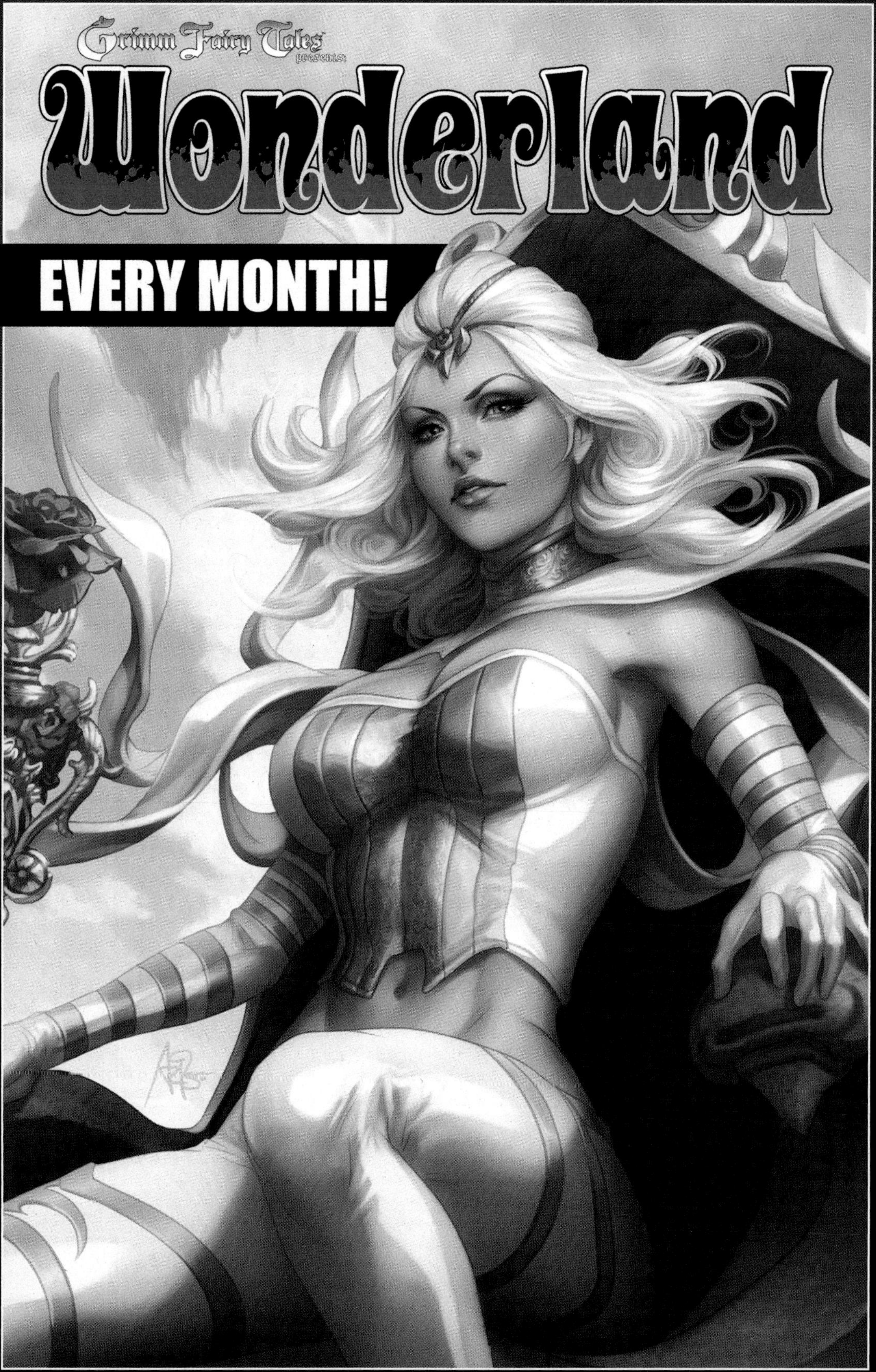
Grimm Fairy Tales presents:
Wonderland
EVERY MONTH!

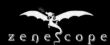

Begin your epic journey down the rabbit hole...

Grimm Fairy Tales presents:

Wonderland

THE OFFICIAL READING ORDER

01 **RETURN TO WONDERLAND** WONDERLAND TRILOGY PART 1

02 **BEYOND WONDERLAND** WONDERLAND TRILOGY PART 2

03 **ESCAPE FROM WONDERLAND** WONDERLAND TRILOGY PART 3

04 **ALICE IN WONDERLAND**

05 **CALL OF WONDERLAND**

06 **MADNESS OF WONDERLAND**

07 **WONDERLAND (ONGOING) VOL. 1**

08 **WONDERLAND (ONGOING) VOL. 2**

09 **WONDERLAND (ONGOING) VOL. 3**

10 **WONDERLAND (ONGOING) VOL. 4**

11 **WONDERLAND (ONGOING) VOL. 5**

12 **WONDERLAND (ONGOING) VOL. 6**

Return to Wonderland
01

Beyond Wonderland
02

Escape from Wonderland
03

Alice in Wonderland
Gregory · Gill · Embury
04

Call of Wonderland
05

06

Wonderland
07

Wonderland
08

Wonderland
09

Wonderland
10

Wonderland
11

Wonderland
12

THE MADNESS CONTINUES WITH THESE WONDERLAND SUPPLEMENTAL TITLES!

01 **TALES FROM WONDERLAND VOL. 1**

02 **TALES FROM WONDERLAND VOL. 2**

03 **TALES FROM WONDERLAND VOL. 3**

04 **WONDERLAND: HOUSE OF LIDDLE**

05 **WONDERLAND: THROUGH THE LOOKING GLASS**

06 **WONDERLAND: DOWN THE RABBIT HOLE**

07 **WONDERLAND: ASYLUM**

08 **WONDERLAND: CLASH OF QUEENS**

Tales from
Wonderland
Volume 1
01

Tales from
Wonderland
Volume 2
02

Tales from
Wonderland
Volume 3
03

Wonderland
House of Liddle
04

Wonderland
Through the Looking Glass
05

Wonderland
Down the Rabbit Hole
Gregory · Shand · Watson
06

Wonderland
Asylum
Shand · Brescini · Curtado · Camboa
07

Wonderland
Clash of Queens
AGE OF DARKNESS
08

zenescope

COMIC SHOP LOCATOR SERVICE
comicshoplocator.com
888-COMIC-BOOK

GRIMM FAIRY TALES PRESENTS WONDERLAND TITLES ARE CURRENTLY AVAILABLE FOR PURCHASE AT YOUR LOCAL COMIC SHOP AND **SHOP.ZENESCOPE.COM**. TO FIND YOUR NEAREAST RETAILER CALL **1-888-COMIC-BOOK** OR ON THE WEB AT **COMICSHOPLOCATOR.COM**. ALL UPCOMING WONDERLAND BOOKS ARE AVAILABLE FOR PRE-ORDER THROUGH **DIAMOND PREVIEWS**, SEE YOUR LOCAL COMIC RETAILER FOR ORDERING INFO.

Grimm Fairy Tales
presents:
Wonderland